P9-CJF-350

A 1996 HOMETOWN COLLECTION

America's Best Recipes

Oxmoor House®

©1996 by Oxmoor House, Inc.
Book Division of Southern Progress Corporation
P.O. Box 2463, Birmingham, Alabama 35201

All rights reserved.

ISBN: 0-8487-1498-9
ISSN: 0898-9982

Manufactured in the United States of America
First Printing 1996

Editor-in-Chief: Nancy Fitzpatrick Wyatt
Senior Foods Editor: Susan Carlisle Payne
Senior Editor, Editorial Services: Olivia Kindig Wells
Art Director: James Boone

America's Best Recipes: A 1996 Hometown Collection

Editors: Janice Krahn Hanby, Whitney Wheeler Pickering
Assistant Editor: Kathryn L. Matuszak, R.D.
Copy Editor: Donna Baldone
Editorial Assistant: Stacey Geary
Senior Production Designer: Larry Hunter
Director, Test Kitchens: Kathleen Royal Phillips
Assistant Director, Test Kitchens: Gayle Hays Sadler
Test Kitchens Home Economists: Susan Hall Bellows,
   Julie Christopher, Michele Brown Fuller, Heather Irby,
   Natalie E. King, Elizabeth Tyler Luckett, Jan Jacks Moon,
   Iris Crawley O'Brien, Jan A. Smith
Senior Photographer: Jim Bathie
Senior Photo Stylist: Kay E. Clarke
Photo Stylist: Iris Crawley O'Brien
Indexer: Mary Ann Laurens
Production and Distribution Director: Phillip Lee
Associate Production Manager: Theresa L. Beste
Production Coordinator: Marianne Jordan Wilson
Production Assistant: Valerie L. Heard
Project Consultants: Meryle Evans, Audrey P. Stehle

Cover: *Chocolate-Raspberry Truffle Cheesecake (page 118)*

Contents

Introduction

All across America proud cooks preserve family traditions and regional cuisines with quality community cookbooks. *America's Best Recipes* brings you over 400 of the highest-rated recipes, all rigorously taste-tested by our Test Kitchens staff. You'll find the best of regional cuisines as well as cherished family fare. These are the recipes that are swapped and shared with friends in hometowns throughout our country.

With more people eating healthy, we also bring you the best light community recipes in our special "Light Recipes" chapter beginning on page 5. Everyone can benefit from a diet low in fat, sodium, and calories—not just those trying to lose weight. In the light chapter you'll find:

- Recipes low in fat and sodium, but high in flavor
- An analysis of 8 nutritional values including calories, fat, and sodium for each recipe
- A Low-Fat Ingredient Substitution Chart to help you lighten your favorite recipes

In addition, don't miss our "Quick and Easy" chapter beginning on page 45. This chapter features timesaving recipes that are easy to prepare (just 45 minutes or less) and use only a handful of commonly used ingredients.

We're proud to bring you this collection of recipe winners. And if a particular book sparks your interest and you'd like to order a copy, you'll find an alphabetical listing, along with mailing addresses in the Acknowledgments beginning on page 320. When you order copies, you'll receive great recipes and the satisfaction of helping support the local communities and their charitable causes that we salute in *America's Best Recipes*.

The Editors

Light Recipes

Low-Calorie Chicken Oriental, page 15

Light Cooking

Enjoy good food, but save your splurges for special occasions.
Moderation is the key to good health.

Trends toward healthy eating are evident not only in today's growing interest in diet foods and weight loss, but also on the pages of community cookbooks. Recipes collected from volunteer groups across the country reflect the low-fat cooking trend. In this special chapter we've selected the best light recipes from those cookbooks to make it easy for you to adopt new eating habits. So, try these delicious light recipes from your neighbors' kitchens.

Using the nutrient analysis at the end of each recipe is an easy way to bring balance to your eating plan. This information coupled with the handy chart on the next page promises recipes that not only taste good, but help keep you healthy.

Every Recipe Is Analyzed for:

- Calories
- Percent of calories from fat
- Fat
- Saturated Fat
- Carbohydrate
- Protein
- Cholesterol
- Sodium

How the Recipes Are Analyzed

- The values in the nutrient grid of each recipe come from a computer analysis from the U.S. Department of Agriculture.
- All meats are trimmed of fat and skin before cooking.
- Some calories from alcohol evaporate during cooking; the analysis reflects the remaining amount of calories.
- When a marinade is used, only the amount absorbed is calculated.
- Garnishes and optional ingredients are not calculated.

How to Make Our Recipes Work for You

- If you're eating low-fat foods, look for low figures for total fat, saturated fat, and cholesterol to help you stick to your goal.
- If you're trying to shed a few pounds, the amount of fat and calories will be of most interest to you.
- And if you want to maintain good health, notice the carbohydrate, protein, and fat information included in each analysis. Maximizing carbohydrate and minimizing protein and fat play an important role in health and well-being.

LOW-FAT INGREDIENT SUBSTITUTIONS

Recipe calls for	Substitute
Fats and Oils	
Butter and/or margarine	Reduced-calorie margarine or margarine made with safflower, soybean, corn, canola, or peanut oil; reduced-calorie stick margarine in baked products
Mayonnaise	Nonfat or reduced-calorie mayonnaise
Oil	Safflower, soybean, corn, canola, or peanut oil in reduced amount
Salad dressing	Nonfat or oil-free dressing
Shortening	Soybean, corn, canola, or peanut oil in amount reduced by one-third
Dairy Products	
Sour cream	Low-fat or nonfat sour cream or yogurt
Whipping cream	Chilled evaporated skimmed milk, whipped
American, Cheddar, colby, Edam, Swiss	Cheeses with 5 grams of fat or less per ounce
Cottage cheese	Nonfat or 1% low-fat cottage cheese
Cream cheese	Nonfat or light process cream cheese, Neufchâtel cheese
Ricotta cheese	Nonfat, lite, or part-skim ricotta cheese
Milk, whole or 2%	Skim milk, ½% milk, 1% milk
Ice cream	Nonfat or low-fat frozen yogurt, low-fat ice cream, nonfat ice cream, sherbet, sorbet
Meats, Poultry, and Eggs	
Bacon	Canadian bacon, turkey bacon, lean ham
Beef, veal, lamb, pork	Chicken, turkey, or lean cuts of meat trimmed of all visible fat
Ground beef	Extra-lean ground beef, ultra-lean ground beef, ground turkey
Luncheon meat	Skinned, sliced turkey or chicken breast, lean cooked ham, lean roast beef
Poultry	Skinned poultry
Tuna packed in oil	Tuna packed in water
Turkey, self basting	Turkey basted with fat-free broth
Egg, whole	2 egg whites or ¼ cup egg substitute
Miscellaneous	
Chocolate, unsweetened	3 tablespoons unsweetened cocoa plus 1 tablespoon margarine per ounce of chocolate
Fudge sauce	Fat-free fudge sauce or chocolate syrup
Nuts	One-third to one-half less, toasted
Soups, canned	99% fat-free or reduced-sodium condensed cream soups

Fat-Free Mexican Dip

This nonfat, heart-smart dip is also good dolloped on a baked potato instead of sour cream.

1 (24-ounce) carton nonfat cottage cheese
⅔ cup sliced green onions
1 teaspoon garlic powder
½ teaspoon chili powder
1 (12-ounce) package nonfat process American cheese slices, chopped

1 (12-ounce) jar picante sauce
¼ cup skim milk
Garnish: sliced green onions

Position knife blade in food processor bowl; add first 4 ingredients. Process 30 seconds or until smooth, stopping once to scrape down sides; set aside.

Combine American cheese, picante sauce, and milk in a microwave-safe bowl. Microwave at HIGH 6 minutes or until cheese melts, stirring after every minute. Add to cottage cheese mixture in processor bowl; cover and process 30 seconds or until smooth, stopping once to scrape down sides. Cover and chill thoroughly. Garnish, if desired. Serve dip with fresh raw vegetables or no-oil baked tortilla chips. Yield: 5 cups.

Peg Kottke

Simple Elegance
Our Lady of Perpetual Help Women's Guild
Germantown, Tennessee

Per Tablespoon

Calories 13 (0% from Fat)	Carbohydrate 1.0 g	Cholesterol 0 mg
Fat 0.0 g (Saturated Fat 0.0 g)	Protein 2.2 g	Sodium 138 mg

Alice's Stuffed Artichokes

Make soft breadcrumbs by tearing fresh or slightly stale bread into small pieces. If you need a large amount of soft breadcrumbs, process bread slices in the food processor to make fluffy crumbs.

4 small artichokes (about 1½ pounds)
2 tablespoons lemon juice
Vegetable cooking spray
1 teaspoon olive oil
1 (4-ounce) jar sliced mushrooms, drained and chopped
4 cloves garlic, chopped

1 cup chopped onion
1 cup soft whole wheat breadcrumbs
4 sun-dried tomatoes (packed without oil), chopped
1 teaspoon dried basil
¼ cup chopped fresh parsley
2 tablespoons grated Parmesan cheese

Wash artichokes by plunging up and down in cold water. Cut off stem ends; trim about ½ inch from top of each artichoke. Remove any loose bottom leaves. With scissors, trim away about one-fourth of each outer leaf.

Place artichokes in a Dutch oven; add water to depth of 1 inch. Add lemon juice. Bring to a boil; cover, reduce heat, and simmer 25 minutes or until almost tender. Drain; let cool. Spread leaves apart; scrape out fuzzy thistle center (choke) with a spoon.

Coat a large nonstick skillet with cooking spray; add oil. Place skillet over medium-high heat until hot. Add mushrooms, garlic, and onions; cook, stirring constantly, until onion is tender. Add breadcrumbs; stir well. Remove from heat, and add tomato and remaining 3 ingredients; stir well.

Spoon mixture evenly into center and between leaves of artichokes. Place stuffed artichokes in a 13- x 9- x 2-inch baking dish. Bake, uncovered, at 350° for 15 minutes. Serve immediately. Yield: 4 servings.

The Impossible Diet Cookbook
The Recovery Alliance
Milford, Connecticut

Per Serving

Calories 64 (15% from Fat)	Carbohydrate 12.5 g	Cholesterol 1 mg
Fat 1.1 g (Saturated Fat 0.3 g)	Protein 3.1 g	Sodium 137 mg

Mint Tea

This summer sipper keeps calories and fat low, while providing lots of vitamin C.

4 cups water
8 regular-size tea bags
5 fresh mint sprigs
½ cup sugar
1 (46-ounce) can pineapple
  juice

1 (6-ounce) can frozen
  lemonade concentrate,
  thawed and undiluted
4 cups cold water

Bring 4 cups water to a boil in a large saucepan. Add tea bags, mint sprigs, and sugar; remove from heat. Cover and steep 12 minutes. Remove and discard tea bags and mint sprigs, squeezing tea bags gently. Add pineapple juice and lemonade concentrate, stirring until blended. Stir in cold water. Serve over ice. Yield: 16 (1-cup) servings.

Today's Traditional: Jewish Cooking with a Lighter Touch
Congregation Beth Shalom
Carmichael, California

Per Serving

Calories 90 (1% from Fat)   Carbohydrate 22.7 g   Cholesterol 0 mg
Fat 0.1 g (Saturated Fat 0.0 g) Protein 0.3 g   Sodium 3 mg

Confetti Muffins

1⅓ cups all-purpose flour
⅓ cup yellow cornmeal
1 teaspoon baking powder
½ teaspoon baking soda
2 teaspoons sugar
¼ teaspoon ground red pepper
1 large egg, lightly beaten

1⅓ cups buttermilk
1 cup (4 ounces) shredded Cheddar cheese
½ cup finely chopped sweet red pepper
⅓ cup thinly sliced green onions

Combine first 6 ingredients in a large bowl; make a well in center of mixture.

Combine egg and buttermilk; add to dry ingredients, stirring just until moistened. Stir in cheese, sweet red pepper, and green onions. Spoon into greased muffin pans, filling three-fourths full. Bake at 425° for 20 to 22 minutes or until golden. Remove from pans immediately. Yield: 1 dozen.

Cindy Falk

Essence of Kansas: 4-H Cookbook, Taste Two
Kansas 4-H Foundation
Manhattan, Kansas

Per Muffin

Calories 125 (29% from Fat)   Carbohydrate 16.3 g   Cholesterol 29 mg
Fat 4.0 g (Saturated Fat 2.3 g) Protein 5.6 g   Sodium 146 mg

Oatmeal-Honey Bread

1 package active dry yeast
1 teaspoon sugar
½ cup warm water (105° to 115°)
1 cup plain nonfat yogurt
1 cup quick-cooking oats
3 tablespoons honey

1 teaspoon salt
¼ teaspoon baking soda
2⅓ cups all-purpose flour
2 tablespoons all-purpose flour, divided
Vegetable cooking spray
1 tablespoon honey

Combine first 3 ingredients in a 1-cup liquid measuring cup; let stand 5 minutes.

Cook yogurt over medium heat until warm. Combine warm yogurt, oats, and next 3 ingredients in a large mixing bowl; beat at medium speed of an electric mixer until well blended.

Add yeast mixture to oat mixture; mix until blended. Gradually stir in enough flour to make a soft dough.

Sprinkle 1 tablespoon flour over work surface. Turn dough out onto floured surface; knead until smooth and elastic (about 5 minutes). Place in a bowl coated with cooking spray, turning to coat top. Cover and let rise in a warm place (85°), free from drafts, 45 minutes or until doubled in bulk.

Punch dough down. Sprinkle remaining 1 tablespoon flour over work surface. Turn dough out onto floured surface, and knead lightly 4 or 5 times; roll into a 12- x 5-inch rectangle.

Roll up dough, starting at short side, pressing to eliminate air pockets; pinch ends to seal. Place dough, seam side down, in a 7½- x 3- x 2-inch loafpan coated with cooking spray.

Cover and let rise in a warm place, free from drafts, 30 minutes or until doubled in bulk. Bake at 400° for 15 minutes. Reduce heat to 350°; bake 20 minutes or until loaf sounds hollow when tapped. Remove from pan immediately; brush with 1 tablespoon honey, and let cool on a wire rack. Yield: 12 (½-inch slice) servings.

A Slice of Paradise
The Hospital Service League of Naples Community Hospital
Naples, Florida

Per Serving

Calories 155 (5% from Fat)	Carbohydrate 31.9 g	Cholesterol 0 mg
Fat 0.8 g (Saturated Fat 0.1 g)	Protein 5.1 g	Sodium 237 mg

Chicken Curry, Low Calorie

We left the peel on the apple to give it extra color, but if you prefer, peel it.

1 tablespoon vegetable oil
2 cups diced apple
½ cup chopped celery
½ cup chopped onion
1 clove garlic, minced
1 tablespoon curry powder
½ teaspoon ground cinnamon
¼ teaspoon ground ginger
¼ teaspoon ground white
   pepper

2 tablespoons cornstarch
2 cups canned chicken broth,
   undiluted
2 cups cubed cooked chicken
¼ cup raisins
3 cups cooked long-grain rice
   (cooked without salt or fat)

Heat oil in a large nonstick skillet over medium heat until hot. Add apple and next 7 ingredients. Cook 5 minutes, stirring occasionally.

Combine cornstarch and chicken broth, stirring until smooth; add to apple mixture. Stir in chicken and raisins. Bring to a boil; cook over medium heat, stirring constantly, until thickened. Serve over rice. Yield: 6 servings.   Eva Mooney

Not by Bread Alone
Catholic Committee on Scouting and Camp Fire for the Diocese of
Lake Charles, Louisiana

Per Serving

Calories 293 (21% from Fat)	Carbohydrate 39.1 g	Cholesterol 43 mg
Fat 6.8 g (Saturated Fat 1.6 g)	Protein 18.3 g	Sodium 312 mg

Santa Fe Chicken "Steam-Fry"

A "steam-fry" is created by simmering the chicken in its marinade until done and infused with flavor.

½ cup canned chicken broth,
   undiluted
¼ cup fresh lime juice
1 tablespoon sugar
1 tablespoon chili powder
1 tablespoon vegetable oil
1 teaspoon garlic powder

¼ teaspoon salt
¼ teaspoon pepper
2 teaspoons Dijon mustard
4 (4-ounce) skinned, boned
   chicken breast halves
1 teaspoon chopped fresh
   cilantro

Combine first 9 ingredients in a shallow dish; add chicken. Cover and marinate in refrigerator up to 30 minutes.

Place chicken and marinade in a large nonstick skillet; bring marinade to a boil. Reduce heat, and simmer, uncovered, 5 to 6 minutes or until chicken is done. Sprinkle chicken with chopped cilantro. Yield: 4 servings. Lanelle Brown

Amazing Graces: Meals and Memories from the Parsonage
Texas Conference United Methodist Minister's Spouses Association
Palestine, Texas

Per Serving		
Calories 188 (26% from Fat)	Carbohydrate 6.4 g	Cholesterol 66 mg
Fat 5.5 g (Saturated Fat 1.1 g)	Protein 27.2 g	Sodium 411 mg

Low-Calorie Chicken Oriental

1 (15¼-ounce) can pineapple chunks in juice, undrained
8 (4-ounce) skinned, boned chicken breast halves
1 medium-size green pepper, seeded and cut into thin strips
1 medium-size sweet red pepper, seeded and cut into thin strips
3 tablespoons white wine vinegar
1 tablespoon soy sauce
½ teaspoon salt
½ teaspoon dry mustard
¼ teaspoon pepper
1 tablespoon cornstarch
2 tablespoons water
3 cups cooked long-grain rice (cooked without salt or fat)

Drain pineapple, reserving juice. Place pineapple, chicken, and pepper strips in a 13- x 9- x 2-inch baking dish. Set aside.

Combine reserved pineapple juice, vinegar, and next 4 ingredients in a small bowl; stir well. Pour over chicken mixture. Bake, uncovered, at 325° for 40 minutes.

Combine cornstarch and water in a small bowl; stir into chicken mixture. Bake, uncovered, 25 to 30 additional minutes or until thickened. Serve over rice. Yield: 6 servings.   Gloria E. Richter

Gaspee Days Cookbook
Gaspee Days Committee
Warwick, Rhode Island

Per Serving

Calories 339 (6% from Fat)	Carbohydrate 39.0 g	Cholesterol 88 mg
Fat 2.3 g (Saturated Fat 0.5 g)	Protein 37.5 g	Sodium 435 mg

Orange and Spinach-Stuffed Chicken Breasts

6 (4-ounce) skinned, boned
   chicken breast halves
1 (10-ounce) package frozen
   chopped spinach, thawed
1 (11-ounce) can mandarin
   oranges in light syrup,
   undrained
¾ cup cooked orzo (cooked
   without salt or fat)
¼ cup chopped onion
1 clove garlic, pressed

½ teaspoon salt
¼ teaspoon pepper
Vegetable cooking spray
1 tablespoon cornstarch
¾ cup unsweetened orange
   juice
2 teaspoons chopped fresh
   tarragon
¼ teaspoon salt
Garnish: fresh tarragon sprigs

Place chicken between two sheets of heavy-duty plastic wrap; flatten to ¼-inch thickness, using a meat mallet or rolling pin. Set aside.

Drain spinach, and press between paper towels to remove excess moisture. Drain oranges, reserving ½ cup liquid. Combine spinach, oranges, orzo, and next 4 ingredients, stirring well. Spoon about ⅓ cup spinach mixture in center of each chicken breast. Roll up, starting with short end; secure with wooden picks. Place chicken, seam side down, in an 11- x 7- x 1½-inch baking dish coated with cooking spray.

Combine cornstarch, ½ cup mandarin orange liquid, and next 3 ingredients in a small saucepan, stirring well. Bring to a boil over medium heat, stirring constantly. Cook, stirring constantly, 1 minute or until mixture is thickened. Pour sauce over chicken. Bake, uncovered, at 350° for 35 minutes or until done. Garnish, if desired. Yield: 6 servings.

Sheliah Hines

Simply Irresistible
The Junior Auxiliary of Conway, Arkansas

Per Serving

Calories 219 (7% from Fat)   Carbohydrate 20.6 g   Cholesterol 66 mg
Fat 1.8 g (Saturated Fat 0.4 g)   Protein 28.6 g   Sodium 392 mg

Gingerroot-Turkey Stir-Fry

1 pound turkey tenderloins
Vegetable cooking spray
1 tablespoon vegetable oil
2 cups small cauliflower
  flowerets
1 cup diagonally sliced green
  onions
¼ cup peeled julienne-sliced
  gingerroot
1½ tablespoons cornstarch
1 tablespoon sugar

¼ teaspoon dry mustard
⅔ cup canned chicken broth,
  undiluted
3 tablespoons low-sodium soy
  sauce
2 tablespoons dry sherry
1 medium Granny Smith apple,
  thinly sliced
3 medium zucchini, coarsely
  shredded

Slice turkey diagonally across grain into ¼-inch-thick strips. Set aside.

Coat a wok or large nonstick skillet with cooking spray; drizzle oil around top of wok, coating sides. Heat at medium-high (375°) until hot. Add cauliflower, and stir-fry 2½ minutes. Add green onions and gingerroot; stir-fry 1½ minutes. Remove from wok.

Add turkey to wok, and stir-fry 3 to 4 minutes or until turkey is no longer pink.

Combine cornstarch and next 5 ingredients; stir well. Add cornstarch mixture to turkey in wok; cook, stirring constantly, until thickened and bubbly. Add cauliflower mixture and apple; cook, stirring constantly, until thoroughly heated. Remove from wok, and keep warm.

Add zucchini to wok, and stir-fry 1½ minutes. Spoon zucchini onto a serving platter; spoon turkey mixture over zucchini. Serve immediately. Yield: 4 servings. Jeanie Duerr

Altus "Wine Capital of Arkansas" Cookbook
Altus Chamber of Commerce
Altus, Arkansas

Per Serving

Calories 281 (20% from Fat)	Carbohydrate 25.1 g	Cholesterol 68 mg
Fat 6.2 g (Saturated Fat 1.6 g)	Protein 31.3 g	Sodium 525 mg

Beef Salad Stir-Fry

Enhanced by a zesty dressing, this Chinese-inspired medley of vegetables and lean beef is sure to be a hit at your house.

¾ pound lean, boneless top round steak
2 tablespoons water
1 tablespoon unsweetened orange juice
1 tablespoon low-sodium soy sauce
2 tablespoons white vinegar
1 tablespoon low-sodium soy sauce
1 tablespoon unsweetened orange juice

2 teaspoons dark sesame oil
¼ teaspoon dried crushed red pepper
1 clove garlic, minced
4 ounces whole wheat spaghetti, uncooked
2 cups chopped fresh broccoli
1 small sweet red pepper, seeded and chopped
4 cups shredded Chinese cabbage
⅓ cup sliced green onions

Trim fat from steak; cut steak into thin strips.

Combine water, 1 tablespoon orange juice, and 1 tablespoon soy sauce in a heavy-duty, zip-top bag. Add steak; seal bag, and shake until steak is well coated. Marinate in refrigerator 1 hour, turning bag once.

Combine vinegar and next 5 ingredients in a small bowl; set aside.

Cook pasta according to package directions, omitting salt and fat. Drain and set aside.

Remove beef strips from marinade, discarding marinade.

Place a large nonstick skillet over medium-high heat until hot. Add beef strips, and stir-fry 2 minutes. Add broccoli and chopped pepper; stir-fry 2 minutes or until beef is browned and vegetables are tender.

Combine beef mixture, cooked pasta, cabbage, and green onions. Pour vinegar mixture over salad; toss lightly. Serve immediately. Yield: 4 servings.

Mary Beth Harja

Simple Elegance
Our Lady of Perpetual Help Women's Guild
Germantown, Tennessee

Per Serving

Calories 272 (22% from Fat)	Carbohydrate 28.0 g	Cholesterol 47 mg
Fat 6.5 g (Saturated Fat 1.7 g)	Protein 25.1 g	Sodium 242 mg

Light Beef Stroganoff

1 pound lean boneless top round steak
Vegetable cooking spray
1 teaspoon reduced-calorie margarine
½ cup chopped onion
1 clove garlic, minced
2 cups sliced fresh mushrooms
3 tablespoons dry red wine
¾ cup canned beef broth, undiluted, and divided
3 tablespoons all-purpose flour, divided
1 (8-ounce) carton low-fat yogurt
½ teaspoon salt
¼ teaspoon pepper
2 tablespoons minced fresh parsley
2 cups cooked egg noodles (cooked without salt or fat)

Trim fat from steak. Slice steak diagonally across grain into 3- x ½-inch strips. Set aside.

Coat a large nonstick skillet with cooking spray; add margarine, and place over medium-high heat until hot. Add onion and garlic; cook 3 minutes, stirring constantly. Add steak and mushrooms; cook until steak is browned and liquid is evaporated, stirring frequently. Add wine and ½ cup beef broth; cover, reduce heat, and simmer 30 minutes or until tender. Combine remaining ¼ cup beef broth and 2 tablespoons flour; stir well. Add flour mixture to beef mixture, stirring well. Cook over medium heat until thickened and bubbly. Remove from heat.

Combine remaining 1 tablespoon flour and yogurt; stir well. Stir yogurt mixture, salt, and pepper into beef mixture. Combine parsley and noodles; toss gently. Spoon noodles onto a serving platter; top with beef mixture. Yield: 4 servings.   Debra Conklin

Celebrated South Carolinians!
American Cancer Society
Columbia, South Carolina

Per Serving

Calories 361 (19% from Fat)	Carbohydrate 33.4 g	Cholesterol 103 mg
Fat 7.6 g (Saturated Fat 2.7 g)	Protein 36.2 g	Sodium 710 mg

Veal with Snow Peas

Splash this stir-fry combo with a little extra low-sodium soy sauce for a bolder flavor.

1 tablespoon low-sodium soy
  sauce
2 teaspoons dry sherry
2 teaspoons cornstarch
1 pound veal cutlets, cut into
  ½-inch strips
1 pound fresh snow pea pods
1 tablespoon corn oil
2 cloves garlic, minced
1 teaspoon peeled, minced
  gingerroot
1½ cups sliced fresh
  mushrooms

2 green onions, sliced into
  ½-inch pieces
½ cup fresh bean sprouts
½ cup canned low-sodium
  chicken broth, undiluted
¼ teaspoon sugar
¼ teaspoon salt
2 teaspoons cornstarch
1 tablespoon dry sherry
4 cups cooked long-grain rice
  (cooked without salt or fat)

Combine first 3 ingredients in a small bowl; stir until smooth.

Place veal in a large heavy-duty, zip-top plastic bag. Pour soy sauce mixture over veal. Seal bag securely. Marinate in refrigerator 30 minutes, turning occasionally.

Wash snow peas; trim ends, and remove strings. Set aside.

Remove veal from marinade, discarding marinade.

Drizzle oil around top of wok, coating sides. Heat at medium-high (375°) until hot. Add veal, and stir-fry 3 minutes or until lightly browned. Remove from wok, and set aside.

Add garlic and ginger to wok; stir-fry 30 seconds. Add snow peas; stir-fry 2 minutes. Add mushrooms, green onions, and bean sprouts; stir-fry 2 minutes. Add chicken broth; bring to a boil. Return veal to wok; stir-fry 1 minute. Combine sugar and next 3 ingredients; mix well. Add sugar mixture to veal; stir-fry 1 minute or until thickened. Serve over rice. Yield: 4 servings.

The William & Mary Cookbook
College of William and Mary, Alumni Society
Williamsburg, Virginia

Per Serving		
Calories 457 (15% from Fat)	Carbohydrate 61.8 g	Cholesterol 94 mg
Fat 7.5 g (Saturated Fat 1.5 g)	Protein 31.8 g	Sodium 360 mg

Oven-Fried Pork Chops

Now here's an easy dish. Just dip the pork chops in an egg white mixture, dredge them in seasoned breadcrumbs, and relax while they bake.

4 (6-ounce) lean center-cut loin pork chops
1 egg white
2 tablespoons unsweetened pineapple juice
1 tablespoon low-sodium soy sauce
¼ teaspoon ground ginger
¼ teaspoon paprika
⅛ teaspoon garlic powder
⅓ cup Italian-seasoned breadcrumbs
Vegetable cooking spray

Trim fat from pork chops. Combine egg white and next 5 ingredients in a shallow bowl, and whisk gently. Dip pork chops in egg mixture, and dredge in breadcrumbs.

Place chops on a rack in a roasting pan coated with cooking spray. Bake at 350° for 25 minutes; turn and bake 25 additional minutes or until pork chops are done. Yield: 4 servings.   Libby Siskron

Traditions
First United Methodist Church/United Methodist Women
Tallassee, Alabama

Per Serving

Calories 351 (33% from Fat)   Carbohydrate 14.7 g   Cholesterol 107 mg
Fat 12.8 g (Saturated Fat 4.4 g)   Protein 41.1 g   Sodium 705 mg

Pork Chops with Apples

Rome apples, in season from November through May, are preferred for this recipe because they hold their shape well when cooked.

Vegetable cooking spray
4 (4-ounce) lean, boned
   center-cut loin pork chops
   (¼ inch thick)
1 cup chopped onion
⅔ cup water

1 teaspoon chicken-flavored
   bouillon granules
½ teaspoon ground cinnamon
¼ teaspoon pepper
3 medium Rome apples,
   peeled and sliced

Coat a large nonstick skillet with cooking spray; place over medium-high heat until hot. Add pork chops and onion. Cook chops 6 minutes on each side or until browned.

Combine water, bouillon granules, cinnamon, and pepper; stir well. Add to pork mixture, and bring to a boil. Cover, reduce heat, and simmer 20 to 25 minutes. Add apple slices; cover and simmer 15 additional minutes or until apple is tender. Serve immediately. Yield: 4 servings.

By Special Request, Our Favorite Recipes
Piggly Wiggly Carolina Employees
Charleston, South Carolina

Per Serving

Calories 256 (32% from Fat)	Carbohydrate 19.7 g	Cholesterol 68 mg
Fat 9.2 g (Saturated Fat 3.1 g)	Protein 24.1 g	Sodium 278 mg

Roasted Halibut

Olive oil-flavored vegetable
  cooking spray
1 tablespoon olive oil
3 cups thinly sliced onion
1 cup chopped celery
1 cup julienne-sliced carrot
½ cup chopped sweet red
  pepper
½ cup chopped sweet yellow
  pepper
1 cup dry white wine

1 (14½-ounce) can no-salt-
  added whole tomatoes,
  undrained and chopped
½ cup chopped fresh parsley
1 tablespoon brown sugar
1 (4-pound) halibut fillet,
  skinned
½ teaspoon salt
¼ teaspoon pepper
Garnish: fresh parsley sprigs

Coat a large nonstick skillet with cooking spray; add oil. Place over medium-high heat until hot. Add onion and next 4 ingredients; sauté until vegetables are crisp-tender. Add wine and next 3 ingredients; cook 2 minutes.

Pour half of vegetable mixture into a 13- x 9- x 2-inch baking dish coated with cooking spray. Place halibut over vegetable mixture; sprinkle evenly with salt and pepper. Pour remaining vegetable mixture evenly over halibut. Cover and bake at 350° for 55 to 60 minutes or until fish flakes easily when tested with a fork. Garnish, if desired. Yield: 6 servings.

Edith Bloom

A Celebration of Food
Sisterhood Temple Beth David
Westwood, Massachusetts

Per Serving

Calories 344 (20% from Fat)	Carbohydrate 14.9 g	Cholesterol 100 mg
Fat 7.5 g (Saturated Fat 1.0 g)	Protein 46.1 g	Sodium 350 mg

Sea Captain

2½ cups finely chopped onion
2 cups chopped green pepper
2 cloves garlic, chopped
1 tablespoon vegetable oil
2 teaspoons curry powder
½ teaspoon salt
½ teaspoon ground white
   pepper
2 (16-ounce) cans whole
   tomatoes, undrained and
   chopped
1 tablespoon lemon juice

1 teaspoon chopped fresh
   parsley
½ teaspoon ground thyme
1½ teaspoons prepared
   horseradish
¼ teaspoon pepper
4 cups water
1 pound unpeeled medium-size
   fresh shrimp
4 cups cooked long-grain rice
   (cooked without salt or fat)

Cook first 3 ingredients in oil in a Dutch oven over medium-high heat, stirring constantly, until tender. Add curry powder, salt, and white pepper; stir well. Add tomatoes and next 5 ingredients, stirring well. Bring to a boil; reduce heat, and simmer, uncovered, 5 minutes.

Bring water to a boil; add shrimp, and cook 3 to 5 minutes or until shrimp turn pink. Drain well; rinse with cold water. Peel and devein shrimp. Add cooked shrimp to tomato mixture; stir well. Cook over medium heat until thoroughly heated. Place 1 cup rice in each individual serving bowl; spoon shrimp mixture evenly over rice. Yield: 4 servings.

A Southern Collection, Then and Now
The Junior League of Columbus, Georgia

Per Serving		
Calories 452 (12% from Fat)	Carbohydrate 68.3 g	Cholesterol 221 mg
Fat 5.8 g (Saturated Fat 1.1 g)	Protein 31.4 g	Sodium 923 mg

Rotini with Shrimp in Creamy Lemon Sauce

Looking for something elegant, but light to serve guests? Then this is the recipe for you. No one will ever guess the creamy lemon sauce is low fat.

1½ pounds unpeeled medium-size fresh shrimp
8 ounces rotini pasta, uncooked
1 tablespoon margarine
2 tablespoons all-purpose flour
1½ cups skim milk
½ cup dry white wine
1 tablespoon grated lemon rind
1 teaspoon dried dillweed
½ teaspoon salt
⅛ teaspoon pepper
2 cloves garlic, crushed
¼ cup minced green onions
Garnish: lemon wedges

Peel and devein shrimp. Cook pasta according to package directions, omitting salt and fat. Add shrimp during last 3 minutes of cooking time. Drain; cover and set aside.

Melt margarine in a small heavy saucepan over medium heat; add flour. Cook 1 minute, stirring constantly with a wire whisk. Gradually add milk, stirring constantly. Cook, stirring constantly, until mixture is thickened and bubbly. Stir in wine and next 5 ingredients.

Combine pasta mixture and sauce. Sprinkle with green onions. Garnish, if desired. Yield: 4 servings.   Peggy Pressler Fasing

Stephens Remembered, Recollections & Recipes
Stephens College Denver Area Club
Lakewood, Colorado

Per Serving		
Calories 379 (12% from Fat)	Carbohydrate 51.8 g	Cholesterol 107 mg
Fat 5.2 g (Saturated Fat 1.0 g)	Protein 25.1 g	Sodium 483 mg

Nonfat Red and White Soup

Sweet red pepper and potato form the base of this tangy, savory soup.

4 cups water
4 cups peeled, chopped baking
   potato
3 cups chopped sweet red
   pepper
2 cups chopped green pepper
2 cups chopped purple onion
2 (15-ounce) cans tomato sauce
1 cup dry white wine

½ cup chopped fresh cilantro
1 teaspoon ground cumin
1 teaspoon ground cinnamon
½ teaspoon ground red pepper
½ teaspoon salt
¾ cup plus 2 tablespoons plain
   nonfat yogurt
Garnish: fresh cilantro sprigs

Combine first 5 ingredients in a Dutch oven; bring to a boil. Cover, reduce heat, and simmer 30 minutes.

Add tomato sauce and next 6 ingredients; bring to a boil. Cover, reduce heat, and simmer 15 additional minutes.

Position knife blade in food processor bowl; add one-fourth of soup mixture. Process 30 seconds or until smooth. Spoon into a large bowl. Repeat procedure 3 times with remaining soup mixture.

To serve, ladle soup into individual soup bowls, and top each serving with 1 tablespoon yogurt. Garnish, if desired. Yield: 14 (1-cup) servings.

Holly A. Fluty

The Best of Wheeling
The Junior League of Wheeling, West Virginia

Per Serving		
Calories 97 (5% from Fat)	Carbohydrate 18.8 g	Cholesterol 0 mg
Fat 0.5 g (Saturated Fat 0.1 g)	Protein 3.4 g	Sodium 469 mg

Low-Fat Corn and Potato Chowder

Instant potato flakes thicken this low-fat chowder, creating a creamy, rich indulgence.

1½ cups peeled, cubed baking
    potato
¾ cup chopped onion
½ cup chopped celery
½ cup chopped carrot
1 cup water
½ teaspoon salt
½ teaspoon dried parsley
    flakes

1 teaspoon chicken-flavored
    bouillon granules
¼ teaspoon ground white
    pepper
1 (15¼-ounce) can whole
    kernel corn, undrained
2½ cups 2% low-fat milk
1 cup instant potato flakes

Combine first 6 ingredients in a medium saucepan. Bring to a boil; reduce heat, and simmer, uncovered, 15 minutes or until vegetables are tender, stirring occasionally. Stir in parsley flakes and next 4 ingredients. Cook over low heat until thoroughly heated (do not boil). Stir in potato flakes. Serve immediately. Yield: 5 (1½-cup) servings.

A Slice of Paradise
The Hospital Service League of Naples Community Hospital
Naples, Florida

Per Serving

Calories 237 (21% from Fat)
Fat 5.6 g (Saturated Fat 2.1 g)

Carbohydrate 41.3 g
Protein 8.3 g

Cholesterol 17 mg
Sodium 858 mg

Beef Stew in-a-Pumpkin

Select a medium pumpkin that is no larger than 10 inches in diameter (about 14 to 16 pounds), so that it will fit in a pan and in the oven.

2 pounds boneless top round
  steak, cut into 1-inch
  pieces
2 tablespoons margarine,
  melted
2½ cups chopped tomato
2 cups chopped onion
2 cups chopped green pepper
1 clove garlic, chopped
1 teaspoon sugar
1 teaspoon salt
½ teaspoon pepper
¼ teaspoon garlic powder

8 dried peach halves, coarsely
  chopped
6 small round red potatoes,
  quartered
3 cups cubed sweet potato
2 cups canned beef broth, undiluted
2 (10-ounce) packages frozen
  whole kernel corn
½ cup Madeira
1 medium pumpkin (14 to 16
  pounds)
1 tablespoon margarine, melted

Cook beef in 2 tablespoons melted margarine in a Dutch oven over medium-high heat until browned, stirring frequently. Add tomato and next 7 ingredients. Bring to a boil; cover, reduce heat, and simmer 20 minutes, stirring frequently. Add peaches and next 3 ingredients; bring to a boil. Cover, reduce heat, and simmer 45 minutes or until meat and vegetables are tender. Stir in corn and wine.

Cut off pumpkin top; reserve top. Scrape out and discard membranes, removing and reserving pumpkin seeds for another use. Brush inside of pumpkin with 1 tablespoon melted margarine.

Spoon stew mixture into pumpkin shell; cover with reserved pumpkin top. Place pumpkin in an ungreased 15- x 10- x 1-inch jellyroll pan. Bake on lowest position of oven rack at 325° for 1 hour. To serve, ladle stew into individual bowls. Yield: 10 (1-cup) servings.

Great Recipes from Great Gardeners
The Pennsylvania Horticultural Society
Philadelphia, Pennsylvania

Per Serving

Calories 344 (20% from Fat) Carbohydrate 43.8 g Cholesterol 61 mg
Fat 7.6 g (Saturated Fat 2.1 g) Protein 27.7 g Sodium 656 mg

Black Bean and Roasted Corn Salad

Black beans and corn provide ample protein to make this flavorful salad a main dish. Serve it with crusty French bread to soak up the extra juices, and supper's ready.

4 cups dried black beans
2 quarts water
1½ cups fresh corn cut from cob (about 3 ears)
Vegetable cooking spray
1 cup diced sweet red pepper
1 cup diced purple onion
1 cup diced celery
½ cup low-sodium soy sauce
½ cup balsamic vinegar
1 cup tightly packed fresh cilantro, finely chopped
2 tablespoons finely chopped fresh marjoram

Wash and sort beans. Bring water to a boil in a Dutch oven; add beans. Cover and remove from heat. Let stand 1 hour. Bring to a boil; cover, reduce heat, and simmer 1 hour or until beans are tender. Drain and set aside.

Place corn in a large nonstick skillet coated with cooking spray. Cook over high heat about 5 minutes or until corn is browned, stirring often. Remove from heat, and let cool.

Combine beans, corn, sweet pepper, and remaining ingredients in a large bowl; toss well. Yield: 10 (1-cup) servings.   Mary Lindsey

Flavors of Fredericksburg
St. Barnabas Episcopal Church
Fredericksburg, Texas

Per Serving

Calories 302 (5% from Fat)	Carbohydrate 56.3 g	Cholesterol 0 mg
Fat 1.6 g (Saturated Fat 0.4 g)	Protein 18.0 g	Sodium 332 mg

Creamy Caesar Salad

Toss grilled marinated chicken strips into this salad for an easy one-dish meal.

½ cup nonfat mayonnaise
¼ cup freshly grated Parmesan
   cheese
2 tablespoons fresh lemon
   juice
2 tablespoons water
1 teaspoon Worcestershire
   sauce

1 teaspoon Dijon mustard
½ teaspoon freshly ground
   pepper
¾ teaspoon anchovy paste
½ teaspoon minced garlic
14 cups torn romaine lettuce
2 cups fat-free seasoned
   croutons

Combine first 9 ingredients in a small bowl, stirring with a wire whisk until blended.

Place lettuce and croutons in a large bowl. Pour dressing over lettuce mixture; toss well. Place lettuce mixture on chilled individual salad plates. Yield: 8 (1½-cup) servings.

West of the Rockies
The Junior Service League of Grand Junction, Colorado

Per Serving

Calories 38 (26% from Fat)	Carbohydrate 5.0 g	Cholesterol 2 mg
Fat 1.1 g (Saturated Fat 0.6 g)	Protein 2.0 g	Sodium 345 mg

Red Lettuce Spears

You can substitute orange sections, rind, and juice for tangerines, if necessary, but tangerines offer a wonderful flavor.

½ cup nonfat mayonnaise
¼ teaspoon grated tangerine rind
2 tablespoons fresh tangerine juice
1 clove garlic, crushed
⅛ teaspoon ground white pepper
1 head red leaf lettuce

2 cups frozen Italian green beans, thawed
½ teaspoon olive oil
1 cup julienne-sliced sweet red pepper
2 tablespoons fresh tangerine juice
2 medium tangerines, peeled and sectioned

Combine first 5 ingredients in a small bowl; stir well. Cover and chill at least 1 hour.

Slice lettuce vertically into eighths. Trim core, but keep leaves attached. Rinse and drain; set aside.

Cook beans in boiling water to cover 3 minutes; rinse in cold water to stop the cooking process, and drain. Combine beans and olive oil in a small bowl; set aside.

To serve, arrange lettuce leaves evenly on individual salad plates. Top with beans and pepper strips. Sprinkle each salad evenly with 2 tablespoons tangerine juice. Spoon dressing evenly over each salad. Serve with tangerine wedges. Yield: 8 servings.

Great Recipes from Great Gardeners
The Pennsylvania Horticultural Society
Philadelphia, Pennsylvania

Per Serving

Calories 73 (9% from Fat)	Carbohydrate 16.8 g	Cholesterol 0 mg
Fat 0.7 g (Saturated Fat 0.1 g)	Protein 2.3 g	Sodium 198 mg

Mexican Coleslaw

This side dish makes a perfect accompaniment to chicken fajitas and Spanish rice.

2½ cups shredded cabbage
1 (15-ounce) can black beans, drained
½ cup shredded carrot
½ cup diced purple onion
¼ cup chopped fresh flat-leaf parsley

½ cup plain low-fat yogurt
½ cup salsa
1 tablespoon plus 1 teaspoon reduced-calorie mayonnaise
2 teaspoons red wine vinegar
2 teaspoons fresh lime juice

Combine first 5 ingredients in a large bowl; toss gently. Set cabbage mixture aside.

Combine yogurt, salsa, mayonnaise, vinegar, and lime juice in a small bowl, stirring with a wire whisk until blended. Pour over cabbage mixture; toss gently. Serve immediately, or cover and chill 2 hours. Yield: 5 (1-cup) servings.   Judith Joseph

Timeless Treasures
The Junior Service League of Valdosta, Georgia

Per Serving

Calories 160 (12% from Fat) | Carbohydrate 27.5 g | Cholesterol 3 mg
Fat 2.2 g (Saturated Fat 0.6 g) | Protein 9.8 g | Sodium 354 mg

Curried Chicken Salad

2¼ cups cubed cooked chicken (skinned before cooking and cooked without salt)
2 cups seedless green grapes, halved
¾ cup thinly sliced green onions
¼ cup chopped walnuts, toasted

¼ cup reduced-calorie mayonnaise
¼ cup plain nonfat yogurt
1 teaspoon curry powder
5 green leaf lettuce leaves
¼ cup plus 1 tablespoon mango chutney

Combine first 7 ingredients in a large bowl, tossing well. Cover and chill at least 2 hours.

Spoon 1 cup chicken mixture onto each individual lettuce-lined salad plate. Top each serving with 1 tablespoon mango chutney. Yield: 5 (1-cup) servings.   Shug Lockett

River Road Recipes III: A Healthy Collection
The Junior League of Baton Rouge, Louisiana

Per Serving

Calories 282 (30% from Fat)	Carbohydrate 26.5 g	Cholesterol 62 mg
Fat 9.3 g (Saturated Fat 1.0 g)	Protein 24.3 g	Sodium 187 mg

"Lite" Dill Dressing

This low-fat herb dressing is thick enough to serve as a dip.

½ **cup plain nonfat yogurt**
½ **cup nonfat buttermilk**
2 **tablespoons reduced-calorie mayonnaise**
¼ **cup finely chopped fresh parsley**
¼ **cup finely chopped fresh chives**

1 **teaspoon dried dillweed**
1 **teaspoon sugar**
½ **teaspoon onion powder**
¼ **teaspoon dried basil**
¼ **teaspoon dried savory**
¼ **teaspoon dried marjoram**

Combine first 3 ingredients, stirring until smooth. Add parsley and remaining ingredients, stirring well. Cover and chill at least 2 hours. Serve with salad greens. Yield: 1⅓ cups.

Taste the Good Life
The Assistance League of Omaha, Nebraska

Per Tablespoon

Calories 12 (23% from Fat)	Carbohydrate 1.5 g	Cholesterol 0 mg
Fat 0.3 g (Saturated Fat 0.0 g)	Protein 0.6 g	Sodium 21 mg

White Beans with Tomato and Garlic

1½ cups dried navy beans
6 cups water
1 clove garlic, chopped
1 tablespoon vegetable oil
2 large tomatoes, chopped
¼ cup water
1 tablespoon chopped fresh
   basil
½ teaspoon salt
¼ teaspoon freshly ground
   pepper
1 tablespoon white vinegar
2 tablespoons minced fresh
   parsley
3 tablespoons freshly grated
   Romano cheese

Wash and sort beans. Bring water to a boil in a Dutch oven; add beans. Cover and remove from heat. Let stand 1 hour. Bring to a boil; cover, reduce heat, and simmer 1 hour or until tender. Drain.

Cook garlic in oil in a large skillet over medium heat 30 seconds or until tender. Add tomato, and cook 1 minute. Add ¼ cup water; cover and cook 1 minute. Add beans, basil, and next 3 ingredients. Cook 4 minutes or until thoroughly heated. Sprinkle with parsley and Romano cheese. Yield: 10 (½-cup) servings.   Joyce Villella

St. Catherine of Siena Celebration Cookbook
St. Catherine of Siena Church
DuBois, Pennsylvania

Per Serving

Calories 141 (17% from Fat)   Carbohydrate 22.4 g   Cholesterol 2 mg
Fat 2.6 g (Saturated Fat 0.7 g)   Protein 8.3 g   Sodium 153 mg

Colorful Roasted Potatoes, Italian Style

8 large round red potatoes,
   quartered
3 medium onions, quartered
1 medium-size sweet red
   pepper, cut into 1-inch pieces
1 medium-size sweet yellow
   pepper, cut into 1-inch pieces
Vegetable cooking spray
1 teaspoon salt
¼ teaspoon pepper
1 teaspoon chopped fresh
   oregano
1 teaspoon chopped fresh basil
1 teaspoon chopped fresh
   parsley

Combine first 4 ingredients in a large roasting pan; coat vegetables well with cooking spray. Bake at 400° for 1 hour and 15 minutes or until tender. Sprinkle with salt and remaining ingredients; toss gently. Yield: 9 (1-cup) servings.

We Like It Here
Mukwonago High School
Mukwonago, Wisconsin

Per Serving

Calories 150 (4% from Fat)	Carbohydrate 33.7 g	Cholesterol 0 mg
Fat 0.6 g (Saturated Fat 0.1 g)	Protein 4.1 g	Sodium 272 mg

Vegetable Couscous

1 clove garlic, minced
¾ cup chopped onion
1 tablespoon olive oil
1 large sweet red pepper, cut into thin strips
4 carrots, scraped and cut into very thin strips
2¼ cups canned no-salt-added chicken broth, undiluted, and divided
2 medium-size yellow squash, cut into 1-inch pieces

1 cup golden raisins
½ teaspoon ground cinnamon
¼ teaspoon salt
¼ teaspoon ground white pepper
¼ teaspoon ground black pepper
¼ teaspoon ground turmeric
⅛ teaspoon saffron
1½ cups couscous, uncooked

Cook garlic and onion in olive oil in a large saucepan over medium-high heat 5 minutes or until tender. Add red pepper, carrot, and ¼ cup chicken broth; bring to a boil, reduce heat to medium, and cook 5 minutes. Add squash, and cook 5 minutes. Add remaining 2 cups chicken broth, raisins, and next 6 ingredients. Bring to a boil; slowly stir in couscous. Remove from heat; cover and let stand 10 minutes. Yield: 8 (1-cup) servings.

Claude Barrilleaux

River Road Recipes III: A Healthy Collection
The Junior League of Baton Rouge, Louisiana

Per Serving

Calories 163 (15% from Fat)	Carbohydrate 33.3 g	Cholesterol 0 mg
Fat 2.7 g (Saturated Fat 0.4 g)	Protein 3.9 g	Sodium 128 mg

Vegetable-Quinoa Pilaf

A delicate-flavored, rice-like grain, quinoa is a rich source of vital nutrients like protein. Substitute this tiny, bead-shaped grain for rice in soups, side dishes, salads, main dishes, and even pudding.

1 cup quinoa, uncooked
1¾ cups canned low-sodium chicken broth, undiluted
2 teaspoons olive oil
2 medium leeks, finely chopped
¼ cup chopped sweet red pepper
¼ cup chopped yellow pepper
¾ cup finely chopped carrot

½ cup finely chopped celery
2 teaspoons minced garlic
2 tablespoons freshly grated Parmesan cheese
¼ teaspoon salt
¼ teaspoon freshly ground pepper
¼ cup chopped fresh flat-leaf parsley

Rinse quinoa with cold water according to package directions; drain. Combine quinoa and broth in a medium saucepan; bring to boil. Cover, reduce heat, and simmer 15 minutes or until quinoa is tender and liquid is absorbed.

Heat oil in a medium skillet over medium-high heat. Add leeks and next 4 ingredients. Cook 6 minutes or until vegetables are tender, stirring occasionally. Stir in garlic; cook 1 minute. Combine vegetable mixture and quinoa. Stir in cheese, salt, and pepper. Sprinkle with parsley. Yield: 6 (½-cup) servings.

Taste Without Waist
The Service League of Hickory, North Carolina

Per Serving

Calories 167 (24% from Fat)	Carbohydrate 27.1 g	Cholesterol 2 mg
Fat 4.4 g (Saturated Fat 0.8 g)	Protein 6.1 g	Sodium 196 mg

No-Fat Crème Anglaise

Serve this creamy sauce warm over low-fat pound cake, angel food cake, or fresh fruit for a sweet finish.

2 cups skim milk
¼ cup sugar
3 tablespoons cornstarch

¼ cup frozen egg substitute, thawed
1 teaspoon vanilla extract

Combine first 4 ingredients in a small saucepan. Cook over medium heat, stirring constantly, until thickened and bubbly. Stir in vanilla. Serve warm. Yield: 2⅓ cups.

West of the Rockies
The Junior Service League of Grand Junction, Colorado

Per Tablespoon		
Calories 12 (0% from Fat)	Carbohydrate 2.7 g	Cholesterol 0 mg
Fat 0.0 g (Saturated Fat 0.3 g)	Protein 0.6 g	Sodium 9 mg

Low-Fat Chocolate Sauce

¾ cup sugar
⅓ cup unsweetened cocoa
1 tablespoon plus ½ teaspoon cornstarch

¾ cup water
1 tablespoon margarine
1 teaspoon vanilla extract

Combine first 3 ingredients in a medium saucepan, and stir well. Stir in water. Bring mixture to a boil over medium heat, stirring constantly. Reduce heat, and cook, uncovered, 1 minute, stirring constantly. Remove from heat; stir in margarine and vanilla. Serve warm or chilled. Yield: 1 cup.

A Quest for Good Eating
Cape Cod Questers
Yarmouth Port, Massachusetts

Per Tablespoon		
Calories 50 (18% from Fat)	Carbohydrate 11.0 g	Cholesterol 0 mg
Fat 1.0 g (Saturated Fat 0.3 g)	Protein 0.4 g	Sodium 9 mg

Jersey Peach Dreams

Use fresh, ripe peaches for this naturally sweet dessert.

3 fresh ripe peaches
1½ cups skim milk
1 pint vanilla low-fat ice cream
¼ cup orange juice
½ teaspoon vanilla extract
¼ teaspoon almond extract
5 (¼-inch-thick) orange slices

Peel and slice peaches. Combine peaches, milk, ice cream, orange juice, and flavorings in container of an electric blender; cover and process 30 seconds or until smooth, stopping once to scrape down sides. Pour ice cream mixture evenly into chilled glasses. Top each serving with an orange slice, and serve immediately. Yield: 5 (1-cup servings).   Rutgers, State University of New Jersey

A Ukrainian-American Potpourri
St. Stephen Ukrainian Catholic Church
Dover Township, New Jersey

Per Serving

Calories 163 (14% from Fat)	Carbohydrate 31.3 g	Cholesterol 9 mg
Fat 2.5 g (Saturated Fat 1.5 g)	Protein 5.6 g	Sodium 83 mg

Elegant Poached Pears with Raspberries

1 (10-ounce) package frozen
  raspberries, thawed
2 tablespoons honey
6 ripe pears
3 cups water

1 cup sugar
1 (3-inch) stick cinnamon
1 cup fresh raspberries
¼ (1-ounce) square semisweet
  chocolate, shaved

Combine thawed raspberries and honey in container of an electric blender; cover and process until smooth, stopping once to scrape down sides. Spoon puree into a wire-mesh strainer over a bowl; press with back of spoon against the sides of strainer to extract juice. Discard pulp and seeds remaining in strainer. Cover and chill puree.

Peel and core pears; cut each in half lengthwise. Combine water, sugar, and cinnamon in a large skillet; bring to a boil. Cook, stirring constantly, until sugar dissolves; add pear halves. Reduce heat, and simmer, uncovered, 12 minutes or until tender, turning occasionally. Spoon pear halves and liquid into a 13- x 9- x 2-inch dish; let cool. Cover and chill thoroughly.

To serve, spoon raspberry puree evenly onto 6 individual serving plates. Place 2 pear halves, cut side up, on each plate. Fill centers with fresh raspberries, and top with shaved chocolate. Yield: 6 servings.

Sensational Seasons: A Taste & Tour of Arkansas
The Junior League of Fort Smith, Arkansas

Per Serving

Calories 290 (3% from Fat)   Carbohydrate 73.7 g   Cholesterol 0 mg
Fat 1.1 g (Saturated Fat 0.2 g)   Protein 1.2 g   Sodium 1 mg

Low-Fat Mocha Cake

Place a doily on top of this cake before sprinkling it with the powdered sugar mixture to create a whimsical design.

Vegetable cooking spray
1 cup all-purpose flour
⅓ cup plus 2 tablespoons
   unsweetened cocoa, divided
1 teaspoon instant espresso
   coffee granules
1 teaspoon baking powder
1 teaspoon baking soda

6 large egg whites
1⅓ cups firmly packed brown
   sugar
1 cup coffee-flavored nonfat
   yogurt
1 teaspoon vanilla extract
1 tablespoon powdered sugar
½ teaspoon ground cinnamon

Line a 9-inch round cakepan with wax paper; coat with cooking spray, and set aside.

Combine flour, ⅓ cup plus 1 tablespoon cocoa, espresso granules, baking powder, and baking soda; set aside.

Beat egg whites and next 3 ingredients at medium speed of an electric mixer 2 minutes or until blended. Gradually add flour mixture; beat at medium speed 2 minutes.

Pour batter into prepared pan. Bake at 350° for 35 minutes or until a wooden pick inserted in center comes out clean. Cool in pan on a wire rack 15 minutes; remove from pan, and let cool completely on wire rack.

Combine remaining 1 tablespoon cocoa, powdered sugar, and cinnamon, and sprinkle mixture evenly over cake before serving. Yield: 8 servings.

Linda Zehnder

Flavors of Fredericksburg
St. Barnabas Episcopal Church
Fredericksburg, Texas

Per Serving

Calories 247 (3% from Fat)	Carbohydrate 53.5 g	Cholesterol 1 mg
Fat 0.8 g (Saturated Fat 0.4 g)	Protein 5.6 g	Sodium 231 mg

Heart-Healthy Chocolate Cupcakes

1½ cups all-purpose flour
1 teaspoon baking soda
½ teaspoon salt
½ cup sugar
¼ cup unsweetened cocoa
½ cup unsweetened orange
  juice

⅓ cup water
3 tablespoons vegetable oil
1 tablespoon white vinegar
1 teaspoon vanilla extract
1 teaspoon powdered sugar

    Combine first 5 ingredients in a medium bowl; make a well in center of mixture. Combine orange juice and next 4 ingredients; add to dry ingredients, stirring just until dry ingredients are moistened.
    Spoon batter into paper-lined muffin pans, filling two-thirds full. Bake at 375° for 12 to 14 minutes or until a wooden pick inserted in center comes out clean. Remove from pans immediately, and let cool on a wire rack. Sprinkle powdered sugar evenly over cooled cupcakes. Yield: 1 dozen.   Sister Marguerite Charette

Not by Bread Alone
Catholic Committee on Scouting and Camp Fire for the Diocese of
Lake Charles, Louisiana

Per Cupcake

Calories 134 (26% from Fat)	Carbohydrate 22.6 g	Cholesterol 0 mg
Fat 3.8 g (Saturated Fat 0.8 g)	Protein 2.2 g	Sodium 204 mg

Guilt-Free Cheesecake

About 14 graham cracker squares, finely crushed, yield 1 cup crumbs for this crust. Butter adds flavor to this crust, and, incredibly, the cheesecake remains "guilt free."

1 cup graham cracker crumbs
3 tablespoons sugar
3 tablespoons butter, melted
2 (8-ounce) packages nonfat
  cream cheese, softened
½ cup sugar
1½ tablespoons all-purpose
  flour

½ cup frozen egg substitute,
  thawed
½ cup low-fat sour cream
1½ teaspoons vanilla extract
1 (20-ounce) can lite cherry pie
  filling

Combine first 3 ingredients in a small bowl, stirring well. Press mixture evenly in bottom and up sides of a 9-inch pieplate. Bake at 300° for 5 minutes.

Beat cream cheese at medium speed of an electric mixer until creamy; gradually add ½ cup sugar and flour, beating well. Add egg substitute; mix well. Stir in sour cream and vanilla.

Pour mixture into crust; bake at 300° for 40 minutes or until set, shielding crust with aluminum foil, if necessary. Remove cheesecake from oven, and let cool on a wire rack. Cover and chill 8 hours. Top with cherry pie filling. Yield: 8 servings.   Ronda Krasowski

The Feast
St. Mary's Catholic Community
Caldwell, Idaho

Per Serving

Calories 261 (25% from Fat)	Carbohydrate 37.2 g	Cholesterol 27 mg
Fat 7.3 g (Saturated Fat 4.0 g)	Protein 11.3 g	Sodium 485 mg

Happy Gingerbread Cookies

Just a little shortening gives these cookies the flavor of a richer tasting gingerbread cookie. And yet, the calories and fat are still very low.

¼ cup shortening
1 large egg, lightly beaten
½ cup molasses
1 tablespoon white vinegar
¼ cup skim milk
2½ cups all-purpose flour
¾ teaspoon baking soda
¼ teaspoon salt
1 teaspoon ground ginger
½ teaspoon ground cinnamon
½ teaspoon ground cloves
1 teaspoon all-purpose flour, divided

Vegetable cooking spray
2 cups sifted powdered sugar
1 tablespoon margarine, softened
2 tablespoons skim milk
¼ teaspoon lemon extract (optional)
5 drops of yellow liquid food coloring (optional)
¼ cup raisins, chopped

Beat shortening at medium speed of an electric mixer until fluffy. Add egg and next 3 ingredients; beat well.

Combine 2½ cups flour and next 5 ingredients. Gradually add to shortening mixture, mixing well. Shape into a ball; cover and chill at least 2 hours.

Sprinkle ½ teaspoon flour evenly over work surface. Divide dough in half. Roll 1 half of dough to ⅛-inch thickness on floured surface; cut with a 3-inch round cookie cutter. Place on a cookie sheet coated with cooking spray. Repeat procedure with remaining ½ teaspoon flour and dough. Bake at 375° for 8 to 10 minutes or until lightly browned. Remove from cookie sheets, and let cool on wire racks.

Combine sugar and margarine; beat at medium speed until blended. Gradually add milk; beat until smooth. If desired, stir in extract and food coloring. Spread cookies with frosting; decorate with raisins to form smiling faces. Yield: 24 cookies.   Susan Hagins White

Ribbon Winning Recipes
South Carolina State Fair
Columbia, South Carolina

Per Cookie

Calories 134 (18% from Fat)	Carbohydrate 26.1 g	Cholesterol 9 mg
Fat 2.7 g (Saturated Fat 0.3 g)	Protein 1.8 g	Sodium 77 mg

Lo-Cal Version of Spanish Flan

Flan is a Spanish baked custard with a caramelized sugar glaze. This one's topped with fresh strawberry halves, but any fruit adds flair.

½ cup sugar, divided
½ cup skim milk
1 (12-ounce) can evaporated
  skimmed milk
¾ cup frozen egg substitute,
  thawed

⅛ teaspoon salt
½ teaspoon almond extract
2 cups fresh strawberry halves

Place ¼ cup sugar in a medium saucepan. Cook over medium heat, stirring constantly, until sugar melts and turns light brown. Pour evenly into six 6-ounce custard cups, tilting to coat bottoms of cups.

Combine milks in a medium saucepan. Cook over medium heat, stirring constantly, until thoroughly heated.

Combine egg substitute, remaining ¼ cup sugar, salt, and almond extract in a medium bowl. Beat at medium speed of an electric mixer until blended. Gradually stir 1 cup hot milk into egg substitute mixture; add to remaining hot milk, stirring constantly. Pour evenly into prepared custard cups.

Place custard cups in a 13- x 9- x 2-inch baking pan; pour hot water into pan to depth of 1 inch. Bake at 325° for 50 to 55 minutes or until a knife inserted in center comes out clean. Remove cups from water, and let cool on a wire rack.

Cover and chill at least 4 hours. Loosen edges of custards with a knife; invert onto individual serving plates. Top evenly with fresh strawberry halves. Yield: 6 servings.   Ann Van Cott

Historic Spanish Point: Cooking Then and Now
Gulf Coast Heritage Association
Osprey, Florida

Per Serving

Calories 144 (2% from Fat)   Carbohydrate 27.4 g   Cholesterol 3 mg
Fat 0.3 g (Saturated Fat 0.1 g)   Protein 8.2 g   Sodium 170 mg

Quick & Easy Recipes

Chicken Piccata, page 58

Parson's Piña Colada

The refreshing tropical flavors of this nonalcoholic piña colada are enhanced by the vanilla ice cream.

½ cup pineapple juice
¼ cup cream of coconut

2 cups vanilla ice cream

   Combine all ingredients in container of an electric blender; cover and process until smooth, stopping once to scrape down sides. Serve immediately. Yield: 2¾ cups.   Camille Mele

Watt's Cooking
Oasis Southern Company Services
Atlanta, Georgia

Peanut Butter-Banana Milk Shake

For a shake with fewer calories, substitute skim milk for regular milk, ice milk or frozen yogurt for ice cream, and reduced-fat peanut butter spread for the peanut butter.

¾ cup milk
2 cups vanilla ice cream
1 small banana, cut into 1-inch
  pieces

1 tablespoon creamy peanut
  butter

   Combine all ingredients in container of an electric blender; cover and process until smooth, stopping once to scrape down sides. Serve immediately. Yield: 3 cups.   Sarah Sampson

Angel Food
St. Vincent de Paul School
Salt Lake City, Utah

Lime Sherbet and Mint Punch

There's a subtle mint flavor in this punch. If you're a fan of fresh mint, toss a few more leaves into the sugar mixture. For the limeade, we diluted a can of frozen limeade concentrate.

1 cup water
½ cup sugar
4 fresh mint leaves, coarsely chopped

2 cups limeade
1 quart lime sherbet, softened
Garnish: fresh mint sprigs

Combine first 3 ingredients in a small saucepan. Bring to a boil; reduce heat, and simmer, uncovered, 10 minutes. Remove and discard mint leaves. Cover and chill.

Combine sugar mixture and limeade in a medium bowl; stir well. Add sherbet, and mix well. Serve immediately. Garnish, if desired. Yield: 6 cups.
Margo Davis

Recipes from a New England Green
Middlebury Congregational Church
Middlebury, Connecticut

Fresh Fruit Dip

This dip is so thick and creamy it can double as a yummy spread for quick breads. If you prefer a thinner dip, add a little of the juice from the crushed pineapple.

1 (8-ounce) package cream cheese, softened
1 (7-ounce) jar marshmallow cream
½ cup canned crushed pineapple, drained

1 teaspoon grated orange rind
½ teaspoon Triple Sec or other orange-flavored liqueur
⅛ teaspoon ground ginger

Combine all ingredients in a small bowl; stir well. Cover and chill. Serve with fresh fruit. Yield: 2 cups.

Virginia Fare
The Junior League of Richmond, Virginia

Crunchy Grecian Dip

1 cup crumbled feta cheese
1 (8-ounce) carton sour cream
½ cup chopped pecans or
   walnuts, toasted

⅓ cup milk
¼ cup raisins
¼ teaspoon ground allspice

Combine all ingredients in a small bowl; stir well. Serve with apple slices. Yield: 1½ cups.   Shelly Louden

Recipes & Remembrances
Hospice at Grady Memorial Hospital
Delaware, Ohio

Guacamole

Seed the fresh jalapeño pepper before chopping it to cut down on the fiery flavor of the guacamole.

1 cup chopped tomato
3 ripe avocados, peeled and
   mashed
¼ cup chopped onion

1 jalapeño pepper, chopped
1 tablespoon lemon juice
1 teaspoon salt

Reserve 1 tablespoon chopped tomato for garnish; place remaining chopped tomato in a medium bowl. Add avocado and next 4 ingredients; stir well. Sprinkle with reserved tomato. Serve with tortilla chips. Yield: 4 cups.   Kay Bauer

Angel Food
St. Vincent de Paul School
Salt Lake City, Utah

Stuffed Mushrooms

For a flavor-teaser, substitute ground turkey sausage or mild or hot Italian sausage for the pork sausage.

36 fresh mushroom caps
1 pound ground pork sausage

1 (8-ounce) package cream
    cheese, softened

Clean mushroom caps with damp paper towels; set aside.

Brown sausage in a large skillet, stirring until it crumbles; drain well. Place sausage in a medium bowl; add cream cheese, and stir well. Spoon sausage mixture evenly into mushroom caps. Place mushrooms on an ungreased baking sheet. Bake, uncovered, at 350° for 10 minutes. Broil 5½ inches from heat (with electric oven door partially opened) 3 minutes or until lightly browned. Serve immediately. Yield: 3 dozen.
                                                Janette Garland

Recipes on Parade
Calloway County Band Boosters
Murray, Kentucky

Hot Chili Peanuts

If you have unsalted dry roasted peanuts in your pantry and prefer to use them instead of salted peanuts, simply add 1 to 2 tablespoons of salt instead of the ½ teaspoon called for in this recipe.

9 cups salted dry roasted
    peanuts (about 2½ pounds)
¼ cup plus 2 tablespoons
    butter or margarine,
    melted

2 tablespoons ground red
    pepper
1 tablespoon plus ½ teaspoon
    chili powder
½ teaspoon salt

Spread peanuts in a single layer in an ungreased 15- x 10- x 1-inch jellyroll pan. Combine butter and next 3 ingredients; stir well. Pour butter mixture over peanuts; toss gently. Bake at 350° for 15 minutes, stirring often. Yield: 9 cups.
                                              Karen Kohut

Tri-State Center for the Arts Celebrity Cookbook
Tri-State Center for the Arts
Pine Plains, New York

Sweet Mustard-Sauced Fish

You can substitute any mild-flavored fish for the orange roughy.

1½ pounds orange roughy
    fillets
½ cup salsa
2 tablespoons mayonnaise

2 tablespoons honey
2 tablespoons prepared
    mustard

Cut fish into 6 portions; place in an ungreased 13- x 9- x 2-inch baking dish. Bake, uncovered, at 450° for 6 to 7 minutes or until fish flakes easily when tested with a fork. Drain well.

Combine salsa and next 3 ingredients; spoon evenly over fish. Bake, uncovered, 2 to 3 additional minutes or until thoroughly heated. Remove fish to individual serving plates; spoon sauce over fish. Yield: 6 servings.

Carol DeLoach

Treasured Gems
Hiddenite Center Family
Hiddenite, North Carolina

Shrimp and Asparagus Stir-Fry

2 pounds unpeeled medium-
    size fresh shrimp
½ pound fresh asparagus
    spears
1 medium onion, thinly sliced

1 tablespoon butter or
    margarine, melted
2 tablespoons soy sauce
¼ cup sesame seeds, toasted

Peel shrimp, and devein, if desired. Set aside.

Snap off tough ends of asparagus. Remove scales from stalks with a vegetable peeler, if desired. Cut into 1½-inch pieces. Set aside.

Cook onion in butter in a large skillet over medium-high heat, stirring constantly, until onion is tender. Add shrimp, asparagus, and soy sauce; cook, stirring constantly, 1 to 2 minutes or until shrimp turn pink. Remove mixture to a serving platter, and sprinkle with sesame seeds. Yield: 4 servings.

Beth Hedrick

Tempting Southern Treasures Cookbook
Riverchase Women's Club
Hoover, Alabama

Grilled Rib-Eye Steak with Crispy Gorgonzola Crust and Grilled Scallions

Kosher salt is coarsely grained. Some food lovers prefer its texture and flavor. You can prepare this recipe without kosher salt by substituting ³/₄ teaspoon regular salt per teaspoon of kosher salt.

1 tablespoon minced garlic
1 tablespoon minced shallot
1 tablespoon olive oil
1 teaspoon kosher salt
¼ teaspoon ground white
   pepper
4 (8-ounce) rib-eye steaks

8 ounces Gorgonzola cheese
¼ cup fine, dry breadcrumbs
8 large green onions
1 tablespoon olive oil
½ teaspoon kosher salt
¼ teaspoon ground white
   pepper

Combine first 5 ingredients; stir well. Brush mixture evenly over both sides of steaks. Cook, covered with grill lid, over medium-hot coals (350° to 400°) 6 to 8 minutes on each side or to desired degree of doneness.

Remove steaks from grill, and place on a rack in a broiler pan. Crumble cheese evenly over steaks; sprinkle breadcrumbs evenly over cheese. Place green onions around steaks on rack. Combine olive oil, ½ teaspoon kosher salt, and ¼ teaspoon white pepper; brush over green onions. Broil 5½ inches from heat (with electric oven door partially opened) 3 minutes or until cheese is lightly browned and green onions are heated. Yield: 4 servings. Charles Bistro

Cooking in the Litchfield Hills
The Pratt Center
New Milford, Connecticut

Beef and Bean Enchiladas

The corn tortillas in this recipe are softened by lightly frying them in oil. If you'd prefer to soften them in water, bring water to a simmer in a medium skillet. Dip tortillas in water, one at a time, 1 to 2 seconds on each side or just until softened.

1½ pounds ground chuck
1 medium onion, chopped
1 (16-ounce) can refried beans
1 teaspoon salt
⅛ teaspoon garlic powder
3 (10-ounce) cans enchilada
   sauce

Vegetable oil
12 (6-inch) corn tortillas
3 cups (12 ounces) shredded
   Cheddar cheese, divided

Brown ground chuck and onion in a large skillet, stirring until meat crumbles; drain. Return meat mixture to skillet. Add beans, salt, and garlic powder; cook over medium heat, stirring constantly, until thoroughly heated. Set aside.

Place enchilada sauce in a medium saucepan. Cook over medium heat until thoroughly heated. Pour 1 cup sauce into a lightly greased 13- x 9- x 2-inch baking dish; set dish and remaining sauce aside.

Pour vegetable oil to depth of ½ inch into a large heavy skillet. Fry tortillas, 1 at a time, in hot oil over medium heat 3 to 5 seconds on each side or just until softened. Brush tortillas lightly on each side with 1 cup sauce. Spoon ⅓ cup bean mixture down center of each tortilla; sprinkle each with 1 tablespoon cheese. Roll up tortillas; place, seam side down, in prepared dish. Pour remaining sauce evenly over tortillas; sprinkle with remaining cheese. Bake at 350° for 15 minutes or until cheese melts and enchiladas are thoroughly heated. Yield: 6 servings.

Dorothy Harrison

Recipes on Parade
Calloway County Band Boosters
Murray, Kentucky

Mexican Hot Dish

1 pound ground beef
1 small onion, chopped
2 cups elbow macaroni,
   uncooked
1 (15-ounce) can kidney beans,
   undrained
1 (11-ounce) can whole kernel
   corn, undrained
1 (8-ounce) can tomato sauce
2 cups water
2 teaspoons chili powder
½ teaspoon salt

Brown ground beef and onion in a large skillet, stirring until meat crumbles; drain. Add macaroni and remaining ingredients; bring to a boil. Cover, reduce heat, and simmer 18 minutes, stirring occasionally. Yield: 10 servings.   Arletta Wanstedt Lynch

Heavenly Recipes
Rosebud WELCA, Lemmon Rural Lutheran Parish
Lemmon, South Dakota

Cheesy Cheeseburgers

Flavorful pockets of Monterey Jack cheese and ripe olives are nestled in these hearty burgers.

1½ cups (6 ounces) shredded
   Monterey Jack cheese
¼ cup plus 2 tablespoons
   chopped ripe olives
⅛ teaspoon hot sauce
1¾ pounds ground chuck
¼ cup chopped onion
1 teaspoon salt
½ teaspoon pepper

Combine first 3 ingredients; stir well. Shape cheese mixture into 6 balls. Set aside.

Combine ground chuck and next 3 ingredients in a large bowl; stir well, and shape into 12 patties.

Place a cheese ball in center of 6 patties; flatten cheese balls slightly. Top with remaining patties, pressing edges to seal. Cook, covered with grill lid, over medium-hot coals (350° to 400°) 5 to 6 minutes on each side or until done. Yield: 6 servings.   Mark J. Religa

Essence of Kansas: 4-H Cookbook, Taste Two
Kansas 4-H Foundation
Manhattan, Kansas

Pork Tenderloin with Orange Marmalade

Low-sugar marmalade plays an important role in this recipe. The low-sugar content helps keep the glaze from burning.

1 tablespoon plus 1½ teaspoons coarse-grained mustard
1 clove garlic, minced
¼ teaspoon chopped fresh rosemary
⅛ teaspoon freshly ground pepper
2 (8-ounce) pork tenderloins
¼ cup low-sugar orange marmalade, divided
½ cup water
¼ cup chicken broth

Combine first 4 ingredients in a small bowl; stir well, and set aside.

Slice tenderloins lengthwise to, but not through, the center, leaving one long side connected.

Spread mustard mixture evenly into opening of each tenderloin. Fold top sides over mustard mixture, and tie securely with string at 2-inch intervals. Place tenderloins, seam side down, on a lightly greased rack in a roasting pan. Brush each with 1 tablespoon marmalade. Add water to pan. Bake, uncovered, at 400° for 35 minutes or until meat thermometer inserted in thickest part of tenderloins registers 160° (medium).

Combine remaining 2 tablespoons marmalade and chicken broth in a small saucepan. Bring to a boil; reduce heat, and simmer, uncovered, 2 to 3 minutes or until thickened.

To serve, slice tenderloins, and arrange on a serving platter. Spoon marmalade mixture over slices. Yield: 4 servings.   Linda Bullock

Our Favorite Recipes, Seasoned with Love
Neighborhood Bible Studies
Houston, Texas

Fruited Pork Chops

You can save on calories by using a fat-free dressing.

4 (½-inch-thick) bone-in pork
   loin chops, trimmed
1 (8¼-ounce) can pineapple
   chunks, drained

1 cup pitted prunes
½ cup dried apricot halves
½ cup commercial spicy sweet
   French dressing

Brown pork chops in a large nonstick skillet over medium-high heat. Place pineapple, prunes, and apricots over pork chops. Pour dressing over fruit. Bring to a boil; cover, reduce heat, and simmer 20 minutes or until pork chops are done. Yield: 4 servings.　　　Sandra Dierks

Fabulous Foods
Children's Miracle Network, St. John's Hospital and
Southern Illinois University School of Medicine
Springfield, Illinois

Grilled Lamb Chops

¼ cup butter or margarine,
   softened
1½ tablespoons lemon juice
1 teaspoon paprika
1 teaspoon minced green
   onion

½ teaspoon minced garlic
¼ teaspoon salt
⅛ teaspoon pepper
4 (4-ounce) lamb chops

Combine first 7 ingredients in a small bowl; rub butter mixture on both sides of lamb chops. Cook, covered with grill lid, over medium coals (300° to 350°) 5 minutes on each side or to desired degree of doneness. Yield: 2 servings.　　　Stacey E. Pickering

Saints Alive!
The Ladies' Guild of St. Barnabas Anglican Church
Atlanta, Georgia

Chicken Cutlets with Artichoke Cream Sauce

The marinade from the artichoke hearts gives this cream sauce its rich flavor.

4 skinned and boned chicken breast halves
¼ cup plus 1 tablespoon all-purpose flour, divided
¼ cup butter or margarine, divided
1 (6-ounce) jar marinated quartered artichoke hearts, undrained
1 cup milk

Place chicken between two sheets of heavy-duty plastic wrap, and flatten to ¼-inch thickness, using a meat mallet or rolling pin. Dredge chicken in 2 tablespoons flour. Melt 2 tablespoons butter in a large skillet over medium heat; add chicken, and cook 5 minutes on each side or until done. Remove chicken to a serving platter; set aside, and keep warm.

Drain artichoke hearts, reserving liquid. Set artichoke hearts and liquid aside.

Melt remaining 2 tablespoons butter in a heavy saucepan over low heat; add remaining 3 tablespoons flour, stirring until smooth. Cook 1 minute, stirring constantly. Gradually add milk and reserved artichoke liquid; cook over medium heat, stirring constantly, until mixture is thickened and bubbly. Stir in artichoke hearts; pour mixture over chicken. Yield: 4 servings.   Mario R. Bucacci

Gaspee Days Cookbook
Gaspee Days Committee
Warwick, Rhode Island

Irish Cream Chicken

4 skinned and boned chicken
  breast halves
½ teaspoon salt
½ teaspoon ground white
  pepper
3 tablespoons butter or
  margarine, melted
2 tablespoons Irish whiskey

1 cup whipping cream
2 tablespoons minced green
  onions
2 teaspoons chopped fresh
  tarragon
Garnishes: lemon slices, fresh
  tarragon sprigs

Place chicken between two sheets of heavy-duty plastic wrap, and flatten to ½-inch thickness, using a meat mallet or rolling pin. Sprinkle with salt and pepper. Cook chicken in butter in a large skillet over medium-high heat 5 to 7 minutes on each side or until done. Remove chicken to a serving platter, reserving drippings in skillet. Set chicken aside, and keep warm.

Add whiskey to drippings in skillet; cook over high heat, deglazing skillet by scraping particles that cling to bottom. Cook until whiskey is reduced by half. Add whipping cream, green onions, and chopped tarragon; bring to a boil. Cook, stirring constantly, until thickened. Spoon sauce over chicken. Garnish, if desired. Serve immediately. Yield: 4 servings.   Lee McCullough

Candlelight and Wisteria
Lee-Scott Academy
Auburn, Alabama

Chicken Piccata

Using fresh lemon juice will make this chicken recipe extra special.

1 large egg
1 tablespoon lemon juice
⅓ cup all-purpose flour
⅛ teaspoon garlic powder
⅛ teaspoon paprika
4 skinned and boned chicken
   breast halves

¼ cup butter or margarine,
   melted
1½ to 2 teaspoons chicken-
   flavored bouillon granules
½ cup hot water
2 tablespoons lemon juice
Garnish: lemon slices

Combine egg and 1 tablespoon lemon juice in a small bowl; beat well with a wire whisk.

Combine flour, garlic powder, and paprika in a small bowl; stir well. Dip chicken in egg mixture; dredge in flour mixture. Brown chicken in butter in a large skillet over medium-high heat 4 to 5 minutes on each side.

Dissolve bouillon granules in hot water; add bouillon mixture and 2 tablespoons lemon juice to chicken. Bring to a boil; cover, reduce heat, and simmer 20 to 25 minutes or until chicken is done. Garnish, if desired. Yield: 4 servings.

Lori Jean Miller

Gaspee Days Cookbook
Gaspee Days Committee
Warwick, Rhode Island

Macaroni and Cheese Soufflé

This dish doesn't rise like a traditional soufflé, probably because it's so rich with cheese. You'll love it all the same.

1 (8-ounce) package shell
   macaroni
2 large eggs, separated
½ cup milk
½ cup finely chopped
   onions

2 tablespoons minced fresh
   parsley
¼ teaspoon salt
¼ teaspoon pepper
4 cups (16 ounces) shredded
   Cheddar cheese, divided

Cook shell macaroni according to package directions, and drain macaroni well.

Combine pasta, egg yolks, and next 5 ingredients in a large bowl; stir in 2 cups cheese.

Beat egg whites at high speed of an electric mixer until stiff peaks form. Fold egg white into pasta mixture. Spoon into a greased 11- x 7- x 1½-inch baking dish; sprinkle with remaining 2 cups cheese. Bake at 350° for 20 minutes. Yield: 6 servings.

Sheridan School Brown Bag Cookbook
Sheridan School
Houston, Texas

Rosa's Artichoke Pasta

Fresh mint adds an unexpected flavor to this pasta dish. However, if you don't have fresh mint, try basil.

1 (12-ounce) package angel hair pasta
⅓ cup chopped garlic
¼ cup olive oil
2 (6-ounce) jars marinated quartered artichoke hearts, undrained

½ cup grated Parmesan cheese
½ cup grated Romano cheese
½ cup chopped fresh mint

Cook pasta according to package directions; drain well, and place in a large bowl. Set aside, and keep warm.

Cook garlic in olive oil in a large skillet over medium-high heat, stirring constantly, until tender. Add artichoke hearts, and cook until thoroughly heated. Pour artichoke mixture over pasta; add cheeses, and toss well. Sprinkle with mint, and serve immediately. Yield: 8 servings.

Carla Gerami

Tell Me More
The Junior League of Lafayette, Louisiana

Elegant Pimiento Soup

Serve this delicately colored soup as an elegant first course at a special meal.

5 cups chicken broth, divided
2 (7-ounce) jars diced
  pimientos, drained
¼ cup plus 1 tablespoon butter
  or margarine
¼ cup all-purpose flour

3 cups half-and-half
Salt and freshly ground pepper
  to taste
Garnishes: sour cream, fresh
  dill sprigs

Combine 2 cups chicken broth and pimiento in a medium saucepan; bring to a boil. Remove from heat, and let cool slightly. Pour pimiento mixture into container of an electric blender; cover and process until smooth, stopping once to scrape down sides.

Melt butter in a saucepan over low heat. Add flour, stirring until smooth. Cook 1 minute, stirring constantly. Gradually add half-and-half; cook over medium heat, stirring constantly, until mixture is thickened and bubbly. Reduce heat to low; add remaining 3 cups broth, pimiento mixture, and salt and pepper to taste. Cook until heated, stirring occasionally.

To serve, ladle into individual soup bowls. Serve immediately, or cover and chill. Garnish, if desired. Yield: 9 cups.   Toni Kennedy

Simple Elegance
Our Lady of Perpetual Help Women's Guild
Germantown, Tennessee

Fresh Tomato Soup

If you prefer, you can replace the wine in this recipe with an equal amount of no-salt-added chicken broth.

2 cups peeled, diced ripe
  tomato
3 tablespoons butter or
  margarine
2 tablespoons all-purpose flour

1 teaspoon salt
⅛ teaspoon pepper
1 cup half-and-half
¼ teaspoon baking soda
¼ to ½ cup dry white wine

Combine tomato and butter in a large saucepan. Bring to a boil; reduce heat, and simmer, uncovered, 5 minutes. Pour mixture into container of an electric blender; cover and process until smooth, stopping once to scrape down sides. Add flour, salt, and pepper; cover and process until blended.

Return mixture to saucepan; bring to a boil. Reduce heat, and simmer 2 to 3 minutes, stirring constantly. Add half-and-half and soda; cook until slightly thickened, stirring often. Stir in wine, and bring just to a boil. Yield: 3 cups.   Lori Jean Miller

Gaspee Days Cookbook
Gaspee Days Committee
Warwick, Rhode Island

Asparagus, Quick and Easy

1 **tablespoon cornstarch**	2 **pounds fresh asparagus**
¾ **cup chicken broth**	2 **tablespoons olive oil**
2 **tablespoons soy sauce**	¼ **teaspoon salt**
1 **tablespoon water**	⅛ **teaspoon pepper**
1 **clove garlic, minced**	

Combine first 5 ingredients in a small saucepan. Cook over medium heat, stirring constantly, until mixture thickens and boils. Boil 1 minute, stirring constantly. Remove from heat, and set aside.

Snap off tough ends of asparagus. Remove scales from stalks with a vegetable peeler, if desired. Cut asparagus into 1-inch pieces. Cook asparagus in olive oil in a large skillet over medium-high heat, stirring constantly, 6 to 8 minutes or until crisp-tender. Add chicken broth mixture to asparagus; cook, stirring constantly, 1 minute or until thoroughly heated. Stir in salt and pepper. Serve immediately. Yield: 4 servings.   Chris Woolley

Family Favorites
Optimist Clubs of Alabama/Mississippi District
Montgomery, Alabama

Deviled Carrots

Hot sauce and dry mustard add the devilish flavor kick to these quick, easy carrots.

8 large carrots, scraped (about 1 pound)
½ cup butter or margarine, melted
2 tablespoons brown sugar
2 teaspoons dry mustard
2 drops of hot sauce
½ teaspoon salt
Freshly ground pepper to taste

Cut carrots into 3-inch pieces, and quarter. Cook carrot in butter in a large skillet over medium-high heat 5 minutes, stirring constantly. Stir in brown sugar and remaining ingredients; cook 5 minutes or until tender. Serve immediately. Yield: 4 servings.   Debbe Shipman

Feeding Our Flocks
The Shepherd's Fund
Hollis, New Hampshire

Crunchy Celery Casserole

4 cups diced celery
¼ cup butter or margarine, melted and divided
1 (10¾-ounce) can cream of chicken soup, undiluted
1 (8-ounce) can sliced water chestnuts, drained
1 (2-ounce) jar diced pimiento, drained
½ cup soft breadcrumbs
¼ cup sliced almonds

Cook celery in 2 tablespoons butter in a large skillet over medium-high heat, stirring constantly, 2 minutes or until crisp-tender.

Combine celery, soup, water chestnuts, and pimiento; stir well. Spoon into a greased 1½-quart casserole.

Combine breadcrumbs and remaining 2 tablespoons butter. Sprinkle evenly over celery mixture; top with almonds. Bake, uncovered, at 350° for 25 to 30 minutes or until bubbly. Yield: 8 servings.

Pass It On . . . A Treasury of Tastes and Traditions
Delta Delta Delta National Fraternity
Arlington, Texas

Summer Squash and Cherry Tomatoes in Basil Butter

If you have Basil Butter to spare or are inspired to make a double batch, try slathering it on corn on the cob or a baked potato.

1 pound yellow squash, thinly sliced	⅔ cup Basil Butter, divided
8 ounces cherry tomatoes, halved	

Cook squash and tomato in 2 tablespoons Basil Butter in a large skillet over medium-high heat, stirring constantly, 10 minutes or until squash is tender. Serve with remaining Basil Butter. Yield: 6 servings.

Basil Butter

3 cloves garlic, minced	½ cup butter or margarine, softened
1 shallot, minced	
¾ cup tightly packed fresh basil leaves	Freshly ground pepper to taste

Position knife blade in food processor bowl; add all ingredients. Process until smooth, stopping once to scrape down sides. Cover and chill until firm. Yield: ⅔ cup.

Dining by Fireflies: Unexpected Pleasures of the New South
The Junior League of Charlotte, North Carolina

Asparagus and Goat Cheese Salad

1 pound fresh asparagus
2 tablespoons cider vinegar
½ teaspoon salt
¼ teaspoon pepper
¼ cup plus 2 tablespoons
  vegetable oil

1 large head Boston lettuce,
  torn
2 ounces goat cheese

Snap off tough ends of asparagus. Remove scales from stalks with a vegetable peeler, if desired. Cook asparagus in a small amount of boiling water 3 minutes or until crisp-tender. Drain well, and set aside.

Combine vinegar, salt, and pepper in a small bowl; add oil in a thin stream, whisking until blended. Pour dressing over asparagus; toss gently to coat.

To serve, divide lettuce evenly among six individual salad plates. Spoon asparagus evenly over lettuce; crumble cheese evenly over asparagus. Yield: 6 servings.   Pat Miree

New Additions and Old Favorites
Canterbury United Methodist Church
Birmingham, Alabama

Raspberry Salad

If you don't want to buy a package of baby salad greens, use 8 cups of any mixture of torn lettuces.

½ cup olive oil
¼ cup raspberry vinegar
2 tablespoons honey
½ teaspoon pepper
¼ teaspoon salt

1 clove garlic, minced
1 (6½-ounce) package mixed
  baby salad greens
2 cups fresh raspberries

Combine first 6 ingredients in a jar. Cover tightly, and shake vigorously. Pour dressing over lettuce; toss gently to coat. Top with raspberries. Yield: 8 servings.   Joyce Sloop

Silver Selections
Catawba School Alumni
Rock Hill, South Carolina

Easy Cheddar Biscuits

1½ cups all-purpose flour
1 tablespoon baking powder
½ teaspoon salt
1 tablespoon sugar

1 cup (4 ounces) shredded
   sharp Cheddar cheese
⅓ cup shortening
½ cup milk

Position knife blade in food processor bowl; add first 4 ingredients. Pulse 4 or 5 times or until mixture is blended. Add cheese and shortening; pulse 4 or 5 times or until mixture is crumbly. Add milk, and pulse just until mixture forms dough.

Turn dough out onto a lightly floured surface; shape into a ball. Pat to ½-inch thickness. Cut with a 2-inch round biscuit cutter. Place biscuits on an ungreased baking sheet. Bake at 425° for 10 minutes or until golden. Yield: 15 biscuits.   Laura C. Robelen

What's Cooking in Delaware
American Red Cross in Delaware
Wilmington, Delaware

Millstone Farm Maple-Walnut Scones

3½ cups all-purpose flour
1 tablespoon plus 1 teaspoon
   baking powder
1 teaspoon salt
⅔ cup butter or margarine

1 cup chopped walnuts
1 cup milk
⅓ cup maple syrup
Maple syrup

Combine first 3 ingredients in a bowl; stir. Cut in butter with pastry blender until mixture is crumbly. Stir in walnuts. Combine milk and ⅓ cup syrup; add to dry ingredients, stirring just until moistened.

Turn dough out onto a lightly floured surface; knead lightly 5 or 6 times. Divide dough in half. Shape each portion into a ball, and place on ungreased baking sheets. Pat dough to a 2-inch thickness. Cut each round into 6 wedges, using a sharp knife; separate wedges slightly. Brush with maple syrup. Bake at 375° for 20 to 22 minutes or until lightly browned. Serve warm. Yield: 1 dozen.   Avery Larned

Cooking in the Litchfield Hills
The Pratt Center
New Milford, Connecticut

Spinach-Topped French Bread

1 (10-ounce) package frozen
  chopped spinach, thawed
  and well drained
½ teaspoon garlic powder
2 cups (8 ounces) shredded
  Cheddar cheese

2 cups (8 ounces) shredded
  mozzarella cheese
½ cup butter or margarine,
  melted
1 (1-pound) loaf French bread,
  cut in half lengthwise

Combine first 5 ingredients in a large bowl; stir well. Spread mixture evenly on bread halves. Place on an ungreased baking sheet. Bake, uncovered, at 350° for 15 minutes or until cheeses melt. Yield: 8 servings.

Daynese Haynie

Tell Me More
The Junior League of Lafayette, Louisiana

Peach Butter

Peach Butter's great for topping breakfast breads or ice cream. The "butter" in the title refers to its texture; there's no butter in it.

3 cups sliced fresh peaches
  (about 4 large)
¼ cup orange juice
¾ cup sugar

2 tablespoons honey
½ teaspoon grated orange rind
⅛ teaspoon ground allspice

Combine peaches and orange juice in a saucepan; bring to a boil. Cover, reduce heat, and simmer 8 minutes or until tender, stirring occasionally. Place mixture in container of an electric blender or food processor; cover and process until smooth, stopping once to scrape down sides.

Return peach mixture to saucepan; add sugar and remaining ingredients. Bring to a boil; reduce heat, and simmer, uncovered, 25 minutes or until thickened, stirring occasionally. Spoon into jars; cover and store in refrigerator. Serve with pancakes, biscuits, or toast. Yield: 1½ cups.

Sande Knapp

Flavors of Fredericksburg
St. Barnabas Episcopal Church
Fredericksburg, Texas

Bachelor's Chocolate Torte

8 ounces sweet baking
  chocolate, chopped
1 (8-ounce) carton sour cream
2 teaspoons vanilla extract
1 teaspoon instant coffee
  granules

⅛ teaspoon salt
1 (16-ounce) frozen pound
  cake, thawed
¼ cup plus 2 teaspoons
  Cognac, divided

Combine first 5 ingredients in top of a double boiler; bring water to a boil. Reduce heat to low; cook until chocolate melts, stirring often.

Slice cake horizontally into 4 layers. Place bottom layer, cut side up, on a serving platter; drizzle with 1½ teaspoons Cognac. Spread 3 tablespoons chocolate mixture over Cognac. Repeat procedure twice; top with remaining cake layer. Spread remaining chocolate mixture on top and sides of cake. Cover and chill 8 hours. Cut into slices to serve. Yield: 12 servings.   Mrs. W. Brewer Grant

Meals on Wheels Southwest Collection Cookbook
Meals on Wheels
Albuquerque, New Mexico

Rocky Road Clusters

2 cups (12 ounces) semisweet
  chocolate morsels
1 cup miniature marshmallows

½ cup slivered almonds,
  toasted

Place chocolate morsels in top of a double boiler; bring water to a boil. Reduce heat to low; cook until chocolate melts, stirring occasionally. Set aside, and let cool.

Add marshmallows and almonds to chocolate; stir well. Drop by teaspoonfuls onto wax paper. Chill 15 minutes or until firm. Store in an airtight container in the refrigerator. Yield: 3 dozen.

The Roaring Fork
Gloria J. Deschamp Donation Fund
Grand Junction, Colorado

Peppermint Pie

If you can't find peppermint ice cream, substitute mint chocolate chip ice cream.

2 cups (12 ounces) semisweet
    chocolate morsels, divided
¼ cup plus 2 tablespoons
    butter or margarine, divided
2 cups crisp rice cereal
½ cup chopped walnuts,
    toasted

1 quart peppermint ice cream,
    softened
½ cup milk
Crushed peppermint candy

Cook 1 cup chocolate morsels and 2 tablespoons butter in a large saucepan over medium heat until chocolate and butter melt, stirring occasionally. Remove from heat. Stir in cereal and walnuts. Firmly press cereal mixture in bottom and up sides of a greased 9-inch pieplate. Chill until firm.

Spoon softened ice cream into prepared crust. Cover and freeze until firm.

Combine remaining 1 cup chocolate morsels, remaining ¼ cup butter, and milk in a small saucepan. Cook over low heat, stirring constantly, until chocolate and butter melt. Set aside, and let cool.

Let pie stand at room temperature 5 minutes before serving. Drizzle chocolate mixture evenly over pie; sprinkle with candy. Yield: one 9-inch pie.

Donna Jones

Happy Memories and Thankful Hearts:
Traditions Kept and Blessings Shared
St. Christina's Catholic Church
Parker, South Dakota

Appetizers & Beverages

Mike's Christmas Nog, page 84

Roasted Corn and Avocado Dip

For maximum heat from the jalapeños, you can chop the peppers, seeds and all.

1 cup frozen whole kernel corn, thawed	3 tablespoons chopped fresh cilantro
2 teaspoons olive oil	2 tablespoons minced onion
1 ripe avocado, peeled and mashed	2 small canned jalapeño peppers, seeded and diced
1 ripe avocado, peeled and chopped	2 cloves garlic, minced
¾ cup seeded, diced tomato	½ teaspoon salt
3 tablespoons lime juice	¼ teaspoon ground cumin

Combine corn and oil in a shallow pan. Bake at 400° for 15 minutes or until corn is lightly browned, stirring occasionally. Let cool.

Combine corn, mashed avocado, chopped avocado, and remaining ingredients, stirring well. Cover and chill at least 8 hours before serving. Serve with tortilla chips. Yield: 2¾ cups.   Charlie Ward

Pepper Lovers Club Cookbook, Volume I
Pepper Lovers Club of Virginia Beach, Virginia

Spicy Peanut Dip

You can purchase Chinese rice wine and Chinese black vinegar from an Asian market. We found 2 teaspoons Worcestershire sauce to be a good substitute for the black vinegar.

2 cups roasted peanuts, chopped	1½ tablespoons sugar
3 large cloves garlic	3 tablespoons soy sauce
1 (2-inch) piece peeled gingerroot	2 tablespoons Chinese rice wine or sake
¼ cup water	1½ tablespoons Chinese black vinegar
¼ cup dark sesame oil	1 teaspoon hot chili paste

Position knife blade in food processor bowl; add first 3 ingredients. Process 2 minutes, stopping once to scrape down sides. Add water and remaining ingredients. Process until blended. Serve with fresh snow peas, carrot and celery sticks, and sweet red pepper strips. Yield: 2⅓ cups. Paige Gilchrist Blomgren

Stephens Remembered, Recollections & Recipes
Stephens College Denver Area Club
Lakewood, Colorado

Goat Cheese Spread with Fresh Spinach and Basil

Reserve the shapeliest basil leaf for a garnish before chopping what you need.

¼ cup plain low-fat yogurt
8 ounces goat cheese
3 tablespoons olive oil
2 cups tightly packed torn
  fresh spinach

3 tablespoons fresh basil leaves
¼ teaspoon dried crushed red
  pepper

Spoon yogurt onto several layers of heavy-duty paper towels; spread yogurt to ½-inch thickness. Cover with additional paper towels; let stand 5 minutes.

Position knife blade in food processor bowl; scrape yogurt into bowl, using a rubber spatula. Add goat cheese and olive oil; process until smooth, stopping once to scrape down sides. Add spinach, basil, and red pepper; process until spinach is chopped. Spoon mixture into a bowl; cover and chill at least 2 hours. Serve with assorted crackers. Yield: 1½ cups. Janet Kemp

Cooking Up a Storm, Florida Style
Brookwood Guild
St. Petersburg, Florida

Wild Mushroom-Walnut Spread on Garlic Toasts

To substitute dried herbs for fresh, use only one-third the amount.

3 ounces dried wild
   mushrooms
1½ cups hot water
1 cup whipping cream
3 tablespoons Cognac
½ cup minced green onions
2 large cloves garlic, minced
¼ cup olive oil
1 (3-ounce) package cream
   cheese, softened
¾ cup toasted walnuts, minced
1 cup chopped fresh parsley
3 tablespoons chopped fresh
   thyme

3 tablespoons chopped fresh
   chives
2 tablespoons chopped fresh
   tarragon
1½ teaspoons salt
¾ teaspoon freshly ground
   pepper
¼ cup plus 1 tablespoon butter
   or margarine, melted
1 clove garlic, minced
1 French baguette, cut into
   ¼-inch slices

Rinse mushrooms thoroughly with cold water; drain well. Combine mushrooms and hot water in a medium bowl; let stand 2 hours. Drain well. Coarsely chop mushrooms; set aside.

Combine whipping cream and Cognac in a heavy saucepan. Bring almost to a boil; reduce heat, and simmer, uncovered, 20 to 30 minutes or until reduced to ¾ cup, stirring occasionally.

Cook green onions and 2 cloves minced garlic in hot oil in a large skillet over medium-high heat, stirring constantly, until tender. Add mushrooms; cook 5 minutes, stirring constantly. Add whipping cream mixture and cream cheese, stirring until cream cheese melts. Remove from heat; stir in walnuts and next 6 ingredients. Set aside.

Combine melted butter and 1 clove minced garlic. Brush both sides of bread slices with garlic butter; place on an ungreased baking sheet. Bake at 350° for 6 to 8 minutes; turn and bake 5 additional minutes or until golden.

Spread about 1 tablespoon mushroom mixture on each piece of toast. Yield: about 40 appetizers.

Entertaining in Kingwood
Kingwood Women's Club
Kingwood, Texas

June's Cheese Ball

1 (2¼-ounce) jar dried beef, finely chopped
1 (8-ounce) package cream cheese, softened
½ cup chopped ripe olives
½ cup chopped green onions
¼ teaspoon garlic powder
⅛ to ¼ teaspoon hot sauce
¼ cup chopped pecans, toasted

Combine all ingredients except pecans; stir well. Cover and chill at least 1 hour.

Shape cheese mixture into a ball; roll in pecans. Wrap cheese ball in heavy-duty plastic wrap, and chill up to 3 days. Serve with unsalted crackers. Yield: one 4½-inch ball.   Mary Johnson

Cottonwood Cookbook
Cottonwood Elementary School
Fernley, Nevada

Cranberry-Glazed Brie

1 (12-ounce) package fresh cranberries
¾ cup firmly packed brown sugar
⅓ cup currants
⅓ cup water
⅛ teaspoon dry mustard
⅛ teaspoon ground ginger
⅛ teaspoon ground cardamom
⅛ teaspoon ground allspice
⅛ teaspoon ground cloves
1 (35.2-ounce) round Brie
Garnish: fresh fruit

Combine first 9 ingredients in a medium saucepan. Cook over medium heat, stirring constantly, 8 minutes or until cranberry skins pop. Set aside, and let cool.

Remove rind from top of Brie, cutting to within ½ inch of outside edges. Place cheese on a baking sheet; spoon cranberry mixture over top of Brie. Bake at 300° for 20 to 25 minutes or until cheese is softened, but not melted.

Transfer cheese to a serving platter; garnish, if desired. Serve with assorted crackers. Yield: 18 appetizer servings.   Alice Smith

What's Cooking in Delaware
American Red Cross in Delaware
Wilmington, Delaware

Pesto-Cheese Pie

This savory cheesecake promises to be the star attraction at your next party.

Vegetable cooking spray
¼ cup Italian-seasoned breadcrumbs
2 tablespoons grated Parmesan cheese
2 (8-ounce) packages cream cheese, softened
1 cup ricotta cheese
½ cup grated Parmesan cheese
¼ teaspoon salt
⅛ teaspoon ground red pepper
3 large eggs
½ cup pesto sauce
¼ cup pine nuts

Coat an 8-inch springform pan with cooking spray. Combine breadcrumbs and 2 tablespoons Parmesan cheese; sprinkle breadcrumb mixture evenly on bottom and up sides of pan. Set aside.

Beat cream cheese and next 4 ingredients at medium speed of an electric mixer until creamy. Add eggs, one at a time, beating after each addition. Spoon half of cheese mixture into a small bowl; set aside. Stir pesto sauce into remaining cheese mixture; pour into prepared pan. Pour reserved cheese mixture over pesto mixture; sprinkle with pine nuts.

Bake at 325° for 1 hour and 5 minutes or until almost set. Let cool completely in pan on a wire rack. Carefully remove sides of springform pan. Serve at room temperature, or cover and chill thoroughly. Serve with French baguette slices. Yield: 24 appetizer servings.

Great Recipes from Great Gardeners
The Pennsylvania Horticultural Society
Philadelphia, Pennsylvania

Salmon Tart with Parmesan-Dill Crust

1 cup all-purpose flour
1 tablespoon chopped fresh dill
¼ teaspoon salt
⅓ cup shortening
½ cup grated Parmesan cheese
3 to 4 tablespoons cold water
1 (15½-ounce) can red salmon, drained
¾ cup finely chopped onion
1 tablespoon butter or margarine, melted

1 (8-ounce) package cream cheese, softened
3 large eggs
2 tablespoons white wine vinegar
1 tablespoon chopped fresh dill
Garnishes: sour cream, fresh dill sprigs, salmon caviar

Combine first 3 ingredients; cut in shortening with pastry blender until mixture is crumbly. Stir in Parmesan cheese. Sprinkle cold water, 1 tablespoon at a time, evenly over surface; stir with a fork until dry ingredients are moistened. Shape into a ball.

Gently press dough into a 4-inch circle on heavy-duty plastic wrap; cover with additional heavy-duty plastic wrap, and chill 15 minutes. Roll dough, still covered, into an 11-inch circle. Uncover dough, and fit into a 9-inch tart pan with removable bottom. Line pastry shell with aluminum foil; fill with dried beans or pie weights. Bake at 450° for 10 minutes. Carefully remove beans and foil; bake 4 to 5 additional minutes or until lightly browned. Let cool on a wire rack.

Remove and discard skin and bones from salmon, if desired. Cook onion in butter in a small saucepan over medium-high heat, stirring constantly, until tender.

Position knife blade in food processor bowl; add salmon, onion mixture, cream cheese, and next 3 ingredients. Process until smooth, stopping once to scrape down sides.

Pour salmon mixture into prepared pastry shell. Bake at 325° for 30 minutes or until center is almost set. Let cool to room temperature in pan on wire rack; cover and chill at least 4 hours. Garnish, if desired. Yield: 16 appetizer servings.

Marlene Naumann

Good to the Core
The Apple Corps of the Weller Center for Health Education
Easton, Pennsylvania

Shrimp and Gruyère Cheesecake

1¼ cups round buttery cracker crumbs

¼ cup butter or margarine, melted

½ pound unpeeled medium-size fresh shrimp

⅓ cup minced green pepper

⅓ cup minced sweet red pepper

¼ cup minced onion

1 large clove garlic, minced

3 tablespoons butter or margarine, melted

2 (8-ounce) packages cream cheese, softened

½ cup mayonnaise

4 large eggs

⅓ cup milk

1¼ cups (5 ounces) shredded Gruyère or Swiss cheese

1 teaspoon ground white pepper

Garnishes: sweet red pepper strips, fresh cooked shrimp, fresh basil leaves

Italian Tomato Sauce

Combine cracker crumbs and ¼ cup butter. Firmly press crumb mixture on bottom of an ungreased 9-inch springform pan. Set aside.

Peel, devein, and chop shrimp. Cook shrimp, green pepper, and next 3 ingredients in 3 tablespoons butter in a skillet over medium-high heat, stirring constantly, 4 to 5 minutes. Drain well; set aside.

Beat cream cheese and mayonnaise at high speed of an electric mixer until light and fluffy. Add eggs, one at a time, beating after each addition. Gradually add milk, beating at low speed just until blended. Stir in shrimp mixture, Gruyère, and white pepper. Pour into pan.

Bake at 300° for 1 hour or until set. Turn oven off. Partially open oven door, and let cheesecake cool in oven 1 hour. Let cool to room temperature in pan on a wire rack; cover and chill at least 8 hours. Carefully remove sides of springform pan. Garnish, if desired. Serve with Italian Tomato Sauce. Yield: 16 appetizer servings.

Italian Tomato Sauce

¼ cup chopped onion

1 clove garlic, minced

1 tablespoon olive oil

2 (14-ounce) cans whole tomatoes, drained and chopped

1½ teaspoons dried Italian seasoning

1 bay leaf

Cook chopped onion and garlic in hot oil in a medium saucepan over medium-high heat, stirring mixture constantly, until tender. Add tomatoes and remaining ingredients. Bring to a boil; reduce heat, and simmer, uncovered, 20 minutes or until most of liquid evaporates, stirring occasionally. Remove and discard bay leaf. Serve warm. Yield: 1½ cups.

Be Our Guest
Trianon
Baton Rouge, Louisiana

Parmesan Cheese Puffs

If you're running short on time, serve these puffs immediately after the first baking without splitting them and adding the Gruyère cheese.

1 cup water	5 large eggs, divided
⅓ cup butter	1 cup grated Parmesan cheese
1 cup all-purpose flour	1 teaspoon water
1 teaspoon salt	1½ tablespoons sesame seeds
Dash of nutmeg	8 ounces sliced Gruyère cheese
Dash of pepper	

Combine 1 cup water and butter in a medium saucepan; bring to a boil. Combine flour and next 3 ingredients; stir well. Add to butter mixture, all at once, stirring vigorously over medium heat until mixture leaves sides of pan and forms a smooth ball. Remove from heat, and let cool 2 minutes.

Add 4 eggs, one at a time, beating thoroughly with a wooden spoon after each addition; beat until dough is smooth. Add Parmesan cheese; stir until smooth.

Drop dough by rounded teaspoonfuls, 2 inches apart, onto ungreased baking sheets. Combine remaining egg and 1 teaspoon water; beat well. Brush egg mixture on top of dough; sprinkle with sesame seeds.

Bake at 425° for 15 minutes or until golden; place on wire racks. Split each puff in half horizontally; let cool completely.

Cut Gruyère into 1-inch pieces; place 1 piece in each puff. Place on baking sheets; bake at 375° for 8 to 10 additional minutes or until cheese melts. Serve immediately. Yield: 5½ dozen.

The Bountiful Arbor
The Junior League of Ann Arbor, Michigan

Blue Cheese-Walnut Wafers

If you're tempted to substitute margarine for butter in this recipe, don't. The butter makes these wafers wonderfully short and the dough easier to handle. Store the wafers in an airtight container up to one week.

1 (4-ounce) package blue
   cheese, softened
½ cup butter, softened

1¼ cups all-purpose flour
⅛ teaspoon salt
⅓ cup finely chopped walnuts

   Position knife blade in food processor bowl; add first 4 ingredients. Process until blended, stopping once to scrape down sides. (Mixture will be sticky.) Transfer mixture to a bowl; stir in walnuts. Cover and chill 5 minutes. Divide dough in half. Shape each portion of dough into an 8-inch log. Wrap in heavy-duty plastic wrap, and chill 1 hour or until firm.
   Slice dough into ¼-inch slices; place on ungreased baking sheets. Bake at 350° for 12 minutes or until lightly browned. Yield: about 4 dozen.

Judy Bryson

Georgia Hospitality
Georgia Elks Aidmore Auxiliary
Conyers, Georgia

Sunflower Crisps

For easier slicing, use dental floss to cut the dough for these thick crackers.

2 cups (8 ounces) shredded
   Cheddar cheese
½ cup grated Parmesan cheese
½ cup margarine, softened
3 tablespoons water
1 cup all-purpose flour

¼ teaspoon salt
1 cup quick-cooking oats,
   uncooked
⅔ cup roasted salted sunflower
   kernels

   Combine first 4 ingredients in a large mixing bowl. Beat well at medium speed of an electric mixer. Gradually add flour and salt to cheese mixture; mix at low speed until blended. Add oats and sunflower kernels, mixing well. Shape dough into 2 (8-inch) rolls. Cover and chill 3½ to 4 hours.

Slice dough into ¼-inch slices; place on lightly greased baking sheets. Bake at 400° for 12 minutes or until lightly browned. Yield: about 3½ dozen.   Ellen Aronheim

Recipes from a New England Green
Middlebury Congregational Church
Middlebury, Connecticut

Mandarin-Style Meat Dumplings

1 **pound ground pork**
2 **cups finely chopped Chinese cabbage**
1 **cup finely chopped onion**
1 **(4-ounce) can mushroom stems and pieces, drained and chopped**
⅓ **cup canned shrimp, drained and chopped**
2 **tablespoons soy sauce**
2 **teaspoons grated gingerroot**
1 **teaspoon salt**
1 **teaspoon dark sesame oil**
75 **small round wonton wrappers**
½ **cup vegetable oil, divided**
2⅔ **cups water, divided**
2 **tablespoons soy sauce**
2 **tablespoons rice vinegar**

Combine first 9 ingredients in a large bowl, stirring well. Place 1 heaping teaspoon pork mixture in center of wonton wrapper. Moisten edges of wonton wrapper with water; fold in half over filling, and seal edges. Repeat procedure with remaining pork mixture and wonton wrappers.

Heat 2 tablespoons vegetable oil in a large skillet over medium-high heat. Add one-fourth of dumplings, and brown on all sides. Add ⅔ cup water to dumplings in skillet; bring to a boil. Cover, reduce heat, and simmer 10 minutes or until water evaporates. Repeat procedure with remaining vegetable oil, dumplings, and water. Combine 2 tablespoons soy sauce and rice vinegar; serve with dumplings. Yield: 75 dumplings.   Gladys Wilson

300th Anniversary Cookbook
All Hallows' Episcopal Church
Davidsonville, Maryland

President's House Miniature Crab Cakes with Pepper Sauce

This ingredient list may seem long, but we think this coastal favorite is worth it. If you don't have time to make the Pepper Sauce, substitute a commercial pepper sauce.

1 large egg, lightly beaten
1 tablespoon mayonnaise
½ teaspoon paprika
¼ teaspoon salt
¼ teaspoon dry mustard
¼ teaspoon curry powder
⅛ teaspoon ground red pepper
⅛ teaspoon freshly ground black pepper

1 tablespoon hot sauce
1 tablespoon fresh lemon juice
1 teaspoon Worcestershire sauce
1 pound fresh lump crabmeat, drained
⅓ cup fine, dry breadcrumbs
¼ cup corn oil, divided
Pepper Sauce

Combine first 11 ingredients; stir well. Stir in crabmeat and breadcrumbs. Shape mixture into 12 (2-inch) patties; cover and chill at least 30 minutes. Heat 2 tablespoons oil in a large skillet over medium heat; cook half of patties on each side until golden. Drain on paper towels. Repeat procedure with remaining oil and patties.

Arrange crab cakes on plates, and spoon Pepper Sauce over top. Serve immediately. Yield: 6 servings.

Pepper Sauce

½ large sweet red pepper
½ large sweet yellow pepper
½ jalapeño pepper
1 cup cold unsalted butter, divided
½ cup chopped fresh mushrooms
2 shallots, chopped
1 sprig fresh thyme, chopped

¼ cup dry white wine
¼ cup white wine vinegar
½ cup chicken broth
¼ cup whipping cream
1 tablespoon fresh lemon juice
¼ teaspoon freshly ground pepper

Remove and discard seeds and membranes from peppers; place peppers, skin side up, on an aluminum foil-lined baking sheet, and flatten with palm of hand. Broil peppers 5½ inches from heat (with electric oven door partially opened) 15 to 20 minutes or until charred. Place peppers in ice water until cool. Remove peppers from water; peel and discard skins. Chop peppers, and set aside.

Melt 1 tablespoon butter in a large skillet over medium heat. Add mushrooms, shallot, and thyme; cook, stirring constantly, until tender. Stir in wine, vinegar, and broth; cook over medium-high heat until mixture is reduced to ½ cup, stirring occasionally. Add whipping cream; cook over medium-high heat until mixture is reduced to ½ cup, stirring occasionally. Reduce heat; add remaining butter, one tablespoon at a time, stirring constantly with a wire whisk until sauce is thickened and smooth.

Pour sauce through a wire-mesh strainer into a small bowl, discarding mushrooms, shallot, and thyme. Stir in lemon juice, pepper, and chopped peppers. Yield: 1 cup.

The William & Mary Cookbook
College of William and Mary, Alumni Society
Williamsburg, Virginia

Lime-Garlic Shrimp with Mango-Mint Salsa

You'll love this recipe as a main dish as well as an appetizer. Just double the amount of shrimp to serve four for an entrée—the salsa recipe makes plenty.

12 unpeeled jumbo fresh
    shrimp
2 tablespoons fresh lime juice
2 cloves garlic, crushed
1 teaspoon hot chili oil

½ teaspoon salt
¼ teaspoon pepper
Vegetable cooking spray
Mango-Mint Salsa

Peel and devein shrimp; set aside.

Combine lime juice and next 4 ingredients in a medium bowl. Add shrimp, tossing to coat. Cover and chill 45 minutes.

Remove shrimp from marinade, discarding marinade. Coat grill rack with cooking spray; place on grill over medium-hot coals (350° to 400°). Place shrimp on rack, and cook, uncovered, 3 minutes on each side or until shrimp turn pink.

To serve, spoon Mango-Mint Salsa onto the center of six individual serving plates. Arrange 2 shrimp on salsa on each plate. Yield: 6 appetizer servings.

Mango-Mint Salsa

2 cups diced mango (about 2
    large)
¾ cup minced purple onion
2 jalapeño peppers, seeded
    and minced

1 medium-size sweet red
    pepper, seeded and diced
1 tablespoon plus 1 teaspoon
    chopped fresh mint
3 tablespoons fresh lime juice

Combine all ingredients in a medium bowl, and toss well. Yield: 3½ cups.

West of the Rockies
The Junior Service League of Grand Junction, Colorado

Orange-Lemon Rind Tea

The ginger ale adds a little fizz to this tea, so add it just before serving.

2 teaspoons grated lemon rind
2 tablespoons grated orange rind
2 cups water
1 teaspoon loose tea
½ cup sugar

3 tablespoons fresh lemon juice
⅓ cup fresh orange juice
2 cups ginger ale, chilled
Garnishes: lemon and orange slices

Place lemon and orange rind on a 4-inch square of cheesecloth; tie with string, and set aside.

Bring water to a boil in a large saucepan; add tea, sugar, and cheesecloth bag. Remove from heat; cover and steep 10 minutes. Remove and discard cheesecloth bag. Cover and steep tea 2½ hours.

Add lemon and orange juices to tea mixture. Strain and chill.

Stir in ginger ale just before serving. Serve tea over ice. Garnish, if desired. Yield: 4½ cups.

Perfectly Splendid: One Family's Repasts
McFaddin-Ward House
Beaumont, Texas

Pineapple Percolated Punch

To make enough of this punch for a crowd (30 cups), use a party-size coffee maker, and increase each ingredient by 5 times.

3 cups water
3 cups pineapple juice
½ cup firmly packed brown sugar

¼ teaspoon salt (optional)
1 tablespoon whole cloves
1½ teaspoons whole allspice
3 (3-inch) sticks cinnamon

Combine first 4 ingredients in an 8-cup percolator. Place spices in percolator basket. Perk through complete cycle of percolator. Yield: 6 cups.

Debra Dobbins Burleson

Homecoming: Special Foods, Special Memories
Baylor University Alumni Association
Waco, Texas

Albritton Deep-Freeze Daiquiri

It's not necessary to thaw these fruit juice concentrates before using them in the recipe. Just spoon the icy mixture straight from the cans.

1 (12-ounce) can frozen pink lemonade concentrate, undiluted
1 (6-ounce) can frozen limeade concentrate, undiluted

1 (750-milliliter) bottle light rum
5¼ cups water, divided

Combine half each of lemonade and limeade concentrates, rum, and water in container of an electric blender. Cover and process until smooth. Pour mixture into a large freezer container. Repeat procedure with remaining concentrates, rum, and water. Combine mixtures in freezer container; cover and freeze at least 8 hours or up to 1 month.

Remove daiquiri mixture from freezer, and stir well 30 minutes before serving. Stir again just before serving (mixture should be icy). Yield: 11 cups.   Sara Houstoun Lindsey

Houston Junior League Cookbook
The Junior League of Houston, Texas

Mike's Christmas Nog

3 (½-gallon) cartons vanilla ice cream, softened
1 (750-milliliter) bottle brandy
½ (750-milliliter) bottle Kahlúa or other coffee-flavored liqueur (about 1½ cups)

Ground nutmeg

Spoon softened ice cream into a punch bowl; stir with a spoon until ice cream is smooth. Pour brandy and Kahlúa over ice cream. Stir gently just until blended. (Do not overstir; nog will be too foamy.) Sprinkle with nutmeg. Yield: 6 quarts.   Michael F. Platenyk

A Ukrainian-American Potpourri
St. Stephen Ukrainian Catholic Church
Dover Township, New Jersey

Breads

Sour Cream Cinnamon Buns, page 95

Banana-Chocolate Bread

½ cup butter, softened
1 cup sugar
2 large eggs
1½ cups all-purpose flour
2 tablespoons cocoa
1 teaspoon baking soda
1 teaspoon salt
½ teaspoon ground cinnamon
½ cup sour cream
1 teaspoon vanilla extract
1 cup mashed ripe banana
½ cup chopped pecans
⅓ cup semisweet chocolate
  mini-morsels

Beat butter at medium speed of an electric mixer until creamy; gradually add sugar, beating well. Add eggs, one at a time, beating after each addition.

Combine flour and next 4 ingredients; add to butter mixture alternately with sour cream, beginning and ending with flour mixture. Mix at low speed after each addition until blended. Stir in vanilla and remaining ingredients. Pour batter into two greased and floured 7½- x 3- x 2-inch loafpans.

Bake at 350° for 50 to 55 minutes or until a wooden pick inserted in center comes out clean. Cool in pans on wire racks 10 minutes; remove from pans, and let cool completely on wire racks. Yield: 2 loaves.

Jo Ann Everett

A Taste of the Past and Present
First Baptist and Pastor's Sunday School Class
Philadelphia, Tennessee

Orange-Poppy Tea Bread

½ cup butter or margarine,
  softened
¾ cup sugar
2 large eggs
1 (8-ounce) carton sour cream
1 tablespoon poppy seeds
1 tablespoon grated orange
  rind
2 tablespoons fresh orange
  juice
2 cups all-purpose flour
1 teaspoon baking powder
1 teaspoon baking soda
½ teaspoon salt

Beat butter at medium speed of an electric mixer until creamy; gradually add sugar, beating well. Add eggs and next 4 ingredients, beating until blended.

Combine flour and next 3 ingredients in a medium bowl; add to butter mixture. Mix at low speed until blended.

Pour batter into an ungreased 9- x 5- x 3-inch loafpan. Bake at 325° for 1 hour and 5 minutes or until a wooden pick inserted in center comes out clean. Cool in pan on a wire rack 10 minutes. Remove bread from pan, and let cool completely on wire rack. Yield: 1 loaf.

What's Cooking at Allied
Allied Services Nurse Retention and Recruitment Committee
Scranton, Pennsylvania

Strawberry Jam Coffee Cake

1 (8-ounce) package cream
  cheese, softened
½ cup butter, softened
¾ cup sugar
2 large eggs, lightly beaten
¼ cup milk
1 teaspoon vanilla extract
2 cups all-purpose flour
1 teaspoon baking powder
½ teaspoon baking soda
¼ teaspoon salt
1 (18-ounce) jar strawberry
  preserves
1 tablespoon lemon juice
½ cup chopped pecans
¼ cup firmly packed brown
  sugar

Beat cream cheese and butter at medium speed of an electric mixer until creamy; gradually add ¾ cup sugar, beating well. Combine eggs, milk, and vanilla; add to cream cheese mixture. Beat well.

Combine flour and next 3 ingredients; add to cream cheese mixture, mixing at low speed until blended. Spoon half of batter into a greased and floured 13- x 9- x 2-inch pan. Combine strawberry preserves and lemon juice; spread over batter in pan. Dollop remaining batter over strawberry mixture. Combine pecans and brown sugar; sprinkle over batter in pan.

Bake at 350° for 35 minutes or until a wooden pick inserted in center comes out clean. Let cool 15 minutes before serving. Cut into squares to serve. Yield: 15 servings.   Jeannie Lane

With Special Distinction
Mississippi College Cookbook Committee
Clinton, Mississippi

Tropical Coffee Cake

½ cup chopped pecans
½ cup flaked coconut
¼ cup sugar
2 teaspoons grated orange rind
1 teaspoon ground cinnamon
½ cup butter or margarine, softened
1 cup sugar

2 large eggs
1 (8-ounce) carton sour cream
1 teaspoon vanilla extract
2 cups all-purpose flour
1 teaspoon baking soda
1 teaspoon baking powder
⅛ teaspoon salt

Combine first 5 ingredients in a small bowl; set aside.

Beat butter at medium speed of an electric mixer until creamy; gradually add 1 cup sugar, beating well. Add eggs, one at a time, beating after each addition. Stir in sour cream and vanilla.

Combine flour and next 3 ingredients; add to butter mixture. Mix at low speed until blended.

Spoon half of batter into a greased 9-inch round cakepan. Sprinkle with half of pecan mixture. Top with remaining batter, and sprinkle with remaining pecan mixture. Gently swirl batter with a knife to create a marbled effect. Bake at 350° for 35 to 40 minutes or until a wooden pick inserted in center comes out clean. Let cool completely in pan on a wire rack. Cut into wedges to serve. Yield: 8 to 12 servings.

Virginia Fare
The Junior League of Richmond, Virginia

Oatmeal-Walnut Pancakes

1 cup whole wheat flour
1 cup regular oats, uncooked
½ cup plain cornmeal
½ cup unbleached flour
1 tablespoon baking powder
1 teaspoon salt

1 cup finely chopped walnuts
2 large eggs, lightly beaten
2¼ cups milk
¼ cup honey
¼ cup vegetable oil

Combine first 7 ingredients in a large bowl; make a well in center of mixture.

Combine eggs, milk, honey, and oil in a small bowl; add to dry ingredients, stirring mixture just until moistened. Let mixture stand 10 minutes.

Pour ¼ cup batter for each pancake onto a hot, lightly greased griddle or skillet. Cook until tops are covered with bubbles and edges look cooked; turn and cook other side. Yield: 20 (4-inch) pancakes.   Linda Cardone and Ed Metcalfe

Town Hill Playground Cookbook
Town Hill Playground Committee
Whitingham, Vermont

Sage Cornbread

This moist, dense cornbread with its herb appeal makes a tasty base for a hearty dressing.

1 cup all-purpose flour	2 large eggs
¾ cup cornmeal	1 cup buttermilk
1½ teaspoons baking powder	3 tablespoons butter or
½ teaspoon baking soda	margarine, melted
2 tablespoons chopped fresh sage	2 tablespoons honey

Combine first 5 ingredients in a large bowl; make a well in center of mixture. Combine eggs and next 3 ingredients; beat with a wire whisk until blended. Add to dry ingredients, stirring just until blended.

Pour into a greased 9-inch square pan. Bake at 425° for 20 to 25 minutes or until golden. Cut into squares, and serve warm with honey. Yield: 8 servings.   Cindy Watson Pottehaum

Madison County Cookbook
St. Joseph Church
Winterset, Iowa

Light and Lively Biscuits

You'll enjoy the convenience of these easy ham biscuits. Chopped cooked ham is stirred directly into the biscuit dough.

1½ cups unbleached flour
2 teaspoons baking powder
½ teaspoon baking soda
¼ teaspoon salt
1 teaspoon sugar
2 tablespoons butter or
    margarine

2 tablespoons shortening
¾ cup 1% low-fat cottage
    cheese
1 large egg, lightly beaten
½ cup chopped cooked ham
1 tablespoon butter, melted

Combine first 5 ingredients in a medium bowl; cut in butter and shortening with pastry blender until mixture is crumbly.

Combine cottage cheese and egg, beating well. Add mixture to flour mixture, stirring until dry ingredients are moistened. Stir in ham.

Turn dough out onto a floured surface; knead 4 or 5 times. Roll dough to ½-inch thickness; cut with a 1¾-inch biscuit cutter. Place on greased baking sheets. Brush with melted butter. Bake at 425° for 12 minutes or until golden. Yield: 26 biscuits.   Lottie Mae Franklin

New Additions and Old Favorites
Canterbury United Methodist Church
Birmingham, Alabama

Apricot-Raisin Scones

If you can't find apricot preserves, just substitute jam.

2 cups all-purpose flour
2 tablespoons sugar
1 tablespoon baking powder
½ teaspoon salt
½ cup butter or margarine
2 large eggs, lightly beaten
¼ cup milk

1 cup raisins
½ cup apricot preserves
2 tablespoons butter or
    margarine, melted
¼ cup sugar
1½ teaspoons to 1 tablespoon
    ground cinnamon

Combine first 4 ingredients in a large bowl; cut in ½ cup butter with pastry blender until mixture is crumbly. Add eggs, milk, and raisins, stirring just until moistened.

Press half of dough firmly on bottom and ¼ inch up sides of a greased 9-inch round cakepan. Spread preserves evenly over dough. Top with remaining dough, pressing evenly over preserves. Brush 2 tablespoons melted butter over dough.

Combine ¼ cup sugar and cinnamon, and sprinkle mixture over butter. Bake at 400° for 20 to 25 minutes or until a wooden pick inserted in center comes out clean. Cut into wedges to serve. Yield: 8 servings. Stacy Ekberg

Celebrating California
Children's Home Society of California
San Diego, California

Applesauce-Rhubarb Muffins

The peak growing season for fresh rhubarb is from April to June. If fresh rhubarb is unavailable, you can substitute frozen rhubarb that has been thawed and drained.

2 cups all-purpose flour
1 cup whole wheat flour
2 teaspoons baking powder
½ teaspoon baking soda
½ teaspoon salt
2 teaspoons ground cinnamon
1⅓ cups firmly packed brown
   sugar

1⅓ cups applesauce
½ cup vegetable oil
2 large eggs, beaten
1½ cups coarsely chopped
   fresh rhubarb
⅓ cup sugar
2 teaspoons ground cinnamon

Combine first 6 ingredients in a large bowl; make a well in center of mixture. Combine brown sugar, applesauce, oil, and eggs; add to dry ingredients, stirring just until moistened. Stir in rhubarb.

Spoon batter into greased muffin pans, filling two-thirds full. Combine ⅓ cup sugar and 2 teaspoons cinnamon in a small bowl, stirring well. Sprinkle sugar mixture evenly over batter. Bake at 400° for 18 minutes. Remove from pans immediately. Yield: 2 dozen.

The Bess Collection
The Junior Service League of Independence, Missouri

Orange Streusel Muffins

2 cups all-purpose flour
1 tablespoon baking powder
1 teaspoon salt
⅓ cup sugar
½ cup chopped pecans
1 large egg, lightly beaten
½ cup orange juice
¼ cup milk
¼ cup vegetable oil
1 tablespoon grated orange rind
½ cup orange marmalade
1 tablespoon all-purpose flour
¼ cup sugar
½ teaspoon ground cinnamon
¼ teaspoon ground nutmeg
1 tablespoon butter or margarine, softened

Combine first 5 ingredients in a large bowl; make a well in center of mixture. Set aside.

Combine egg and next 5 ingredients; add to dry ingredients, stirring just until moistened. Spoon batter into greased muffins pans, filling two-thirds full.

Combine 1 tablespoon flour and remaining ingredients; sprinkle over batter. Bake at 375° for 15 minutes or until golden. Remove from pans immediately. Yield: 15 muffins. Overhall Sam

Quilters Guild of Indianapolis Cookbook
Quilters Guild of Indianapolis, Indiana

Whole Wheat Popovers

½ cup all-purpose flour
½ cup whole wheat flour
½ teaspoon salt
1 cup milk
3 large eggs, lightly beaten
3 tablespoons vegetable oil

Combine all ingredients in a mixing bowl; beat at low speed of an electric mixer just until smooth.

Spoon batter into well-greased popover pans, filling three-fourths full. Place in a cold oven. Turn oven on 450°; bake 15 minutes. Reduce heat to 350°; bake 30 additional minutes or until crusty and golden. Serve immediately. Yield: 6 popovers. Karen Walker

Treasured Gems
Hiddenite Center Family
Hiddenite, North Carolina

Tomato, Onion, and Herb Bread

2 cups coarsely chopped tomato	1 tablespoon dried parsley flakes
2 packages active dry yeast	1 teaspoon dried rosemary
1½ tablespoons sugar	½ teaspoon pepper
5½ to 6 cups all-purpose flour	¼ cup plus 2 tablespoons butter or margarine, melted
½ cup minced onion	1 egg white, lightly beaten
1 teaspoon salt	2 teaspoons water
1 teaspoon dried marjoram	Sage leaves
1 teaspoon dried basil	
1 teaspoon celery seeds	

Place tomato in container of an electric blender; cover and process until smooth. Pour into a medium saucepan; heat until warm (105° to 115°). Add yeast and sugar to tomato; let stand 5 minutes.

Combine 2 cups flour and next 8 ingredients in a large mixing bowl. Gradually add yeast mixture and butter to flour mixture, beating at medium speed of an electric mixer until well blended. Gradually stir in enough remaining flour to make a soft dough. (Dough will be sticky.)

Turn dough out onto a well-floured surface, and knead until smooth and elastic (about 5 minutes). Place in a well-greased bowl, turning to grease top.

Cover and let rise in a warm place (85°), free from drafts, 45 minutes or until doubled in bulk.

Punch dough down, and divide in half; shape each portion into a round loaf. Place loaves 4 inches apart on a well-greased baking sheet.

Cover and let rise in a warm place, free from drafts, 15 minutes or until doubled in bulk.

Combine egg white and water; brush over loaves. Dip sage leaves in egg white mixture, and place decoratively on top of loaves.

Bake at 375° for 35 to 40 minutes or until loaves sound hollow when tapped. Remove loaves from baking sheet; let cool completely on wire racks. Yield: 2 loaves.

Joan Ballestrini

Recipes and Remembrances of Tolland
Tolland Historical Society
Tolland, Connecticut

Honey-Cinnamon-Currant Bread

2 packages active dry yeast
2¼ cups warm water (105° to 115°)
2 cups whole wheat flour
4 cups unbleached flour, divided
½ cup instant nonfat dry milk powder

2 tablespoons brown sugar
1 tablespoon salt
1 tablespoon ground cinnamon
⅓ cup vegetable oil
¼ cup honey
¾ cup currants

Combine yeast and warm water in a large mixing bowl; let stand 5 minutes. Add whole wheat flour, 2 cups unbleached flour, and next 6 ingredients to yeast mixture; beat at medium speed of an electric mixer until well blended. Gradually stir in enough remaining unbleached flour to make a soft dough. Stir in currants.

Cover dough, and let rise in a warm place (85°), free from drafts, 15 minutes.

Punch dough down; turn out onto a lightly floured surface, and knead lightly 4 or 5 times. Divide dough in half. Roll 1 portion of dough into a 14- x 7-inch rectangle. Roll up dough, starting at short side, pressing firmly to eliminate air pockets; pinch ends to seal. Place dough, seam side down, in a well-greased 9- x 5- x 3-inch loafpan. Repeat procedure with remaining portion of dough.

Cover and let rise in a warm place, free from drafts, 1 hour or until doubled in bulk.

Bake at 350° for 30 minutes or until loaves sound hollow when tapped. Remove bread from pans immediately; let cool on wire racks. Yield: 2 loaves.   Doris K. Atkinson

Ronald McDonald House of Burlington, Vermont,
Anniversary Edition Cookbook
Ronald McDonald House
Burlington, Vermont

Sour Cream Cinnamon Buns

Our Test Kitchens gave these buns their highest rating–a 3.

1 (8-ounce) carton sour cream	3 cups all-purpose flour, divided
2 tablespoons butter or margarine	2 tablespoons butter or margarine, softened
3 tablespoons sugar	½ cup firmly packed brown sugar
½ teaspoon salt	
⅛ teaspoon baking soda	2 teaspoons ground cinnamon
1 large egg, lightly beaten	1½ cups sifted powdered sugar
1 package active dry yeast	2 tablespoons milk

Heat sour cream in a small saucepan over medium-low heat to 105° to 115°.

Combine warm sour cream, 2 tablespoons butter, 3 tablespoons sugar, salt, and baking soda in a large mixing bowl. Add egg and yeast; blend well. Add 1½ cups flour; beat at medium speed of an electric mixer until well blended. Gradually stir in enough remaining 1½ cups flour to make a soft dough.

Turn dough out onto a lightly floured surface, and knead lightly 4 or 5 times. Cover and let rest 5 minutes.

Roll dough into an 18- x 6-inch rectangle; spread 2 tablespoons softened butter over dough. Sprinkle brown sugar and cinnamon over dough. Roll up dough, starting at short side, pressing firmly to eliminate air pockets; pinch seam to seal.

Slice roll into 12 (1½-inch) slices. Place slices, cut side down, in greased muffin pans. Cover and let rise in a warm place (85°), free from drafts, 30 minutes or until doubled in bulk. Bake at 375° for 12 to 15 minutes or until golden. Remove buns from pan immediately; let cool on a wire rack. Combine powdered sugar and milk; drizzle over buns. Yield: 1 dozen.

Theo F. Bartschi

Montana Celebrity Cookbook
Intermountain Children's Home
Helena, Montana

Buttery Almond Bear Claws

1 cup butter or margarine
2 packages active dry yeast
⅓ cup warm water (105° to 115°)
1 (5-ounce) can evaporated milk
3 egg yolks
¼ cup sugar
½ teaspoon salt
3⅓ cups all-purpose flour
Almond Filling
1 egg white, lightly beaten
¾ cup sliced almonds
1½ tablespoons sugar

Melt butter in a saucepan over medium heat. Cool to 115°.

Combine yeast and warm water in a large mixing bowl; let stand 5 minutes. Add melted butter, milk, and next 3 ingredients; beat at medium speed of an electric mixer until well blended. Gradually add flour; beat 3 minutes at medium speed of electric mixer. Cover and chill at least 8 hours or up to 3 days.

Punch dough down; turn out onto a lightly floured surface, and knead lightly 4 or 5 times. Roll dough into a 27- x 13½-inch rectangle. Cut dough lengthwise into 3 (4½-inch-wide) strips. Divide Almond Filling into 3 portions. Roll 1 portion into a 27-inch rope, and place in center of 1 strip of dough; flatten rope slightly. Fold each long side of dough to center of filling, overlapping edges. Cut filled dough into 6 (4½-inch) pieces; place, seam side down, on a greased baking sheet. Cut 5 (¾-inch) crosswise slits to center of dough; curve each bear claw into a semi-circle. Repeat procedure with remaining Almond Filling and dough. Lightly brush each bear claw with egg white; top with sliced almonds, and sprinkle evenly with 1½ tablespoons sugar.

Cover and let rise in a warm place (85°), free from drafts, 30 minutes or until doubled in bulk.

Bake at 375° for 12 to 13 minutes or until golden. Cool on wire racks. Yield: 1½ dozen.

Almond Filling

½ cup butter, softened
1⅓ cups sifted powdered sugar
⅔ cup all-purpose flour
1 (8-ounce) can almond paste, crumbled
2 egg whites
1 teaspoon grated lemon rind
¾ cup finely chopped blanched almonds

Beat butter at medium speed of an electric mixer until creamy; gradually add sugar, beating well. Add flour and almond paste, stirring until crumbly. Add egg whites and lemon rind, beating at medium speed until blended. Stir in almonds. Cover and chill until firm. Yield: 2⅔ cups.   Mary Minaglia-Cody

Cooking in Alexander Valley: A Tradition of Excellence in
Food, Wine and Education
Alexander Valley Parents Club
Healdsburg, California

Herb Buns

These yummy buns take on an earthy look and flavor from the herbs.

1 **package active dry yeast**	1 **teaspoon salt**
1 **cup warm water (105° to 115°)**	1 **teaspoon caraway seeds**
2¼ **cups all-purpose flour, divided**	½ **teaspoon dried sage leaves**
2 **tablespoons sugar**	¼ **teaspoon ground nutmeg**
2 **tablespoons shortening**	1 **large egg**

Combine yeast and warm water in a large mixing bowl; let stand 5 minutes. Add 1 cup flour, sugar, and next 5 ingredients; beat at medium speed of an electric mixer until well blended. Add egg, beating well. Gradually stir in enough remaining 1¼ cups flour to make a soft dough. Cover and let rise in a warm place (85°), free from drafts, 30 minutes or until doubled in bulk. Stir dough down to remove air bubbles. Spoon into greased muffin pans, filling two-thirds full. Let rise in a warm place, free from drafts, 30 minutes. Bake at 400° for 15 minutes or until golden. Yield: 1 dozen.   Christy Drake

Recipes from the End of the Road
Homer Special Olympics
Anchor Point, Alaska

Gruyère Rolls

If you prefer a milder flavored cheese, substitute Swiss for Gruyère in this recipe.

3 cups all-purpose flour, divided
1 package rapid-rise yeast
1 cup shredded Gruyère cheese
¼ teaspoon sugar
1 teaspoon salt
1¼ cups warm water (120° to 130°)

Combine 2¾ cups flour, yeast, and next 3 ingredients in a large mixing bowl. Gradually add water to flour mixture, beating at high speed of an electric mixer. Beat 2 additional minutes at medium speed. Gradually stir in enough remaining flour to make a soft dough.

Turn dough out onto a floured surface, and knead until smooth and elastic (about 10 minutes). Place in a well-greased bowl, turning to grease top. Cover and let rise in a warm place (85°), free from drafts, 1 hour or until doubled in bulk.

Punch dough down; turn out onto a lightly floured surface, and knead lightly 4 or 5 times. Divide dough in half. Shape each portion of dough into 8 balls. Roll each ball in flour; shape each portion into an oval.

Place rolls 2 inches apart on a greased baking sheet. Cover and let rise in a warm place, free from drafts, 30 minutes or until doubled in bulk. Place rolls in oven; spray rolls with water. Bake at 425° for 5 minutes, spraying after 3 minutes without removing rolls from oven. Reduce heat to 350°; continue to bake, without spraying, 13 additional minutes or until rolls are golden. Remove from baking sheet immediately; let cool on a wire rack. Yield: 16 rolls.   Glenn Davidowich

Ethnic Delights
Our Lady of Perpetual Help Byzantine Catholic Church
Norfolk, Virginia

Mom's Penny Rolls

These bite-size dinner rolls are ideal for an appetizer buffet.

1 **package active dry yeast**
½ **cup warm water (105° to 115°)**
½ **cup hot water**
¼ **cup sugar**

1 **tablespoon vegetable oil**
1 **teaspoon salt**
1 **large egg, beaten**
3 to 3¼ **cups all-purpose flour**

Dissolve yeast in warm water in a 1-cup liquid measuring cup; let stand 5 minutes.

Combine hot water, sugar, oil, and salt in a large mixing bowl, stirring until sugar dissolves. Let cool 5 minutes. Add yeast mixture and egg; beat at medium speed of an electric mixer until blended. Gradually add 2 cups flour, beating at low speed until blended. Beat 2 additional minutes at medium speed. Gradually stir in enough remaining flour to make a soft dough.

Turn dough out onto a lightly floured surface, and knead until smooth and elastic (about 8 minutes). Place in a well-greased bowl, turning to grease top.

Cover and let rise in a warm place (85°), free from drafts, 1 hour and 15 minutes or until doubled in bulk.

Punch dough down, and divide into 30 equal portions. Shape each portion into a ball. Place in greased muffin pans. Cover and let rise in a warm place, free from drafts, 45 minutes or until doubled in bulk. Bake at 375° for 10 minutes or until lightly browned. Remove from pans immediately. Serve warm. Yield: 2½ dozen.   Kay Schell

Our Favorite Recipes, Seasoned with Love
Neighborhood Bible Studies
Houston, Texas

Cornbread-Jalapeño English Muffins

Always wear rubber gloves when seeding and chopping jalapeño peppers.

1¾ cups milk
¼ cup water
1 tablespoon butter or
   margarine
5½ cups all-purpose flour,
   divided
1 cup cornmeal

2 tablespoons sugar
2 teaspoons salt
1 package active dry yeast
6 jalapeño peppers, seeded
   and chopped
1 large egg
Cornmeal

Combine first 3 ingredients in a saucepan; heat until butter melts, stirring occasionally. Cool to 120° to 130°.

Combine 1 cup flour, 1 cup cornmeal, and next 3 ingredients in a large mixing bowl. Gradually add milk mixture to flour mixture, beating at high speed of an electric mixer. Beat 2 additional minutes at medium speed. Add 1 cup flour, jalapeño peppers, and egg; beat well. Gradually stir in enough remaining 3½ cups flour to make a soft dough.

Turn dough out onto a floured surface, and knead until smooth and elastic (about 10 minutes). Place in a well-greased bowl, turning to grease top. Cover and let rise in a warm place (85°), free from drafts, 1 hour or until doubled in bulk. Punch dough down; cover and let rise in a warm place, free from drafts, 45 minutes or until doubled in bulk.

Punch dough down; turn out onto a lightly floured surface, and knead lightly 4 or 5 times. Divide dough in half. Turn 1 portion of dough out onto a smooth surface sprinkled with cornmeal. Roll dough into a ½-inch-thick circle; cut dough into rounds, using a 3¼-inch biscuit cutter. Repeat procedure with remaining half of dough.

Sprinkle baking sheets with cornmeal. Place rounds, cornmeal side down, 2 inches apart on baking sheets (one side should remain free of cornmeal). Cover and let rise in a warm place (85°), free from drafts, 30 minutes or until doubled in bulk. Using a wide spatula, transfer rounds, cornmeal side down, to a preheated, lightly greased electric skillet (350°). Cook 5 to 7 minutes on each side or until golden. Let cool on wire racks. Yield: 16 muffins. Corrine Malopolski

Pepper Lovers Club Cookbook, Volume I
Pepper Lovers Club of Virginia Beach, Virginia

Cakes

Holiday Chocolate Log, page 116

Apple Blossom Cake

2⅓ cups sugar, divided
1¼ cups vegetable oil
2 large eggs
3 cups peeled, chopped
  cooking apples
1½ cups chopped pecans or
  walnuts, divided

1 teaspoon vanilla extract
3 cups all-purpose flour
1½ teaspoons baking soda
½ teaspoon salt
2 teaspoons ground cinnamon,
  divided
1 teaspoon ground nutmeg

Combine 2 cups sugar, oil, and eggs in a large bowl, beating with a wire whisk until blended. Stir in apple, 1 cup pecans, and vanilla.

Combine flour, soda, salt, 1 teaspoon cinnamon, and nutmeg; add to apple mixture, stirring until blended (batter will be thick). Spread batter into a greased and floured 13- x 9- x 2-inch pan. Combine remaining ⅓ cup sugar, ½ cup pecans, and 1 teaspoon cinnamon; sprinkle evenly over batter.

Bake at 350° for 45 to 50 minutes or until a wooden pick inserted in center of cake comes out clean. Cool in pan on a wire rack. Cut into squares. Yield: 15 servings.   Uldene Van Wassenhove

Favorite Recipes
St. Isaac Jogues Senior Guild, St. Mary's of the Hills Catholic Church
Rochester Hills, Michigan

Cider Cake

½ cup butter or margarine,
  softened
1 cup sugar
2 large eggs
¾ cup currants
2¼ cups all-purpose flour,
  divided

1 teaspoon baking soda
½ teaspoon salt
1 teaspoon ground cinnamon
¼ teaspoon ground nutmeg
1 cup apple cider
3 tablespoons brandy

Beat butter at medium speed of an electric mixer until creamy; gradually add sugar, beating well. Add eggs, one at a time, beating after each addition.

Combine currants and ¼ cup flour; toss to coat.

Combine remaining 2 cups flour, soda, and next 3 ingredients; add to butter mixture alternately with cider, beginning and ending with flour mixture. Mix at low speed after each addition until blended. Stir in brandy and currants. Pour batter into a greased 9-inch square pan.

Bake at 350° for 35 minutes or until a wooden pick inserted in center comes out clean. Cool in pan. Cut into squares. Yield: 16 servings.

Cooking with Fire
Fairfield Historical Society
Fairfield, Connecticut

Louisiana Praline Cake

There are no pralines in the cake—just butter, brown sugar, and pecans.

1 cup quick-cooking oats, uncooked
1½ cups boiling water
½ cup butter or margarine, softened
1 cup sugar
1 cup firmly packed brown sugar
2 large eggs
2 cups all-purpose flour

1 teaspoon baking soda
½ teaspoon salt
¾ cup chopped pecans
¾ cup firmly packed brown sugar
3 tablespoons butter or margarine, softened
2 tablespoons whipping cream
¾ cup chopped pecans

Combine oats and water; let stand 15 minutes. Beat ½ cup butter with an electric mixer until creamy; gradually add 1 cup sugar and 1 cup brown sugar, beating well. Add eggs, one at a time, beating after each addition.

Combine flour, soda, and salt; add to butter mixture alternately with oat mixture, beginning and ending with flour mixture. Mix at low speed after each addition until blended. Stir in ¾ cup pecans. Pour into a greased and floured 13- x 9- x 2-inch pan. Bake at 325° for 45 minutes or until a wooden pick inserted in center comes out clean.

Combine ¾ cup brown sugar and remaining 3 ingredients; spoon evenly over top of cake. Broil 5½ inches from heat (with electric oven door partially opened) 2 minutes or until bubbly. Cool in pan on a wire rack. Cut into squares. Yield: 20 servings.   Corliss Ivanyisky

Food for the Spirit
St. Thomas Aquinas Home & School Association
Hammond, Louisiana

Crown Jewel Cranberry-Orange Tea Cake

1 tablespoon sesame seeds
½ cup butter, softened
½ cup sugar
1 large egg
1½ cups all-purpose flour
2 teaspoons baking powder
½ teaspoon salt
1 cup lemon yogurt
2 teaspoons grated orange rind

½ cup finely chopped walnuts
2 cups fresh or frozen cranberries, thawed and coarsely chopped
⅓ cup sugar
1 teaspoon grated orange rind
⅓ cup sifted powdered sugar
1 to 2 teaspoons fresh orange juice

Grease bottom and sides of a 10-inch springform pan. Sprinkle sesame seeds over bottom and 1 inch up sides of pan; set aside.

Beat butter at medium speed of an electric mixer until creamy; gradually add ½ cup sugar, beating well. Add egg, beating well.

Combine flour, baking powder, and salt; add to butter mixture alternately with yogurt, beginning and ending with flour mixture. Mix at low speed after each addition until blended. Stir in 2 teaspoons orange rind and walnuts. Pour batter into prepared pan.

Combine cranberries, ⅓ cup sugar, and 1 teaspoon orange rind in a small bowl. Spoon mixture over batter to within 1 inch of cake edge. Bake at 350° for 50 to 55 minutes or until golden. Remove from oven; run a knife around edge of pan to release sides. Let cool slightly on a wire rack. Remove sides of pan.

Combine powdered sugar and orange juice in a small bowl. Drizzle over warm cake. Serve warm or cool. Yield: 10 servings.   Lisa Keys

Recipes from a New England Green
Middlebury Congregational Church
Middlebury, Connecticut

Old-Fashioned Triple Lemon Cake

Three lemons should give you enough juice and rind for this recipe.

¾ cup butter, softened
¾ cup sugar
3 tablespoons grated lemon rind, divided
3 large eggs
1½ cups all-purpose flour
1 teaspoon baking powder
⅛ teaspoon salt
1 teaspoon lemon extract

⅔ cup sifted powdered sugar
⅓ cup fresh lemon juice
1¾ cups sifted powdered sugar
2 tablespoons fresh lemon juice
1½ tablespoons butter, softened
Fresh strawberries (optional)

Beat ¾ cup butter at medium speed of an electric mixer until creamy; gradually add ¾ cup sugar and 2 tablespoons lemon rind, beating well. Add eggs, one at a time, beating after each addition.

Combine flour, baking powder, and salt; add to butter mixture. Mix at low speed until blended. Stir in lemon extract. Pour batter into a greased and floured 9-inch round cakepan with 2-inch sides.

Bake at 325° for 35 to 40 minutes or until a wooden pick inserted in center comes out clean. Cool in pan on a wire rack 10 minutes; remove from pan. Place cake on wire rack on a baking sheet.

Combine ⅔ cup powdered sugar and ⅓ cup lemon juice in a small bowl, stirring until blended. Drizzle glaze over top of warm cake. Let cake cool completely.

Combine 1¾ cups powdered sugar, 2 tablespoons lemon juice, 1½ tablespoons butter, and remaining 1 tablespoon lemon rind in a medium bowl; beat well. Spread on top of cooled cake. Serve with strawberries, if desired. Yield: one 9-inch cake.   Deb Steiner

We Like It Here
Mukwonago High School
Mukwonago, Wisconsin

Bourbon-Laced Fruit and Nut Cake

Yes, this Lane cake calls for a dozen eggs, but every rich bite is worth it!

1 cup butter or margarine, softened
2 cups sugar
3½ cups sifted cake flour
1 tablespoon plus ½ teaspoon baking powder

¾ teaspoon salt
1 cup milk
1 teaspoon vanilla extract
8 egg whites
Cake Filling
Frosting

Grease four 9-inch round cakepans; line with wax paper. Grease wax paper. Set aside.

Beat butter at medium speed of an electric mixer until creamy; gradually add sugar, beating well.

Combine flour, baking powder, and salt; add to butter mixture alternately with milk, beginning and ending with flour mixture. Mix at low speed after each addition until blended. Stir in vanilla.

Beat egg whites at high speed until stiff peaks form. Gently fold into flour mixture. Pour batter into prepared pans.

Bake at 375° for 20 minutes or until a wooden pick inserted in center comes out clean. Cool in pans on wire racks 10 minutes; remove from pans, and let cool completely on wire racks.

Spread Cake Filling between layers and on top of cake. Spread Frosting on sides of cake. Yield: one 4-layer cake.

Cake Filling

1½ cups raisins
1½ cups red candied cherries, quartered
1½ cups pecans, coarsely chopped
1½ cups flaked coconut

12 egg yolks, lightly beaten
1¾ cups sugar
¾ cup butter
½ teaspoon salt
½ cup bourbon

Place raisins in a small saucepan, and cover with water. Bring to a boil; cover, remove from heat, and let stand 5 minutes. Drain and pat dry. Combine raisins, cherries, chopped pecans, and coconut in a large bowl; set aside.

Combine egg yolks, sugar, butter, and salt in top of a double boiler; bring water to a boil. Reduce heat to medium; cook, stirring constantly, 20 minutes or until butter melts and mixture is very thick. Add bourbon; stir well. Pour over fruit and nut mixture, stirring well; let cool completely. Yield: enough for one 4-layer cake.

Frosting

1½ cups sugar
½ teaspoon cream of tartar
½ cup water

4 egg whites
½ teaspoon vanilla extract

Combine first 3 ingredients in a heavy saucepan. Cook over medium heat, stirring constantly, until mixture is clear. Cook, without stirring, until mixture reaches soft ball stage or until candy thermometer registers 240°.

While syrup cooks, beat egg whites until soft peaks form; continue to beat, adding syrup in a heavy stream. Add vanilla; continue beating just until stiff peaks form and frosting is thick enough to spread. Yield: 7 cups.   Kathy Kyrish

Texas Temptations
Texas Association for Family and Community Education
Burkburnett, Texas

Chocolate-Port Wine Torte

This recipe is more like a cake than a torte. If you can't find raspberry preserves, substitute raspberry jam.

1 cup cocoa
2 cups boiling water
1 cup butter, softened
2½ cups sugar
4 large eggs
2¾ cups sifted cake flour
½ teaspoon baking powder
2 teaspoons baking soda
½ teaspoon salt

1½ teaspoons vanilla extract
½ cup port wine
1 cup red raspberry preserves
1 cup semisweet chocolate morsels
½ cup half-and-half
1 cup butter, softened
2½ cups sifted powdered sugar

Grease three 9-inch round cakepans; line with wax paper. Grease wax paper. Set aside.

Combine cocoa and boiling water in a medium bowl, stirring with a wire whisk until smooth. Let cool.

Beat 1 cup butter at medium speed of an electric mixer until creamy; gradually add 2½ cups sugar, beating well. Add eggs, one at a time, beating until blended after each addition.

Combine flour and next 3 ingredients; add to butter mixture alternately with cocoa mixture, beginning and ending with flour mixture. Mix at low speed after each addition until blended. Stir in vanilla. Pour batter into prepared pans.

Bake at 350° for 25 to 30 minutes or until a wooden pick inserted in center comes out clean. Cool in pans on wire racks 10 minutes; remove from pans, and let cool completely on wire racks.

Spoon wine over bottoms of cake layers. Stir preserves well, and spread between layers. Combine chocolate morsels and half-and-half in top of a double boiler; cook over hot (not boiling) water, stirring constantly, until chocolate melts.

Beat 1 cup butter at medium speed until creamy; gradually add powdered sugar, beating at low speed until blended. Gradually add chocolate mixture; beat until spreading consistency. Spread frosting on top and sides of cake. Yield: one 3-layer cake.

Heard in the Kitchen
The Heard Museum Guild
Phoenix, Arizona

Fudge Walnut Ripple Layer Cake

½ cup shortening
1½ cups sugar
2 large eggs
1⅔ cups all-purpose flour
⅔ cup cocoa
1½ teaspoons baking soda
½ teaspoon salt
1½ cups buttermilk
1 tablespoon plus 1 teaspoon
   vanilla extract, divided
1 (8-ounce) package cream
   cheese, softened

2 tablespoons butter or
   margarine, softened
1 tablespoon cornstarch
1 (14-ounce) can sweetened
   condensed milk
1 large egg
⅔ cup butter, softened
5¾ cups sifted powdered sugar
1⅓ cups cocoa
½ cup milk
¾ cup chopped walnuts, toasted

Grease two 9-inch round cakepans; line with wax paper. Grease and flour wax paper. Set aside.

Beat shortening at medium speed of an electric mixer until fluffy; gradually add 1½ cups sugar, beating well. Add 2 eggs, one at a time, beating until blended after each addition.

Combine flour and next 3 ingredients; add to shortening mixture alternately with buttermilk, beginning and ending with flour mixture. Mix at low speed after each addition until blended. Beat 3 additional minutes at high speed, stopping once to scrape down sides. Stir in 2 teaspoons vanilla. Pour batter into prepared pans. Set aside.

Beat cream cheese, 2 tablespoons butter, and cornstarch at medium speed until creamy; gradually add sweetened condensed milk, beating well. Add 1 egg; beat well. Stir in 1 teaspoon vanilla. Spoon cream cheese mixture evenly over batter.

Bake at 350° for 40 minutes or until a wooden pick inserted in center comes out clean. Cool in pans on wire racks 10 minutes; remove from pans, and let cool completely on wire racks.

Beat ⅔ cup butter at medium speed until creamy. Combine powdered sugar and 1⅓ cups cocoa; add to butter alternately with ½ cup milk, beginning and ending with powdered sugar mixture. Beat until spreading consistency. Stir in remaining 1 teaspoon vanilla. Spread frosting between layers and on top and sides of cake. Sprinkle with toasted walnuts. Yield: one 2-layer cake.   Linda Thomas

Our Best Home Cooking
Citizens of Zion Missionary Baptist Church Women's Ministry
Compton, California

Lemon-Butter Cake

¾ cup butter, softened
1¼ cups sugar
8 egg yolks, lightly beaten
2½ cups sifted cake flour
1 tablespoon baking powder
¼ teaspoon salt

1 cup milk
1 teaspoon grated lemon rind
1 teaspoon fresh lemon juice
1 teaspoon vanilla extract
Lemon Frosting

Beat butter at medium speed of an electric mixer until creamy; gradually add sugar, beating well. Add egg yolks, one at a time, beating until blended after each addition.

Combine flour, baking powder, and salt; add to butter mixture alternately with milk, beginning and ending with flour mixture. Mix at low speed after each addition until blended. Stir in lemon rind, lemon juice, and vanilla. Pour batter into three greased and floured 8-inch round cakepans.

Bake at 375° for 15 to 18 minutes or until a wooden pick inserted in center comes out clean. Cool in pans on wire racks 10 minutes; remove from pans, and let cool completely on wire racks.

Spread Lemon Frosting between layers and on top and sides of cake. Yield: one 3-layer cake.

Lemon Frosting

1 cup butter, softened
8 cups sifted powdered sugar
2 teaspoons grated lemon rind

⅓ cup fresh lemon juice
2 tablespoons half-and-half

Beat butter at medium speed of an electric mixer until creamy. Gradually add sugar and remaining ingredients, beating until blended. Yield: 5 cups.   Lynn Parnell

Ribbon Winning Recipes
South Carolina State Fair
Columbia, South Carolina

Red Velvet Cake

Our Test Kitchens receive many requests for this cake from yesteryear. The coconut frosting is a tasty departure from the usual cream cheese frosting on most red velvet cakes. You can sprinkle the coconut over the top of the cake instead of stirring it into the frosting.

½ cup shortening
1½ cups sugar
2 large eggs
2 cups all-purpose flour
1 tablespoon cocoa
½ teaspoon salt
1 cup buttermilk
2 (1-ounce) bottles red liquid food coloring
1 teaspoon baking soda
1 tablespoon white vinegar

1 cup milk
¼ cup plus 1½ teaspoons all-purpose flour
¾ cup butter, softened
¼ cup plus 1½ teaspoons shortening
1¼ cups sugar
⅛ teaspoon salt
1 tablespoon vanilla extract
⅓ cup flaked coconut (optional)

Beat ½ cup shortening at medium speed of an electric mixer until fluffy; gradually add 1½ cups sugar, beating well. Add eggs, one at a time, beating until blended after each addition.

Combine 2 cups flour, cocoa, and ½ teaspoon salt; add to shortening mixture alternately with buttermilk and coloring, beginning and ending with flour mixture. Mix at low speed after each addition until blended. Combine soda and vinegar; stir until dissolved. Fold into batter. Pour into three greased and floured 8-inch round cakepans.

Bake at 350° for 25 to 27 minutes or until a wooden pick inserted in center comes out clean. Cool in pans on wire racks 10 minutes; remove from pans, and let cool completely on wire racks.

Gradually stir milk into ¼ cup plus 1½ teaspoons flour in a saucepan until smooth. Cook over medium heat, stirring constantly, until thickened and bubbly. Cool.

Beat butter, ¼ cup plus 1½ teaspoons shortening, 1¼ cups sugar, and ⅛ teaspoon salt until creamy; stir in vanilla. Add milk mixture to creamed mixture, stirring with a wire whisk until smooth. Stir in coconut, if desired. Spread frosting between layers and on top and sides of cake. Yield: one 3-layer cake. Elaine Shepard

Look Who's Cooking
Temple Hesed Sisterhood
Scranton, Pennsylvania

Orange Slice Cake

For those who don't like traditional fruitcake, this version with different fruits may be the answer. The wooden pick test for doneness doesn't work with this recipe, though, so watch your cooking time.

1 cup butter, softened	½ pound orange slice candy, chopped
2 cups sugar	½ pound chopped dates
4 large eggs	2 cups chopped firm pear
1 tablespoon orange juice	1 (3½-ounce) can flaked coconut
1 teaspoon baking soda	
½ cup buttermilk	¾ cup chopped walnuts
3½ cups all-purpose flour, divided	

Beat butter at medium speed of an electric mixer until creamy; gradually add sugar, beating well. Add eggs, one at a time, beating after each addition.

Combine orange juice, soda, and buttermilk. Add 2½ cups flour to butter mixture alternately with buttermilk mixture, beginning and ending with flour. Mix at low speed after each addition until blended.

Combine orange candy, dates, pear, coconut, walnuts, and remaining 1 cup flour in a large bowl; toss gently until well coated. Stir fruit mixture into batter. Pour batter into a greased and floured 10-inch tube pan.

Bake at 275° for 2 hours and 45 minutes. Cool in pan on a wire rack 10 minutes; remove from pan, and let cool completely on wire rack. Yield: one 10-inch cake.

Tina Hatcher

An Apple a Day
Knoxville Academy of Medicine Alliance
Knoxville, Tennessee

Best-Ever Chocolate Pound Cake

1 (16-ounce) can chocolate syrup	2 cups sugar
1 (7-ounce) milk chocolate candy bar	4 large eggs
2 teaspoons vanilla extract	2½ cups all-purpose flour
1 cup butter, softened	½ teaspoon baking soda
	1 cup buttermilk
	1 cup chopped pecans

Combine syrup and candy bar in top of a double boiler; bring water to a boil. Reduce heat to low; cook until candy bar melts, stirring occasionally. Remove from heat, and stir in vanilla.

Beat butter at medium speed of an electric mixer 2 minutes or until soft and creamy. Gradually add sugar, beating at medium speed 5 to 7 minutes. Add eggs, one at a time, beating just until yellow disappears. Add chocolate mixture, beating until blended.

Combine flour and soda; add to butter mixture alternately with buttermilk, beginning and ending with flour mixture. Mix at low speed just until blended after each addition. Fold in pecans. Pour batter into a greased and floured 12-cup Bundt or 10-inch tube pan. Bake at 325° for 1 hour and 15 minutes or until a wooden pick inserted in center comes out clean. Cool in pan on a wire rack 10 to 15 minutes; remove from pan, and let cool completely on wire rack. Yield: one 10-inch cake.

Sallie Ruskin

Saints Alive!
The Ladies' Guild of St. Barnabas Anglican Church
Atlanta, Georgia

Peach Brandy Pound Cake

1 cup butter, softened
3 cups sugar
6 large eggs
3 cups all-purpose flour
¼ teaspoon baking soda
Dash of salt
1 cup sour cream

2 teaspoons light rum
1 teaspoon orange extract
1 teaspoon vanilla extract
½ teaspoon lemon extract
¼ teaspoon almond extract
½ cup peach brandy

Beat butter at medium speed of an electric mixer 2 minutes or until soft and creamy; gradually add sugar, beating at medium speed 5 to 7 minutes. Add eggs, one at a time, beating just until yellow disappears.

Combine flour, soda, and salt; add to butter mixture alternately with sour cream, beginning and ending with flour mixture. Mix at low speed just until blended after each addition. Stir in rum, flavorings, and brandy. Pour into a greased and floured 12-cup Bundt pan.

Bake at 325° for 1 hour and 30 minutes or until a wooden pick inserted in center comes out clean. Cool in pan on a wire rack 10 minutes; remove from pan, and let cool completely on wire rack. Yield: one 10-inch cake.

Elizabeth Smith

Tempting Southern Treasures Cookbook
Riverchase Women's Club
Hoover, Alabama

Peanut Butter Pound Cake

1 cup butter or margarine, softened
½ cup creamy peanut butter
2 cups sugar
1 cup firmly packed brown sugar
5 large eggs
3 cups all-purpose flour
½ teaspoon baking powder
¼ teaspoon baking soda

½ teaspoon salt
1 cup milk
1 tablespoon vanilla extract
2 cups sifted powdered sugar
⅓ cup creamy peanut butter
¼ cup butter or margarine, melted
Dash of salt
¼ cup evaporated milk

Beat 1 cup butter and ½ cup peanut butter at medium speed of an electric mixer 2 minutes or until soft and creamy. Gradually add 2 cups sugar and 1 cup brown sugar, beating at medium speed 5 to 7 minutes. Add eggs, one at a time, beating just until yellow disappears.

Combine flour, baking powder, soda, and ½ teaspoon salt; stir well. Add flour mixture to butter mixture alternately with 1 cup milk, beginning and ending with flour mixture. Mix at low speed just until blended after each addition. Stir in vanilla. Pour batter into a greased and floured 10-inch tube pan.

Bake at 350° for 1 hour and 35 minutes or until a wooden pick inserted in center comes out clean. Cool in pan on a wire rack 10 to 15 minutes; remove from pan, and let cool completely on a wire rack.

Beat powdered sugar and next 3 ingredients at low speed until well blended. Add evaporated milk; beat at medium speed until smooth. Drizzle over cake. Yield: one 10-inch cake.   Evelyn Barlowe

Preserving Our Heritage
Church of God Ladies Ministries
Charlotte, North Carolina

Brownie Cupcakes

4 (1-ounce) squares semisweet chocolate
1 cup butter or margarine
1½ cups chopped pecans
4 large eggs, lightly beaten
1¾ cups sugar
1 cup all-purpose flour
1 teaspoon vanilla extract

Combine chocolate and butter in top of a double boiler; bring water to a boil. Reduce heat to low; cook until chocolate melts. Add pecans; stir well. Remove from heat.

Combine eggs, sugar, flour, and vanilla. Stir in chocolate mixture. Spoon batter into paper- or aluminum foil-lined muffin pans, filling two-thirds full. Bake at 325° for 35 minutes or until a wooden pick inserted in center comes out clean. Remove from pans, and let cool completely on wire racks. Yield: 20 cupcakes.

Taste the Good Life
The Assistance League of Omaha, Nebraska

Holiday Chocolate Log

A traditional French Christmas cake, the yule log or bûche de Noël, can be frosted with chocolate frosting and a fork pulled through the frosting to create the appearance of tree bark.

6 large eggs, separated
¾ cup sugar, divided
⅓ cup cocoa
1½ teaspoons vanilla extract
⅛ teaspoon salt
2 to 3 tablespoons powdered sugar
1½ cups whipping cream

⅓ cup sifted powdered sugar
¼ cup cocoa
2 teaspoons instant coffee granules
1 teaspoon vanilla extract
Sifted powdered sugar
Garnish: red candied cherries

Grease a 15- x 10- x 1-inch jellyroll pan. Line bottom of pan with wax paper; grease wax paper. Set aside.

Combine egg yolks and ½ cup sugar in a large mixing bowl; beat at high speed of an electric mixer 3 minutes or until thick and pale. Add ⅓ cup cocoa, 1½ teaspoons vanilla, and salt; beat at low speed until smooth. Set aside.

Beat egg whites at high speed until foamy. Gradually add remaining ¼ cup sugar, 1 tablespoon at a time, beating until stiff peaks form and sugar dissolves (2 to 4 minutes). Gently fold beaten whites into egg yolk mixture. Spread batter evenly in prepared pan. Bake at 375° for 15 minutes.

Sift 2 to 3 tablespoons powdered sugar in a 15- x 10-inch rectangle on a cloth towel. When cake is done, immediately loosen from sides of pan, and turn out onto sugared towel. Peel off wax paper. Starting at narrow end, roll up cake and towel together; let cool completely on a wire rack, seam side down.

Combine whipping cream and next 4 ingredients in a medium bowl; beat at high speed until stiff peaks form. Cover and chill 1 hour.

Unroll cake; spread with whipped cream mixture. Carefully reroll cake without towel. Cover and chill at least 1 hour. Place cake roll, seam side down, on a serving plate; sprinkle with additional powdered sugar. Garnish, if desired. Yield: 10 servings (1 filled cake roll).

Creative Chef 2
Tourette Syndrome Association
Bayside, New York

Applause Cheesecake

We used Pecan Sandies for the shortbread cookies.

1 (16-ounce) package pecan shortbread cookies (about 22 cookies)
1 cup pecan halves, coarsely chopped
½ cup firmly packed brown sugar
3 tablespoons Grand Marnier or other orange-flavored liqueur, divided
1 (7½-ounce) package almond brickle chips
3 (8-ounce) packages cream cheese, softened
1 cup sugar
3 large eggs
½ cup whipping cream
1 tablespoon all-purpose flour
1 tablespoon vanilla extract
1¼ cups semisweet chocolate morsels
¼ cup sour cream
1¼ cups chopped pecans, toasted
½ cup caramel topping

Position knife blade in food processor bowl; add 22 cookies, reserving others for another use, 1 cup pecans, and brown sugar. Process until finely ground. Add 1 tablespoon liqueur; process until well blended, stopping once to scrape down sides. Firmly press crumb mixture on bottom and up sides of a 10-inch springform pan. Sprinkle brickle chips over crust. Set aside.

Beat cream cheese at medium speed of an electric mixer until creamy; gradually add sugar, beating well. Add eggs, one at a time, beating after each addition. Add whipping cream, flour, and vanilla; beat 5 minutes. Pour batter into prepared pan.

Bake at 325° for 1 hour and 15 minutes or until center is almost set. Let cool in pan on a wire rack 15 minutes.

Combine chocolate morsels and sour cream in a heavy saucepan. Cook over low heat, stirring constantly, until chocolate melts. Spread chocolate mixture evenly over cheesecake. Sprinkle 1¼ cups pecans over chocolate. Combine caramel topping and remaining 2 tablespoons liqueur; spread evenly over pecans. Let cool to room temperature in pan on wire rack; cover and chill at least 8 hours. Carefully remove sides of springform pan. Yield: 12 servings.

Sterling Performances
The Guilds of the Orange County Performing Arts Center
Costa Mesa, California

Chocolate-Raspberry Truffle Cheesecake

For ease, look for packaged crushed sandwich cookies in the cake mix section of your local grocer. That way you won't have to crush them.

1½ cups crushed cream-filled chocolate sandwich cookies (about 21 cookies)
¼ cup butter or margarine, melted
4 (8-ounce) packages cream cheese, softened and divided
1¼ cups sugar
3 large eggs
1 (8-ounce) carton sour cream
1 teaspoon vanilla extract
1 cup (6 ounces) semisweet chocolate morsels, melted

⅓ cup seedless raspberry preserves
1 (16-ounce) carton sour cream
¼ cup sugar
1 teaspoon vanilla extract
½ cup (3 ounces) semisweet chocolate morsels
¼ cup whipping cream
Garnishes: whipped cream, fresh raspberries, fresh mint sprigs

Combine cookie crumbs and butter in a medium bowl; stir well. Firmly press crumb mixture on bottom of a 10-inch springform pan. Bake at 400° for 8 minutes; let cool in pan on a wire rack.

Beat 3 packages cream cheese at medium speed of an electric mixer until creamy. Gradually add 1¼ cups sugar, beating well. Add eggs, one at a time, beating after each addition. Stir in 1 (8-ounce) carton sour cream and 1 teaspoon vanilla extract.

Combine remaining package cream cheese, melted chocolate morsels, and raspberry preserves in a medium bowl; stir well.

Spoon two-thirds of batter into prepared crust. Drop chocolate mixture by rounded tablespoonfuls over batter; pour remaining batter over chocolate mixture.

Bake at 325° for 1 hour and 20 minutes or until cheesecake is almost set. (Cheesecake will rise above pan.) Increase oven temperature to 375°.

Combine 16-ounce carton sour cream and ¼ cup sugar; carefully spread over cheesecake. Bake 5 additional minutes. Cool to room temperature in pan on a wire rack.

Combine ½ cup chocolate morsels and whipping cream in a small saucepan; cook over low heat until chocolate melts, stirring occasionally. Carefully remove sides of springform pan. Drizzle chocolate mixture on top and sides of cheesecake. Cover and chill 8 hours. Garnish, if desired. Yield: 12 servings.   Rosemary Baker

Cane River's Louisiana Living
The Service League of Natchitoches
Natchitoches, Louisiana

Espresso Cheesecake

2½ cups graham cracker
   crumbs
½ cup plus 2 tablespoons
   butter or margarine, melted
2 teaspoons almond extract
4 (8-ounce) packages cream
   cheese, softened
⅔ cup sugar

3 large eggs
8 (1-ounce) squares semisweet
   chocolate, melted
⅓ cup milk
2 teaspoons instant espresso
   powder
Garnish: chocolate curls

Combine first 3 ingredients in a medium bowl; stir well. Press mixture on bottom and 2 inches up sides of a 9-inch springform pan. Set aside.

Beat cream cheese at high speed of an electric mixer until creamy. Gradually add sugar, beating well. Add eggs, one at a time, beating after each addition. Add melted chocolate; beat well. Combine milk and espresso powder, stirring until espresso dissolves. Add to cream cheese mixture; beat until smooth. Pour mixture into prepared crust.

Bake at 350° for 45 to 50 minutes or until center is almost set. Let cool to room temperature in pan on a wire rack; cover and chill 8 hours. Carefully remove sides of springform pan. Garnish, if desired. Yield: 12 servings.   Dorie Roscioli

Good to the Core
The Apple Corps of the Weller Center for Health Education
Easton, Pennsylvania

Almond-Ginger Torte with Orange Sauce

½ cup unsalted butter, softened
¾ cup sugar
1 (8-ounce) can almond paste
3 large eggs
½ cup all-purpose flour
¼ teaspoon baking powder
1 tablespoon Triple Sec or other orange-flavored liqueur
3 tablespoons minced crystallized ginger
2 tablespoons minced gingerroot

¼ teaspoon almond extract
1 teaspoon powdered sugar
2 cups milk
6 egg yolks
½ cup sugar
1 teaspoon cornstarch
2 tablespoons Triple Sec or other orange-flavored liqueur
1 tablespoon grated orange rind, divided
1½ teaspoons vanilla extract

Butter an 8-inch round cakepan; line with wax paper. Grease and flour wax paper. Set aside.

Beat butter at medium speed of an electric mixer until creamy; gradually add ¾ cup sugar and almond paste, beating well. Add eggs, one at a time, beating after each addition. Combine flour and baking powder. Add flour mixture to butter mixture; beat well. Stir in 1 tablespoon liqueur, ginger, and almond extract.

Pour batter into pan. Bake at 350° for 35 to 40 minutes or until a wooden pick inserted in center comes out clean. Cool in pan on a wire rack 10 minutes; remove from pan, and let cool completely on wire rack. Sift powdered sugar over cake.

Bring milk just to a boil in a saucepan. Beat 6 yolks and ½ cup sugar until thick and pale. Add cornstarch; beat well. Stir one-fourth of hot milk into yolks; add to remaining hot mixture, stirring constantly. Cook over low heat, stirring constantly, 15 minutes or until thickened. Remove from heat; stir in 2 tablespoons liqueur, 2 teaspoons rind, and vanilla. Chill. Sprinkle with remaining rind. Spoon over torte. Yield: one 8-inch torte.   Suzanne Breckenridge and Marjorie Snyder

Picnic in the Park
Atwood Community Center
Madison, Wisconsin

Cookies & Candies

Peanut Butter Swirls, page 127

Chocolate Macaroons

Two favorites–chocolate and coconut–come together in these cookies that'll have you raving.

1 cup (6 ounces) semisweet chocolate morsels	2 egg whites
1 cup flaked coconut	¼ teaspoon salt
½ cup finely chopped walnuts	½ cup sugar

Place chocolate in top of a double boiler; bring water to a boil. Reduce heat to low; cook until chocolate melts. Let cool to room temperature. Stir in coconut and walnuts.

Beat egg whites and salt at high speed of an electric mixer until foamy. Gradually add sugar, 1 tablespoon at a time, beating until stiff peaks form and sugar dissolves (2 to 4 minutes). Fold egg white mixture into chocolate mixture.

Drop by heaping teaspoonfuls onto cookie sheets lined with aluminum foil. Bake at 350° for 10 minutes. Remove cookies to wire racks, and let cool completely. Yield: 3 dozen.

Today's Traditional: Jewish Cooking with a Lighter Touch
Congregation Beth Shalom
Carmichael, California

Cry Babies

½ cup shortening	½ teaspoon salt
½ cup sugar	1 teaspoon ground ginger
1 large egg	1 teaspoon ground nutmeg
½ cup molasses	2¾ cups sifted powdered sugar
½ cup strong brewed coffee	1 teaspoon butter, softened
3¼ cups all-purpose flour	3 tablespoons hot water
1 teaspoon baking soda	½ to 1 teaspoon lemon extract

Beat shortening at medium speed of an electric mixer until creamy; gradually add ½ cup sugar, beating well. Add egg, beating well. Add molasses and coffee, mixing until blended. Combine flour and next 4 ingredients; add to shortening mixture, beating well.

Drop dough by heaping teaspoonfuls onto greased cookie sheets. Bake at 350° for 9 minutes. Remove to wire racks; cool completely.

Combine powdered sugar and remaining 3 ingredients in a bowl; stir until smooth. Spread frosting evenly over cooled cookies. Yield: 3½ dozen.   Mary Buffinton

Come Savor Swansea
First Christian Congregational Church
Swansea, Massachusetts

Stuffed Date Drops

For a taste-teaser, the dates are stuffed with a pecan in these unusual cookies. The frosting works best with margarine instead of butter.

12 pecan halves	¼ teaspoon baking powder
24 whole pitted dates	¼ teaspoon baking soda
2 tablespoons shortening	⅓ cup sour cream
⅓ cup firmly packed brown sugar	2 tablespoons margarine
	¾ cup sifted powdered sugar
1 egg yolk	⅛ teaspoon vanilla extract
¾ cup all-purpose flour	1 tablespoon milk

Cut pecans in half lengthwise; stuff each date with a pecan piece. Set aside.

Beat shortening and brown sugar at medium speed of an electric mixer until creamy. Add egg yolk, beating well.

Combine flour, baking powder, and baking soda; add to shortening mixture alternately with sour cream, beginning and ending with flour mixture. Mix at low speed after each addition until blended. Stir in stuffed dates.

Drop dough by rounded teaspoonfuls, 1 stuffed date per cookie, onto lightly greased cookie sheets. Bake at 375° for 8 to 10 minutes or until lightly browned. Cool completely on wire racks.

Heat margarine in a small saucepan over medium heat 3 to 5 minutes or until lightly browned. Remove from heat. Gradually stir in powdered sugar and vanilla (mixture will be crumbly). Add milk, and stir until mixture is smooth. Spoon frosting evenly on top of cookies. Yield: 2 dozen.

Dining with Southern Elegance
Terrebonne Association for Family and Community Education
Houma, Louisiana

Colossal Chocolate Chip Cookies

If you don't have a heavy-duty mixer to handle this large amount of stiff dough, cut the recipe in half. If you do cut it in half, use 1½ cups chocolate morsels, and save half the candy bar for the cook!

2 cups butter or margarine, softened
2 cups sugar
2 cups firmly packed brown sugar
4 large eggs
2 teaspoons vanilla extract
4 cups all-purpose flour
2 teaspoons baking powder
2 teaspoons baking soda

1 teaspoon salt
5 cups regular oats, uncooked
2 cups (12 ounces) semisweet chocolate morsels
1 cup (6 ounces) semisweet chocolate morsels
1 (7-ounce) milk chocolate candy bar, coarsely chopped
2 cups chopped walnuts

Beat butter at medium speed of a heavy-duty electric mixer until creamy; gradually add sugars, beating well. Add eggs and vanilla; beat well. Combine flour and next 3 ingredients; gradually add to butter mixture, beating well.

Position knife blade in food processor bowl; add oats. Process until finely ground. Gradually add to butter mixture, beating well. Stir in chocolate morsels, chopped chocolate, and walnuts.

Shape cookie dough into 2-inch balls. Place 3 inches apart on ungreased cookie sheets. Flatten each ball to a 2½-inch circle. Bake at 375° for 8 to 10 minutes or until lightly browned. Cool slightly on cookie sheets; remove to wire racks, and let cool completely. Yield: 4 dozen.

Nikki Baron

Signature Cuisine
Miami Country Day School Parents' Association
Miami, Florida

Chocolate-Dipped Orange Log Cookies

1 cup butter or margarine,
  softened
½ cup sifted powdered sugar
1 teaspoon grated orange rind
1 teaspoon orange extract

2 cups all-purpose flour
1 cup (6 ounces) semisweet
  chocolate morsels
½ cup finely chopped
  almonds, toasted

Beat butter at medium speed of an electric mixer until creamy; gradually add powdered sugar, beating well. Stir in orange rind and orange extract. Gradually add flour, beating well. Divide dough in half; cover and chill 1 hour.

Work with 1 portion of dough at a time, keeping remaining dough chilled. Divide each portion of dough into 24 pieces; shape each piece into a 2½- x ½-inch log on a lightly floured surface. Place logs on ungreased cookie sheets. Flatten three-quarters of each log lengthwise with tines of a fork to ¼-inch thickness. Bake at 350° for 11 to 12 minutes. Cool 1 minute on cookie sheets; remove to wire racks, and let cool completely.

Place chocolate morsels in top of a double boiler; bring water to a boil. Reduce heat to low; cook until chocolate melts. Dip unflattened tips of cookies in chocolate; roll chocolate-coated tips in chopped almonds. Place on wire racks; let stand until chocolate is firm. Yield: 4 dozen.

Lisa Schenk

The Company's Cookin'
Employees of the Rouse Company
Columbia, Maryland

Peanut Butter Temptations

½ cup butter or margarine, softened
½ cup creamy peanut butter
½ cup sugar
½ cup firmly packed brown sugar
1 large egg, beaten

1 teaspoon vanilla extract
1¼ cups all-purpose flour
¾ teaspoon baking soda
½ teaspoon salt
36 miniature peanut butter cup candies

Beat butter and peanut butter at medium speed of an electric mixer until creamy; gradually add sugars, beating well. Add egg and vanilla; beat well. Combine flour, soda, and salt; add to butter mixture, beating well.

Shape cookie dough into 1-inch balls. Place in ungreased miniature (1¾-inch) muffin pans. Bake at 375° for 10 to 12 minutes. Working rapidly, place a peanut butter candy in each cookie. Cool completely in pans on a wire rack. Yield: 3 dozen.   Valerie Mosgaller

Door County Cooking
Bay View Lutheran Church
Sturgeon Bay, Wisconsin

Butter Meltaways with Lemon Frosting

Recipe contributor Susie Walker recommends only butter for her recipe, and we agree. It makes these tea cookies wonderfully short.

1 cup butter, softened
⅓ cup sifted powdered sugar
1¼ cups all-purpose flour

¾ cup cornstarch
Lemon Frosting

Beat butter at medium speed of an electric mixer until creamy; gradually add powdered sugar, beating well.

Combine flour and cornstarch; gradually add to butter mixture, beating well. Shape dough into 2 (6-inch) logs, and wrap in wax paper dusted with powdered sugar. Chill at least 6 hours.

Unwrap dough; cut each log into 18 slices, and place slices 2 inches apart on greased cookie sheets. Bake at 350° for 12 minutes. Remove cookies to a wire rack, and let cool completely. Spread cookies with Lemon Frosting. Yield: 3 dozen.

Lemon Frosting

¼ cup butter, softened
1½ cups sifted powdered sugar
1½ to 2 tablespoons fresh
   lemon juice

1 tablespoon grated lemon rind

Beat butter at medium speed of an electric mixer until creamy; gradually add powdered sugar, beating until blended. Add lemon juice, beating until spreading consistency; stir in lemon rind. Yield: ¾ cup.

Susie Walker

Simply Irresistible
The Junior Auxiliary of Conway, Arkansas

Peanut Butter Swirls

½ cup shortening
1 cup sugar
½ cup chunky peanut butter
1 large egg
2 tablespoons milk

1¼ cups all-purpose flour
½ teaspoon baking soda
½ teaspoon salt
1 cup (6 ounces) semisweet
   chocolate morsels

Beat shortening at medium speed of an electric mixer until creamy; gradually add sugar, beating well. Add peanut butter, egg, and milk; beat well.

Combine flour, baking soda, and salt; add to peanut butter mixture, beating well.

Place chocolate morsels in top of a double boiler; bring water to a boil. Reduce heat to low; cook until chocolate melts. Remove chocolate from heat. Set aside.

Roll dough into a 15- x 8-inch rectangle on floured wax paper. Cover and chill 20 minutes. Spread melted chocolate evenly over dough. Carefully roll up, jellyroll fashion, starting at long side, peeling wax paper from dough while rolling. Cover and chill 30 minutes.

Uncover dough; slice dough into ¼-inch-thick slices, and place on ungreased cookie sheets. Bake at 375° for 8 minutes. Remove cookies to wire racks, and let cool completely. Yield: 5 dozen.

Cafe Oklahoma
The Junior Service League of Midwest City, Oklahoma

Slice of Spice

This recipe says to freeze the logs of dough 1 hour—just until they're firm enough to slice and bake. If you'd like, you can fudge a little, and freeze them up to 3 months. Just let them thaw in the refrigerator until they're soft enough to slice.

½ cup butter or margarine, softened
½ cup shortening
2 cups firmly packed brown sugar
2 large eggs
1 teaspoon vanilla extract
3 cups all-purpose flour

1 teaspoon baking soda
1 teaspoon cream of tartar
½ teaspoon salt
1 cup regular oats, uncooked
½ cup sugar
1 tablespoon plus 1 teaspoon ground cinnamon

Beat butter and shortening at medium speed of an electric mixer until creamy; gradually add brown sugar, beating well. Add eggs and vanilla; beat well.

Combine flour, soda, cream of tartar, and salt; add to butter mixture, beating well. Stir in oats.

Shape dough into 3 (12-inch) logs; wrap in wax paper. Freeze 1 hour.

Unwrap dough, and cut into ¼-inch slices. Combine ½ cup sugar and cinnamon. Dip each slice into sugar mixture, and place each on lightly greased cookie sheets. Bake at 350° for 9 to 11 minutes. Remove cookies to wire racks, and let cool completely. Yield: about 7 dozen.   Mrs. Duane Stoner

Our History, Our Cooks!
Goshen Fire Department Local 1443
Goshen, Indiana

Little Horns Cookies

1 cup butter, softened
1 cup sour cream
2 tablespoons sugar

3¼ cups all-purpose flour
Cranberry-Apple Filling
Sifted powdered sugar

Beat butter and sour cream at medium speed of an electric mixer until creamy; add sugar, beating well. Add flour to butter mixture, beating well. Divide dough into 8 equal portions; cover and chill 30 minutes.

Work with 1 portion of dough at a time, keeping remaining dough chilled. Turn dough out onto a heavily floured surface. Roll each portion into a 9-inch circle; cut into 8 wedges. Spoon ½ teaspoon Cranberry-Apple Filling onto wide end of each wedge. Roll up each wedge, beginning at wide end, and seal points. Place cookies, point side down, on lightly greased cookie sheets, and curve each cookie into a half-moon shape.

Bake at 375° for 15 minutes or until cookies are lightly browned. Cool on cookie sheets 2 minutes. Carefully roll warm cookies in powdered sugar; let cool completely on wire racks. Yield: 64 cookies.

Cranberry-Apple Filling

1⅓ cups fresh cranberries, chopped
½ medium-size cooking apple, peeled and chopped

1 cup sugar
⅓ cup water
1 tablespoon cornstarch
1 tablespoon water

Combine first 4 ingredients in a medium saucepan; bring to a boil. Reduce heat, and simmer, uncovered, 10 minutes.

Combine cornstarch and 1 tablespoon water; add to cranberry mixture, stirring well. Bring to a boil; reduce heat, and simmer, uncovered, 1 hour or until mixture is very thick. Let cool completely. Store in refrigerator until ready to use. Yield: 1 cup.   Lydia Lukina

Flavors of the Russian North
The Archangel, Russia & Greater Portland, Maine
Sister City Committees
Cape Elizabeth, Maine

Almond Biscotti

A twice-baked Italian biscuit, biscotti is perfect for dipping into coffee for an after-dinner treat.

⅓ cup butter or margarine, softened
⅔ cup sugar
2 large eggs
1 teaspoon vanilla extract
2 cups all-purpose flour, divided
2 teaspoons baking powder
1½ cups slivered almonds, finely chopped
1 egg yolk
1 tablespoon water
1 cup (6 ounces) semisweet chocolate morsels
2 tablespoons shortening

Beat butter at medium speed of an electric mixer until creamy; gradually add sugar, beating well. Add eggs, one at a time, beating after each addition. Stir in vanilla.

Combine 1 cup flour and baking powder; add to butter mixture. Gradually stir in enough remaining flour to make a stiff dough. Stir in almonds. Lightly flour hands, and divide dough in half. Shape each portion into a 9-inch log, and place 4 inches apart on a lightly greased cookie sheet. Combine egg yolk and water; brush each log with egg mixture. Bake at 325° for 40 minutes or until lightly browned; remove to wire racks, and let cool completely.

Using a serrated knife, carefully cut each log crosswise into ½-inch slices. Place on ungreased cookie sheets; bake at 300° for 10 minutes on each side. Remove to wire racks, and let cool completely.

Melt chocolate and shortening in a heavy saucepan over low heat, stirring until mixture is smooth; drizzle over top of biscotti. Let cool completely. Yield: 2 dozen.   Stephanie Smith

Daily Bread
Word of Life Women's Ministry
Steubenville, Ohio

Delicious Prune Bars

Even the staffers in our Test Kitchens who loathe prunes admit that these cookies live up to their name.

½ cup butter or margarine, softened
½ cup firmly packed brown sugar
1 cup all-purpose flour
1¼ cups pitted prunes (about 20 prunes)
2 cups water
⅓ cup firmly packed brown sugar

2 tablespoons cornstarch
1 tablespoon grated orange rind
¼ cup orange juice
⅛ teaspoon salt
1 cup coarsely chopped walnuts
2 large eggs
1 (3½-ounce) can flaked coconut

Beat butter at medium speed of an electric mixer until creamy; gradually add ½ cup brown sugar, beating well. Add flour, beating well. Spread in bottom of an ungreased 9-inch square pan. Bake at 350° for 12 minutes or until lightly browned. Let cool at least 15 minutes in pan on a wire rack.

Combine prunes and water in a medium saucepan; bring to a boil. Reduce heat, and simmer, uncovered, 25 to 30 minutes or until prunes are very soft. Drain, reserving 2 tablespoons cooking liquid. Using kitchen shears, finely chop prunes.

Combine chopped prunes, reserved liquid, ⅓ cup brown sugar, and next 4 ingredients in saucepan; bring to a boil. Reduce heat, and simmer, stirring constantly, 2 to 3 minutes or until thickened. Remove from heat, and stir in walnuts.

Spread prune mixture over prepared crust. Beat eggs just until foamy; stir in coconut. Spread coconut mixture over prune mixture. Bake at 350° for 30 minutes or until lightly browned. Let cool slightly before cutting into bars. Yield: 2 dozen.   Kay Crawford

Saxony Sampler
GFWC Saxonburg District Woman's Club
Saxonburg, Pennsylvania

Saucepan Brownies

If you're fond of a fudgy brownie, you'll love these. Just beware—they're so gooey you may have trouble cutting them into squares.

1½ cups sugar
¾ cup butter or margarine
¼ cup water
1 teaspoon instant coffee
    granules
2 cups (12 ounces) semisweet
    chocolate morsels

4 large eggs, lightly beaten
1½ cups all-purpose flour
½ teaspoon baking soda
½ teaspoon salt
1 cup chopped pecans

Combine first 4 ingredients in a large saucepan. Bring to a boil, stirring often. Remove from heat. Add chocolate morsels; stir until chocolate melts. Add eggs, stirring well.

Combine flour, soda, and salt; add to chocolate mixture, stirring well. Add pecans. Spoon into a greased 13- x 9- x 2-inch pan. Bake at 350° for 30 minutes. Let cool completely on a wire rack. Cut into squares. Yield: 1½ dozen. Debbie Salomon

Ronald McDonald House of Burlington, Vermont,
Anniversary Edition Cookbook
Ronald McDonald House
Burlington, Vermont

Really Raspberry Brownies

1 cup unsalted butter,
    softened
1¼ cups sugar
½ cup firmly packed brown
    sugar
4 large eggs
1¼ cups all-purpose flour
½ cup cocoa
¼ teaspoon salt

3 tablespoons framboise or
    other raspberry-flavored
    liqueur, divided
1 teaspoon vanilla extract
2 cups fresh raspberries
4 (1-ounce) squares semisweet
    chocolate
2 teaspoons hot water
Sifted powdered sugar

Beat butter at medium speed of an electric mixer until creamy; gradually add 1¼ cups sugar and ½ cup brown sugar, beating well. Add eggs, one at a time, beating well after each addition.

Combine flour, cocoa, and salt; add to butter mixture, beating well. Stir in 1 tablespoon framboise and vanilla. Spoon batter into a greased 13- x 9- x 2-inch pan. Sprinkle with raspberries. Bake at 325° for 40 minutes or until a wooden pick inserted in center comes out clean. Let cool completely in pan on a wire rack.

Combine chocolate, remaining 2 tablespoons framboise, and water in top of a double boiler; bring water in bottom of double boiler to a boil. Reduce heat to low; cook until chocolate melts, stirring occasionally. Remove from heat, and let cool slightly.

Cut brownies into squares. Sprinkle with powdered sugar. Drizzle with chocolate mixture. Yield: 2 dozen.

Pass It On . . . A Treasury of Tastes and Traditions
Delta Delta Delta National Fraternity
Arlington, Texas

Peanut Butter Fudge

2 **cups sugar**	½ **teaspoon salt**
¾ **cup milk**	¼ **cup creamy peanut butter**
2 **tablespoons butter or margarine**	1 **teaspoon vanilla extract**

Combine first 4 ingredients in a saucepan; cook over medium heat, stirring constantly, until sugar dissolves and mixture comes to a boil. Cover and cook 2 to 3 minutes to wash down sugar crystals from sides of pan. Uncover and cook, without stirring, until mixture reaches soft ball stage or candy thermometer registers 236°.

Combine milk mixture, peanut butter, and vanilla in a large mixing bowl; beat at medium speed of an electric mixer until mixture thickens and begins to lose its gloss (about 6 minutes). Quickly pour into a buttered 8-inch square pan. Let cool completely. Cut into squares. Yield: 1 pound.

Valerie Kennison

Favorite Recipes
National Association of Women in Construction
Tri-County Chapter #317
Vero Beach, Florida

Macadamia Nut Brittle

1 cup sugar
½ cup light corn syrup
¼ cup water
¾ cup whole macadamia nuts
½ cup chopped macadamia
   nuts

1 tablespoon butter or
   margarine
½ teaspoon vanilla extract
⅛ teaspoon baking soda

Combine first 3 ingredients in a large saucepan. Cook over medium heat, stirring constantly, until sugar dissolves. Cover and cook over medium heat 2 to 3 minutes to wash down sugar crystals from sides of pan. Add whole and chopped macadamia nuts; cook until mixture reaches hard crack stage or candy thermometer registers 300°, stirring occasionally. Remove from heat. Stir in butter, vanilla, and soda.

Working rapidly, pour mixture into a buttered 15- x 10- x 1-inch jellyroll pan, spreading thinly. Let cool completely. Break into pieces. Store in an airtight container. Yield: 1 pound.

Another Taste of Aloha
The Junior League of Honolulu, Hawaii

Orange Pecans

1 cup sugar
⅓ cup orange juice
1 teaspoon cream of tartar

2¼ cups pecan halves, toasted
½ teaspoon grated orange rind

Combine first 3 ingredients in a large heavy saucepan. Cook over low heat, stirring constantly, until sugar dissolves and mixture comes to a boil. Cover and cook 2 to 3 minutes to wash down sugar crystals from sides of pan. Uncover and cook, without stirring, until mixture reaches soft ball stage or candy thermometer registers 236°.

Remove from heat; beat with a wooden spoon just until mixture begins to thicken. Stir in pecans and orange rind. Working rapidly, drop by rounded teaspoonfuls onto wax paper. Cool. Yield: 2 dozen.

Dining with Southern Elegance
Terrebonne Association for Family and Community Education
Houma, Louisiana

Desserts

Butter Pecan Ice Cream, page 147

Deep-Fried Bananas

Plunge these banana fritters into your favorite dipper–honey, maple syrup, powdered sugar, or hot fudge.

1 cup all-purpose flour
¼ cup sugar
1 teaspoon salt
¼ teaspoon ground nutmeg
1 large egg, lightly beaten
1 tablespoon vegetable oil

½ cup milk
1 teaspoon vanilla extract
Vegetable oil
9 firm ripe bananas, sliced into
   1-inch pieces

Combine first 4 ingredients in a small bowl. Combine egg, oil, milk, and vanilla in a large bowl. Gradually add flour mixture to egg mixture, stirring until smooth.

Pour oil to depth of 2 inches into a Dutch oven; heat to 375°. Dip banana slices into batter; fry in hot oil 3½ to 4 minutes or until golden. Drain on paper towels. Yield: 12 servings.   Elsie Huser

Conflict-Free Cooking
National Court Reporters Foundation
Vienna, Virginia

Cherry Dumpling Dessert

3 (14½-ounce) cans tart red
   pitted cherries, undrained
1 cup plus 2 tablespoons sugar,
   divided
2 cups all-purpose flour
1 tablespoon plus 1 teaspoon
   baking powder

1 teaspoon salt
¼ cup butter or margarine
¾ cup milk
Half-and-half (optional)

Combine cherries and ½ cup sugar in a large Dutch oven; stir well. Bring to a boil.

Combine flour, baking powder, and salt; cut in butter with pastry blender until mixture is crumbly. Add remaining ½ cup plus 2 tablespoons sugar, stirring just until blended. Add milk, stirring just until moistened.

Carefully drop dough by heaping tablespoonfuls into boiling cherry mixture. Cover and cook over medium heat 25 minutes or until dumplings are done. Serve with half-and-half, if desired. Yield: 8 servings.   Rosemary Braun

Company's Coming
St. Charles Ladies Guild
Morganton, North Carolina

Fig and Pear Crumble

7½ ounces dried figs
5 fresh pears, peeled and cut
  into 8 wedges each
⅓ cup sugar
2 tablespoons unsalted butter
  or margarine, melted
1 tablespoon all-purpose flour
¼ teaspoon salt
¼ teaspoon ground cinnamon

1 cup all-purpose flour
½ cup firmly packed brown
  sugar
¼ cup sugar
¼ teaspoon ground cinnamon
⅓ cup unsalted butter or
  margarine
Whipped cream

Remove stems from figs; quarter figs. Place figs in a small bowl; add hot water to cover. Let stand 20 minutes; drain and set aside.

Place pear wedges in a large bowl. Sprinkle with ⅓ cup sugar, melted butter, 1 tablespoon flour, salt, and ¼ teaspoon cinnamon; toss well. Spoon pear mixture into a buttered 8-inch square baking dish; arrange figs on top of pear mixture. Set aside.

Combine 1 cup flour, brown sugar, ¼ cup sugar, and ¼ teaspoon cinnamon in a medium bowl; stir well. Cut in ⅓ cup butter with pastry blender until mixture is crumbly; sprinkle over figs. Bake at 350° for 45 to 50 minutes or until golden. Serve warm with whipped cream. Yield: 6 servings.   Barbara Arnold

Cooking Up a Storm, Florida Style
Brookwood Guild
St. Petersburg, Florida

Lukshen Kugel with Peaches

Traditionally served on the Jewish Sabbath, kugel is a baked pudding generally served as a side dish. But this sweet version made with peaches is delicious as a dessert.

1 (16-ounce) package wide egg noodles, uncooked
4 large eggs, lightly beaten
1 (16-ounce) carton sour cream
1 (12-ounce) carton small-curd cottage cheese
½ cup butter or margarine, melted
¼ cup sugar
1 teaspoon salt
1 teaspoon vanilla extract
1 (29-ounce) can sliced peaches in heavy syrup, drained

Cook noodles according to package directions; drain. Place in a large bowl; add eggs and next 6 ingredients, stirring well. Spoon mixture into a greased 13- x 9- x 2-inch pan. Place peach slices over mixture. Bake, uncovered, at 375° for 1 hour. Let stand 5 minutes before serving. Yield: 12 servings.   Charles P. Sherman

Today's Traditional: Jewish Cooking with a Lighter Touch
Congregation Beth Shalom
Carmichael, California

Cheese-Filled Pears with Glazed Cranberries

Any leftover Glazed Cranberries can be served as a relish for your favorite meat or poultry.

6 medium-size firm ripe pears
4 cups water
2 tablespoons grated lemon rind
2½ tablespoons fresh lemon juice
2 tablespoons sugar

½ cup ricotta cheese
½ (8-ounce) package cream cheese, softened
1 tablespoon sugar
2 tablespoons half-and-half
Glazed Cranberries

Peel and core pears; cut in half lengthwise, and set aside.

Combine water and next 3 ingredients in a large skillet, stirring until sugar dissolves. Bring to a boil; add pear halves. Cover, reduce heat, and simmer 10 to 15 minutes or until tender. Drain and let cool. Chill pears thoroughly before serving.

Combine ricotta cheese and next 3 ingredients in a small bowl, stirring until smooth. Cover and chill thoroughly.

To serve, place pear halves on individual serving plates. Spoon cheese mixture evenly onto pears. Spoon Glazed Cranberries over cheese mixture. Yield: 12 servings.

Glazed Cranberries

2 cups fresh cranberries
⅔ cup sugar

2 teaspoons grated orange rind
1 (3-inch) stick cinnamon

Combine all ingredients in a 10-inch skillet. Cover and cook over low heat 30 minutes or until sugar dissolves and cranberries are glazed and skins pop. Discard cinnamon stick. Cover and chill thoroughly. Yield: 1½ cups.

Heard in the Kitchen
The Heard Museum Guild
Phoenix, Arizona

Strawberries in Mascarpone Cream

Sliced toasted almonds make a handy substitute for pistachios.

3 egg yolks
⅓ cup sugar
½ teaspoon cornstarch
1 cup whipping cream, divided
½ vanilla bean, split lengthwise
1 cup mascarpone cheese

½ cup firmly packed brown
   sugar
½ cup amaretto
8 cups ripe strawberries,
   halved lengthwise
½ cup shelled pistachios

Combine first 3 ingredients in a medium bowl; beat at medium speed of an electric mixer until thick and pale.

Heat ½ cup whipping cream in a small saucepan over medium heat until very warm.

Gradually beat warmed cream into egg yolk mixture. Pour mixture into saucepan; add vanilla bean, and cook over medium heat, stirring constantly, just until mixture comes to a boil. Remove from heat; remove and discard vanilla bean. Transfer mixture to a bowl; set bowl in a pan of cold water to cool, stirring frequently. Add mascarpone cheese to cooled cream mixture; stir well. Whip remaining ½ cup whipping cream, and fold into mascarpone mixture. Cover and chill.

Reserve 1 tablespoon each of brown sugar and liqueur; sprinkle remaining brown sugar and liqueur over strawberries; stir well. Cover and chill 30 minutes.

Divide berries among six dessert plates or bowls. Top each with mascarpone mixture; sprinkle with reserved brown sugar and liqueur. Top with pistachios. Yield: 8 servings.   Melody Favish

Celebrating California
Children's Home Society of California
San Diego, California

Crème Brûlée with Raspberry Sauce

You can bake this dessert ahead, but wait until just before serving to caramelize the sugar. The crusted sugar will begin to liquefy if the custards sit for more than an hour.

¾ cup sugar	2 teaspoons vanilla extract
3 cups whipping cream	½ cup firmly packed dark
7 egg yolks, lightly beaten	brown sugar

Combine ¾ cup sugar and whipping cream in a heavy saucepan; cook over medium heat, stirring constantly, until sugar melts and mixture comes to a simmer (do not boil). Remove from heat.

Combine egg yolks and vanilla in a small bowl. Gradually stir about one-fourth of hot whipping cream mixture into yolk mixture; add to remaining hot whipping cream mixture, stirring constantly.

Pour custard mixture evenly into eight 4-ounce ramekins. Place ramekins in a 13- x 9- x 2-inch pan; add hot water to pan to depth of 1 inch. Bake at 350° for 35 minutes. Remove ramekins from water; cool slightly on wire racks.

Sprinkle brown sugar evenly over custards. Broil 5½ inches from heat (with electric oven door partially opened) 3 minutes or until sugar melts. Cool on wire racks to allow sugar to harden. Serve with Raspberry Sauce. Yield: 8 servings.

Raspberry Sauce

1 (10-ounce) package frozen raspberries in syrup, thawed and undrained	1 tablespoon lemon juice
	1 to 3 tablespoons sugar

Place 1 cup thawed raspberries with syrup in container of an electric blender or food processor, reserving the prettiest whole raspberries; cover and process 10 seconds or until pureed. Place pureed raspberries in a wire-mesh strainer; press with back of a spoon against sides of strainer to squeeze out juice. Discard pulp and seeds remaining in strainer. Add lemon juice and sugar to puree, stirring until sugar dissolves; add remaining whole raspberries. Yield: 1½ cups.

Appealing Fare
Frost & Jacobs
Cincinnati, Ohio

Peach-Amaretto Bread Pudding

1 (16-ounce) loaf French or
  Italian bread, torn into pieces
1 quart half-and-half
1 tablespoon unsalted butter
3 large eggs, lightly beaten
1½ cups sugar

2 tablespoons almond extract
3 medium-size fresh peaches,
  peeled and thinly sliced
1 cup sliced almonds
Amaretto Sauce

Combine bread and half-and-half in a large bowl. Cover and chill 1 hour. Grease a 13- x 9- x 2-inch baking dish with 1 tablespoon butter; set aside.

Combine eggs, sugar, and almond extract; stir well. Add egg mixture to chilled bread mixture, stirring gently. Gently fold in peaches and almonds. Pour into prepared dish. Bake, uncovered, at 325° for 1 hour or until set and lightly browned. Let stand 15 minutes before serving. Serve with Amaretto Sauce. Yield: 12 servings.

Amaretto Sauce

½ cup unsalted butter
1 cup sifted powdered sugar

1 large egg, lightly beaten
¼ cup amaretto

Combine butter and sugar in a small saucepan; cook, stirring constantly, until butter melts and sugar dissolves. Gradually stir about one-fourth of hot mixture into egg; add to remaining hot mixture, stirring constantly. Cook over medium heat, stirring constantly, until mixture thickens. Remove from heat, and stir in amaretto. Let cool to room temperature, stirring occasionally. Yield: 1 cup.   Dallas Reed

Quilters Guild of Indianapolis Cookbook
Quilters Guild of Indianapolis, Indiana

Cappuccino Soufflé

Butter or margarine
1½ tablespoons sugar
2 cups milk
¼ cup sugar
2 tablespoons instant coffee granules
2 tablespoons Kahlúa or other coffee-flavored liqueur
1 tablespoon brandy
½ (1-ounce) square semisweet chocolate

1 teaspoon vanilla extract
¼ cup unsalted butter
3 tablespoons all-purpose flour
6 large eggs, separated
4 egg yolks
1½ cups milk
3 tablespoons sugar
1½ teaspoons vanilla extract

Cut a piece of aluminum foil long enough to fit around a 2½-quart soufflé dish, allowing a 1-inch overlap; fold foil lengthwise into thirds. Lightly butter one side of foil and bottom of dish. Wrap foil around outside of dish, buttered side against dish, allowing it to extend 3 inches above rim to form a collar; secure with string. Sprinkle bottom with 1½ tablespoons sugar, tilting dish to coat sides. Set aside.

Combine 2 cups milk and next 6 ingredients in a medium saucepan. Cook over medium-low heat, stirring constantly, until chocolate melts. Remove from heat.

Melt ¼ cup butter in a small saucepan over low heat; add flour, stirring until smooth. Cook 1 minute, stirring constantly. Gradually add to milk mixture. Cook over medium heat, stirring constantly, until thickened and bubbly. Remove from heat.

Beat 6 yolks at medium speed of an electric mixer until thick and pale. Gradually stir about one-fourth of hot milk mixture into yolks; add to remaining hot mixture, stirring constantly. Cool completely.

Beat egg whites at high speed until stiff peaks form. Carefully fold into milk mixture. Pour into dish. Bake at 350° for 50 minutes or until puffed and set.

Combine 4 yolks, 1½ cups milk, and 3 tablespoons sugar in a small saucepan. Cook over medium-low heat, stirring constantly, until mixture thickens. Remove from heat, and stir in 1½ teaspoons vanilla. Cover and chill. Serve soufflé immediately with custard sauce. Yield: 10 servings.

Feast of Eden
The Junior League of Monterey County, California

Orange Liqueur Soufflé

½ cup whipping cream
1 tablespoon powdered sugar
½ cup plus 2 tablespoons
   Grand Marnier or other
   orange-flavored liqueur,
   divided
Butter or margarine
2 tablespoons sugar
6 ladyfingers

¼ cup butter
⅓ cup all-purpose flour
2 cups milk
¾ cup sugar
5 large eggs, separated
2 egg whites
⅛ teaspoon salt
¾ teaspoon cream of tartar
1 tablespoon powdered sugar

Beat whipping cream until foamy; gradually add 1 tablespoon powdered sugar, beating until soft peaks form. Stir in 2 tablespoons liqueur. Cover and chill.

Cut a piece of aluminum foil long enough to fit around a 2½-quart soufflé dish, allowing a 1-inch overlap; fold foil lengthwise into thirds. Lightly butter one side of foil and bottom of dish. Wrap foil around outside of dish, buttered side against dish, allowing it to extend 3 inches above rim to form a collar; secure with string. Sprinkle bottom with 2 tablespoons sugar, tilting dish to coat sides. Set aside.

Sprinkle ladyfingers with ¼ cup liqueur; set aside.

Melt ¼ cup butter in a large heavy saucepan over low heat; add flour, stirring until smooth. Cook 1 minute, stirring constantly. Gradually add milk and ¾ cup sugar; cook over medium heat, stirring constantly, until mixture is thickened and bubbly. Remove from heat, and stir in remaining ¼ cup liqueur. Beat egg yolks until thick and pale. Gradually stir about one-fourth of hot mixture into yolks; add to remaining hot mixture, stirring constantly. Beat 7 egg whites and salt in a large bowl at high speed of an electric mixer until foamy. Gradually add cream of tartar, beating until stiff peaks form. Gently fold one-fourth of beaten egg white into milk mixture. Fold in remaining beaten egg white.

Spoon half of mixture into prepared dish. Arrange ladyfingers on top of mixture. Spoon remaining mixture over ladyfingers. Bake at 375° for 38 minutes. Sprinkle soufflé with 1 tablespoon powdered sugar. Bake 2 additional minutes. Serve immediately with sweetened whipped cream. Yield: 6 servings. Donna Ianire

What's Cooking in Delaware
American Red Cross in Delaware
Wilmington, Delaware

Spring Snow Torte

You can make these meringue layers up to 24 hours in advance, and store them in an airtight container. Wait until the last minute to assemble the torte, because the meringues will soften when you add the fruit and filling.

4 egg whites
¼ teaspoon cream of tartar
Dash of salt
1 cup sugar
1 cup (6 ounces) semisweet
   chocolate morsels
3 tablespoons water

3½ cups whipping cream
⅓ cup sugar
1 quart fresh strawberries,
   sliced
Garnish: whole fresh
   strawberries

Combine first 3 ingredients in a large mixing bowl; beat at high speed of an electric mixer until foamy. Gradually add 1 cup sugar, 1 tablespoon at a time, beating until stiff peaks form and sugar dissolves (2 to 4 minutes).

Spread mixture into three 8-inch circles on wax paper on a baking sheet. Bake at 250° for 1 hour and 15 minutes. Let cool completely. Carefully remove meringues from paper.

Combine chocolate morsels and water in top of a double boiler; bring water in bottom of double boiler to a boil. Reduce heat to low; cook until chocolate melts.

Beat whipping cream with electric mixer until foamy; gradually add ⅓ cup sugar, beating until soft peaks form.

Place one meringue circle on a serving plate; drizzle with one-third of chocolate mixture. Spoon one-third of sliced strawberries over chocolate; top with one-third of whipped cream. Repeat layers with remaining meringues, chocolate, strawberries, and whipped cream. Serve immediately. Garnish, if desired. Yield: one 8-inch meringue torte.

Sensational Seasons: A Taste & Tour of Arkansas
The Junior League of Fort Smith, Arkansas

Raspberry Bombe

Vegetable cooking spray
1 (16-ounce) package frozen
  sliced peaches, thawed
  and drained
1 (8-ounce) carton sour cream
½ cup grenadine
½ gallon vanilla ice cream,
  softened
2 (10-ounce) packages frozen
  raspberries in syrup, thawed
  and undrained

1 cup light corn syrup
2 tablespoons frozen orange
  juice concentrate, thawed
  and undiluted
¼ teaspoon orange extract
Garnishes: fresh raspberries,
  fresh mint sprigs

Coat an 11-cup mold with cooking spray. Set aside.

Position knife blade in food processor bowl; add peaches, and process until smooth. Add sour cream and grenadine; process until well blended. Combine peach mixture and ice cream in a large mixing bowl; beat at low speed of an electric mixer until smooth. Pour into prepared mold. Cover and freeze 8 hours or until firm.

Position knife blade in food processor bowl; add thawed raspberries, and process 1 minute. Place raspberry puree in a wire-mesh strainer; press with back of a spoon against sides of strainer to squeeze out juice. Discard pulp and seeds remaining in strainer. Combine raspberry juice, corn syrup, orange juice concentrate, and orange extract; stir well.

To unmold bombe, place a warm, damp towel around mold; run a sharp knife or a small metal spatula around edges. Invert mold onto a chilled serving platter. Serve bombe with raspberry sauce. Garnish, if desired. Yield: 12 servings.

Among the Lilies
Women in Missions, First Baptist Church of Atlanta, Georgia

Butter Pecan Ice Cream

This recipe is so good you may want to double or triple the recipe, and invite your friends over. If you do, make it in a one gallon freezer.

¾ **cup firmly packed brown sugar**
½ **cup water**
⅛ **teaspoon salt**
2 **large eggs, lightly beaten**
2 **tablespoons butter**

1 **cup milk**
1 **teaspoon vanilla extract**
1 **cup whipping cream**
½ **cup finely chopped pecans, toasted**

Combine first 3 ingredients in top of a double boiler; bring water in bottom of double boiler to a boil. Reduce heat to low; cook, stirring constantly, 3 to 4 minutes or until sugar dissolves. Gradually stir a small amount of hot mixture into eggs; add to remaining hot mixture, stirring constantly. Cook over medium heat, stirring constantly, until thermometer registers 160° and mixture thickens (about 4 to 5 minutes). Remove from heat; stir in butter, and let cool. Stir in milk and remaining ingredients.

Pour mixture into freezer container of a 2-quart hand-turned or electric freezer. Freeze according to manufacturer's instructions.

Pack freezer with additional ice and rock salt, and let stand 1 hour before serving. Yield: 1 quart.

A Southern Collection, Then and Now
The Junior League of Columbus, Georgia

Strawberry-Cassis Sherbet

To candy violets, lightly brush petals of fresh violets with egg substitute; lightly sprinkle with superfine sugar. Let violets stand, separated, on wax paper, at least one hour or until they're dry.

1½ pounds fresh strawberries, hulled
1 cup dry red wine
½ cup crème de cassis
½ cup honey
1 tablespoon lemon juice
Crème de cassis
Garnish: candied violets

Position knife blade in food processor bowl; add half of first 5 ingredients. Process until smooth, stopping once to scrape down sides; repeat procedure with remaining half of ingredients.

Pour mixture into freezer container of a 2-quart hand-turned or electric freezer. Freeze according to manufacturer's instructions.

Pack freezer with additional ice and rock salt, and let stand 1 hour before serving. Serve with crème de cassis. Garnish, if desired. Yield: 4 cups.   Francine du Plessix Gray

Cooking in the Litchfield Hills
The Pratt Center
New Milford, Connecticut

Claret Ice

4 cups water
1 cup sugar
1 cup claret
1 cup raspberry syrup
¼ cup plus 3 tablespoons fresh lemon juice
2 tablespoons kirsch
½ teaspoon ground cinnamon

Combine water and sugar in a medium saucepan; bring to a boil. Boil 5 minutes; let cool completely.

Add wine and remaining ingredients; stir well. Pour into a 13- x 9- x 2-inch dish. Cover and freeze until firm. Let stand at room temperature 20 minutes before serving. Yield: 7 cups.

Seasoned Skillets & Silver Spoons
The Columbus Museum Guild
Columbus, Georgia

Eggs & Cheese

Crab, Cream Cheese, and Avocado Omelet, page 154

Poached Eggs in White Wine

For a special occasion top these eggs with our Hollandaise Sauce on page 277 or one of your favorite sauces.

1½ tablespoons unsalted butter	⅛ teaspoon salt
¾ cup dry white wine	⅛ teaspoon pepper
6 large eggs	⅛ teaspoon ground red pepper
3 English muffins, split and toasted	2 teaspoons chopped fresh tarragon

Melt butter in a large nonstick skillet; add wine. Bring to a boil; reduce heat to low, and keep warm. Working with 3 eggs at a time, break eggs, one at a time, into a saucer; slip egg into wine mixture, holding saucer close to wine mixture. Cover and simmer 5 minutes or until cooked. Remove with a slotted spoon; trim edges, if desired, and place on muffin halves. Repeat procedure with remaining eggs and muffin halves. Combine salt and next 3 ingredients; sprinkle over eggs. Yield: 6 servings.   Maria Berton

Signature Cuisine
Miami Country Day School Parents' Association
Miami, Florida

Mexican Scrambled Eggs

Be careful not to overscramble your eggs. Drawing a spatula over the mixture occasionally instead of stirring constantly will prevent the eggs from being dry and crumbly.

8 large eggs, lightly beaten	¼ teaspoon salt
2 tablespoons milk	⅛ teaspoon pepper
1 large tomato, peeled, seeded, and chopped	2 to 3 tablespoons butter or margarine
1 tablespoon chopped green pepper	½ cup chopped cooked ham
1 tablespoon chopped fresh parsley	

Combine first 7 ingredients in a medium bowl, stirring mixture well; set aside.

Melt butter in a large skillet over medium heat. Add ham, and cook 2 minutes, stirring constantly. Add egg mixture to skillet. Cook, without stirring, until egg mixture begins to set on bottom. Draw a spatula across bottom of pan to form large curds. Continue cooking until eggs are firm, but still moist (do not stir constantly). Serve immediately. Yield: 6 servings.   Juanita Ortega

What's Cooking at Cathedral Plaza
Cathedral Plaza
Denver, Colorado

Artichoke Heart Frittata

1 **cup frozen artichoke hearts,**
   thawed, drained, and
   quartered
1 **cup chopped zucchini**
⅔ **cup chopped onion**
⅔ **cup chopped green pepper**
1 **teaspoon minced garlic**
2 **tablespoons vegetable oil**
5 **large eggs, lightly beaten**

⅓ **cup milk**
½ **teaspoon salt**
Dash of pepper
1½ **cups soft bread cubes**
1 **(8-ounce) package cream**
   cheese, cubed
1 **cup (4 ounces) shredded**
   Cheddar cheese

Cook first 5 ingredients in hot oil in a large skillet over medium-high heat, stirring constantly, until vegetables are crisp-tender.

Combine eggs, milk, salt, and pepper in a large bowl; stir well. Gently stir artichoke mixture, bread cubes, cream cheese cubes, and Cheddar cheese into egg mixture. Pour egg mixture into a greased 9-inch pieplate. Bake at 350° for 40 to 45 minutes or until golden. Let stand 5 minutes before serving. Yield: 6 servings.

Sterling Performances
The Guilds of the Orange County Performing Arts Center
Costa Mesa, California

Tapas (Spanish Potato Tortilla)

3 large potatoes
¾ cup olive oil
1½ teaspoons salt, divided
1 large onion, thinly sliced
1 medium-size sweet red
   pepper, sliced into thin rings

4 large eggs
¼ teaspoon freshly ground
   pepper
Red Sauce

Peel potatoes, and cut crosswise into ¼-inch-thick slices.

Heat oil in a 10-inch nonstick skillet over medium-high heat. Add potato slices and ¾ teaspoon salt; cook 15 minutes or until lightly browned, stirring often. Reduce heat; add onion and red pepper rings. Cook 7 to 8 minutes or until vegetables are tender, stirring often. Drain, reserving 3 tablespoons oil. Sprinkle potato mixture with ½ teaspoon salt; set aside.

Combine eggs, remaining ¼ teaspoon salt, and pepper in a large bowl. Beat with a wire whisk until blended; stir in potato mixture.

Heat reserved oil in a large nonstick skillet over medium heat. Add egg mixture, and cook 2 minutes or until set. Carefully invert onto a plate, and then slide off of plate back into skillet; cook 1 to 2 additional minutes or until lightly browned. Cut into wedges. Serve warm with Red Sauce. Yield: 8 servings.

Red Sauce

1 cup chopped onion
1 large clove garlic, minced
1 tablespoon olive oil
1 cup chopped tomato
½ cup water
½ teaspoon salt

⅛ teaspoon freshly ground
   pepper
Dash of saffron
½ cup chopped roasted sweet
   red pepper

Cook onion and garlic in hot oil in a small saucepan over medium-high heat, stirring constantly, until tender. Add tomato and next 4 ingredients. Bring to a boil; reduce heat, and simmer, uncovered, 20 minutes. Stir in roasted pepper, and cook 10 minutes. Bring to a boil, and cook until mixture is thickened. Yield: 1½ cups.

Creative Chef 2
Tourette Syndrome Association
Bayside, New York

Spicy Vegetable-Cheese Omelet

This open-face omelet needs to cook evenly. Make sure you lift the edges of the omelet with a spatula, and tilt the pan so the uncooked egg flows underneath.

8 fresh asparagus spears
2 tablespoons olive oil, divided
1¾ cups chopped fresh broccoli
¾ cup chopped sweet red pepper
¼ cup chopped purple onion
8 large fresh mushrooms, sliced
1½ teaspoons garlic powder
6 large eggs, lightly beaten
1½ cups (6 ounces) shredded Monterey Jack cheese with jalapeño pepper

Snap off tough ends of asparagus; remove scales from stalks with a knife or vegetable peeler, if desired. Cut diagonally into ½-inch slices; set aside.

Heat 1 tablespoon oil in a 10-inch nonstick skillet over medium heat; add asparagus, broccoli, and next 3 ingredients. Cook until crisp-tender; stir in garlic powder. Remove vegetable mixture from pan, and set aside.

Heat skillet over medium heat; add remaining tablespoon oil, and rotate pan to coat bottom. Add eggs. As mixture starts to cook, gently lift edges of omelet with a spatula, and tilt pan so uncooked portion flows underneath. Sprinkle with cheese; top with vegetable mixture. Cover and cook 2 to 3 additional minutes to allow uncooked portion on top to set. Cut into thirds; serve immediately. Yield: 3 servings.

Seaport Savories
TWIG Junior Auxiliary of Alexandria Hospital
Alexandria, Virginia

Crab, Cream Cheese, and Avocado Omelet

4 large eggs, lightly beaten
¼ cup milk
¼ teaspoon salt
⅛ teaspoon paprika
Dash of ground white pepper
1½ tablespoons butter
2 ounces cream cheese, cut into
   1-inch pieces and softened

½ ripe avocado, peeled and
   sliced
½ cup fresh lump crabmeat,
   drained
2 teaspoons lemon juice
Fresh chives

Combine first 5 ingredients; stir with a wire whisk until blended.

Heat a 10-inch nonstick skillet over medium heat until hot enough to sizzle a drop of water. Add butter, and tilt pan to coat bottom evenly. Pour egg mixture into skillet. As mixture starts to cook, gently lift edges of omelet with a spatula, and tilt pan so uncooked portion flows underneath.

Sprinkle cream cheese over half of omelet. Arrange avocado and crabmeat over cheese, and drizzle lemon juice over crabmeat. Fold omelet in half; cover and cook 2 to 3 minutes or until cheese melts. Top with chives. Serve immediately. Yield: 2 servings.

Virginia Fare
The Junior League of Richmond, Virginia

Make-Ahead Brunch Bake

This overnight brunch dish almost qualified for our Quick & Easy chapter in this cookbook. But it was just over the time limit. Still, we think it's super easy.

1 (6-ounce) package garlic-
   flavored croutons
3 cups (12 ounces) shredded
   sharp Cheddar cheese
12 large eggs, lightly beaten

4 cups milk
1 (12-ounce) package bacon,
   cooked and crumbled
½ cup finely chopped green
   pepper (optional)

Place croutons in a single layer in a greased 13- x 9- x 2-inch pan; sprinkle with cheese.

Combine eggs and milk; stir well. Pour egg mixture over croutons. Cover and chill 8 hours. Bake at 350° for 35 minutes. Remove from oven; sprinkle with bacon and, if desired, green pepper. Bake 10 additional minutes or until a knife inserted in center comes out clean. Let stand 10 minutes before serving. Yield: 10 servings.　　　Lisa Plorin

Years and Years of Goodwill Cooking
The Goodwill Circle of New Hope Lutheran Church
Upham, North Dakota

Egg-Cheese Puff

Substitute flavored croutons for plain if you'd like a spicier dish.

4 cups plain croutons
2 cups (8 ounces) shredded
　Cheddar cheese
8 large eggs, lightly beaten
4 cups milk
1½ teaspoons salt

½ teaspoon onion powder
½ teaspoon prepared mustard
¼ teaspoon pepper
8 slices bacon, cooked and
　crumbled

Place croutons in a greased 13- x 9- x 2-inch baking dish. Sprinkle with cheese. Combine eggs and next 5 ingredients; stir well. Pour egg mixture over cheese. Sprinkle with bacon.

Cover and chill 8 hours. Bake at 325° for 55 minutes. Serve immediately. Yield: 8 servings.　　　Curt Fuhro

The Christ Church Cookbook
Christ Episcopal Church
Woodbury, Minnesota

Vegetable Strata

1 cup broccoli flowerets
1 cup cauliflower flowerets
1 teaspoon minced garlic
½ cup sliced green onions
½ cup diced sweet red pepper
½ cup julienne-sliced carrot
2 to 3 tablespoons olive oil
1 cup sliced fresh mushrooms
1 (16-ounce) loaf French bread, cut into 1-inch cubes
1 cup (4 ounces) shredded Cheddar cheese
½ cup grated Parmesan cheese
10 large eggs, lightly beaten
2½ cups milk
½ teaspoon salt
¼ teaspoon ground white pepper
½ teaspoon ground red pepper

Cook broccoli and cauliflower in boiling water to cover 10 seconds; drain immediately. Plunge into ice water to stop cooking process.

Cook garlic and next 3 ingredients in hot oil in a medium saucepan over medium-high heat 2 minutes or until vegetables are crisp-tender. Add mushrooms, and cook 1 minute; remove from heat. Stir in broccoli and cauliflower.

Layer half each of bread cubes, vegetable mixture, and cheeses in a lightly greased 13- x 9- x 2-inch baking dish. Repeat layers, using remaining bread cubes, vegetable mixture, and cheeses.

Combine eggs and remaining 4 ingredients; stir with a wire whisk until blended. Pour egg mixture evenly over cheese layer; cover and chill 8 hours.

Remove from refrigerator; let stand, covered, 1 hour. Uncover and bake at 325° for 1 hour or until set and lightly browned. Let stand 10 minutes before serving. Yield: 8 servings.

Minnesota Times and Tastes, Recipes and Menus Seasoned with History
from the Minnesota Governor's Residence
The 1006 Summit Avenue Society
St. Paul, Minnesota

Apple and Sausage Quiche

Use mild pork sausage for a tamer-flavored quiche. Try hot pork sausage to pump up the flavor.

1 **unbaked 9-inch pastry shell**
1 **cup peeled, chopped cooking apple**
2 **tablespoons sugar**
1 **tablespoon lemon juice**
Dash of salt
Dash of pepper
¾ **cup chopped onion**
3 **tablespoons butter or margarine, melted**

½ **pound ground pork sausage**
4 **large eggs, beaten**
1 **(8-ounce) carton sour cream**
⅛ **teaspoon ground nutmeg**
Dash of ground red pepper
½ **cup (2 ounces) shredded Cheddar cheese**

Prick bottom and sides of pastry with a fork. Bake at 450° for 8 to 10 minutes; let cool on a wire rack.

Combine apple and next 4 ingredients; toss well. Cook apple mixture and onion in butter in a large skillet over medium-high heat, stirring constantly, until onion is tender. Remove from heat, and let cool 20 minutes.

Brown sausage in a large skillet, stirring until it crumbles; drain well. Combine eggs and next 3 ingredients in a large bowl. Add apple mixture and sausage to egg mixture; stir well.

Pour mixture into prepared pastry shell. Bake, uncovered, at 350° for 25 minutes. Sprinkle with cheese, and bake 10 additional minutes or until cheese melts and knife inserted in center comes out clean. Let stand 10 minutes before serving. Yield: one 9-inch quiche.

Among the Lilies
Women in Missions, First Baptist Church of Atlanta, Georgia

Crab and Saga Blue Quiche

Saga blue cheese is a rich, creamy variety from Denmark. It has a mellow flavor with a tender, white edible rind and a texture similar to Brie cheese.

1½ cups all-purpose flour
1 tablespoon sugar
1 teaspoon salt
½ cup unsalted butter or margarine
¼ cup shortening
¼ cup ice water
1 cup grated Gruyère cheese
1 cup fresh lump crabmeat, drained

1 cup crumbled Saga blue cheese
1½ cups whipping cream
3 large eggs, beaten
¼ teaspoon salt
¼ teaspoon pepper
¼ teaspoon ground nutmeg

Combine flour, sugar, and 1 teaspoon salt; cut in butter and shortening with pastry blender until mixture is crumbly. Sprinkle ice water, 1 tablespoon at a time, evenly over surface; stir with a fork until dry ingredients are moistened. Shape into a ball; chill 30 minutes.

Gently press dough into a 4-inch circle on heavy-duty plastic wrap; cover with additional plastic wrap. Roll dough into a 12-inch circle. Remove top sheet of plastic wrap. Invert and fit dough into a 10-inch quiche dish; trim excess pastry along edges.

Line pastry with aluminum foil or wax paper, and fill with pie weights or dried beans. Bake at 425° for 10 minutes.

Sprinkle Gruyère over prepared pastry; top with crabmeat and blue cheese. Combine whipping cream and next 4 ingredients; stir well. Pour over crabmeat mixture. Bake at 350° for 35 to 40 minutes or until a knife inserted in center comes out clean. Let stand 10 minutes before serving. Yield: one 10-inch quiche.   Scott Casky

A Quest for Good Eating
Cape Cod Questers
Yarmouth Port, Massachusetts

Vidalia Onion Pie Supreme

3 cups thinly sliced Vidalia onion
3 tablespoons butter or margarine, melted
1 unbaked deep-dish 9-inch pastry shell
1½ cups sour cream
½ cup milk
3 tablespoons all-purpose flour
2 large eggs, lightly beaten
1 teaspoon salt
3 slices bacon, cooked and crumbled

Cook onion in butter over medium heat 30 minutes or until golden, stirring occasionally. Spoon into pastry shell. Combine sour cream and next 4 ingredients; pour over onion.

Bake at 350° for 30 minutes or until set and lightly browned. Sprinkle with bacon. Yield: one 9-inch pie. Janice Baker

Timeless Treasures
The Junior Service League of Valdosta, Georgia

Orange Blossom French Toast

6 egg yolks
1 tablespoon grated orange rind
½ cup orange juice
⅓ cup whipping cream
1 teaspoon sugar
½ teaspoon ground cinnamon
¼ teaspoon freshly grated nutmeg
1 (16-ounce) loaf French bread, cut into ¾-inch-thick slices
¼ cup butter or margarine, divided
Sifted powdered sugar

Beat egg yolks in a medium bowl with a wire whisk; add orange rind and next 5 ingredients, stirring well.

Dip bread slices into egg yolk mixture, turning to coat. Melt 1 tablespoon butter in a large skillet; add 5 slices bread. Cook over medium heat 1 minute on each side or until golden; remove from skillet, and keep warm. Repeat procedure 3 times, cooking 3 slices the last time. Sprinkle with powdered sugar, and serve immediately with syrup. Yield: 9 servings.

Tasteful Treasures
Docent Guild, Bowers Museum of Cultural Art
Santa Ana, California

Praline French Toast

As a shortcut, combine the melted butter, brown sugar, maple syrup, and pecans, and microwave at HIGH for 30 seconds.

8 large eggs, beaten
1½ cups half-and-half
1 tablespoon brown sugar
2 teaspoons vanilla extract
8 (¾-inch-thick) slices French bread

½ cup butter or margarine
¾ cup firmly packed brown sugar
½ cup maple syrup
¾ cup chopped pecans, toasted

Combine first 4 ingredients in a large bowl, stirring with a wire whisk until blended. Pour 1 cup egg mixture into a greased 13- x 9- x 2-inch baking dish. Place bread in dish; pour remaining egg mixture over bread. Cover and chill 8 hours.

Melt butter in a saucepan over medium heat; add brown sugar and maple syrup, stirring until smooth. Bring to a boil; reduce heat, and simmer 1 minute, stirring constantly. Stir in pecans. Pour over French bread slices in baking dish. Bake at 350° for 30 minutes or until set and golden. Yield: 6 servings.   Tom and Marcia Davis

Here's What's Cooking at Standish Elementary
Standish Elementary PTK
Standish, Michigan

Mrs. Kirven's Cheese Balls

1½ cups (6 ounces) finely shredded sharp Cheddar cheese
1 tablespoon all-purpose flour
⅛ teaspoon ground red pepper

3 egg whites
⅔ cup finely crushed saltine crackers (about 15 crackers)
Vegetable oil

Combine first 3 ingredients in a large bowl. Beat egg whites at high speed of an electric mixer until stiff peaks form; fold into cheese mixture. Drop cheese mixture, one heaping teaspoonful at a time, into crushed crackers. Shape into balls. Place balls on a tray; cover and chill 8 hours.

Pour oil to depth of 1 inch into a Dutch oven, and heat to 375°. Fry cheese balls, in batches, in hot oil 3 to 4 minutes or until golden, turning once. Drain well on paper towels. Serve immediately. Yield: 20 appetizers.

Seasoned Skillets & Silver Spoons
The Columbus Museum Guild
Columbus, Georgia

Phyllo-Cheese Onion Rolls

To save time, slice the onion wedges in your food processor, using a slicing disc. You can also combine the onion and cheeses in the food processor, using the knife blade.

3 large onions
½ cup butter or margarine,
    melted and divided
2 (3-ounce) packages cream
    cheese, softened
1 cup (4 ounces) shredded
    Monterey Jack cheese

1 cup (4 ounces) shredded
    Swiss cheese
12 sheets frozen phyllo pastry,
    thawed in refrigerator

Cut onions into wedges, and slice thinly. Cook sliced onion in 3 tablespoons butter in a large skillet over medium-low heat 15 to 20 minutes or until onion is very tender, stirring frequently. Let cool.

Combine onion and cheeses in a medium bowl; stir well.

Place 1 sheet of phyllo on a damp towel, keeping remaining phyllo covered with a slightly damp towel. Brush phyllo lightly with melted butter. Layer 3 sheets of phyllo over bottom layer, brushing each sheet lightly with butter. Spoon one-third of onion mixture down one long side of phyllo. Starting with long side, carefully roll phyllo, jellyroll fashion; brush roll with butter. Cut roll in half crosswise. Repeat procedure twice with remaining phyllo, butter, and onion mixture. Cover and chill rolls at least 3 hours.

Place rolls, seam side down, on a large ungreased baking sheet. Carefully cut each roll into 1-inch slices. (Do not separate slices.) Bake at 400° for 15 minutes or until rolls are golden and cheese melts. Yield: 3 dozen.   Rick and Chris Mears

Champions: Favorite Foods of Indy Car Racing
Championship Auto Racing Auxiliary
Indianapolis, Indiana

Black Beans and Zucchini Chilaquiles

Chilaquiles is a Mexican entrée that was created as a way to use leftovers. It's sometimes called "poor man's dish." In this version, if time isn't a factor, use dried black beans that have been soaked and cooked according to package directions instead of canned.

12 (6-inch) corn tortillas
1 cup chopped onion
1 medium-size green pepper, finely chopped
2 tablespoons olive oil
1 (28-ounce) can crushed tomatoes
2 teaspoons chili powder

1 teaspoon dried oregano
½ teaspoon ground cumin
2 (15-ounce) cans black beans, rinsed and drained
1 medium zucchini, shredded
2 cups (8 ounces) shredded Cheddar cheese

Place corn tortillas on a large ungreased baking sheet; bake at 350° for 15 minutes or until dry and crisp. Crumble into small pieces. Set aside.

Cook onion and green pepper in oil in a large skillet over medium-high heat, stirring constantly, until tender. Stir in tomatoes and next 3 ingredients. Bring to a boil; reduce heat, and simmer, uncovered, 10 minutes.

Layer half of tortilla pieces, tomato mixture, black beans, zucchini, and cheese in a greased 13- x 9- x 2-inch baking dish. Repeat layers. Bake, uncovered, at 350° for 25 to 30 minutes or until cheese melts and mixture is thoroughly heated. Let stand 5 minutes before serving. Yield: 6 servings.   Betty Stovall Thompson

With Special Distinction
Mississippi College Cookbook Committee
Clinton, Mississippi

Fish & Shellfish

Savory Salmon Steaks, page 169

Catfish with Pecan Sauce

The Seasoning Mix makes enough for three uses—it's delicious on fish or poultry.

8 farm-raised catfish fillets
   (about 3 pounds)
1 cup milk
¾ cup coarsely chopped
   pecans
¼ cup butter or margarine,
   melted

½ cup chopped green onions
1 cup all-purpose flour
Seasoning Mix
½ cup butter or margarine,
   divided
¼ cup fresh lime juice

Combine catfish fillets and milk in a large dish; cover and chill 2 hours.

Cook pecans in ¼ cup melted butter in a large skillet over medium heat, stirring constantly, 5 minutes; add green onions, and cook 2 additional minutes. Remove mixture from skillet; set aside.

Combine flour and 1 tablespoon Seasoning Mix; reserve remaining Seasoning Mix for other uses. Dredge fillets in flour mixture. Melt ¼ cup butter in skillet over medium-high heat. Add 4 fillets, and cook 3 minutes on each side or until browned. Remove fillets to a 4-quart shallow baking dish. Repeat procedure with remaining ¼ cup butter and fillets. Pour lime juice over fillets, and top with pecan mixture. Bake at 350° for 10 to 15 minutes or until fish flakes easily when tested with a fork. Serve immediately. Yield: 8 servings.

Seasoning Mix

1 tablespoon paprika
2½ teaspoons salt
1 teaspoon garlic powder
1 teaspoon onion powder
1 teaspoon ground red pepper

¾ teaspoon ground white
   pepper
¾ teaspoon black pepper
½ teaspoon dried thyme
½ teaspoon dried oregano

Combine all ingredients; stir well. Store in an airtight container. Yield: 3 tablespoons.   Cynthia Holliday

Be Our Guest
Trianon
Baton Rouge, Louisiana

New England Cod Fish Cakes

1½ pounds cod fillets
¾ teaspoon salt
¼ teaspoon pepper
1½ pounds baking potatoes, peeled and cut into 1-inch cubes
¾ cup sliced onion (about 1 small)
½ teaspoon salt
½ teaspoon pepper
1 large egg, beaten
2 teaspoons dry mustard
1 teaspoon Worcestershire sauce
¼ cup grated onion
⅓ cup all-purpose flour
¼ cup vegetable oil, divided

Sprinkle fillets with ¾ teaspoon salt and ¼ teaspoon pepper. Arrange fillets in a steamer basket over boiling water. Cover and steam 5 minutes. Let cool. Flake fish with a fork; set aside.

Place potato, sliced onion, ½ teaspoon salt, and ½ teaspoon pepper in a Dutch oven. Add water to cover, and bring to a boil. Cover, reduce heat, and simmer 15 minutes. Drain and coarsely mash potato mixture.

Place potato mixture in a bowl; add egg, mustard, Worcestershire sauce, and grated onion. Stir well. Gently stir in flaked fish. Cover and chill at least 1 hour.

Shape cod mixture into 12 patties. Dredge in flour. Cook 6 patties in 2 tablespoons hot oil over medium-high heat 3 minutes on each side or until browned. Drain on paper towels. Repeat procedure with remaining oil and patties. Serve with ketchup and tartar sauce. Yield: 4 servings.

Come Savor Swansea
First Christian Congregational Church
Swansea, Massachusetts

Flounder Stuffed with Shrimp

1½ cups water
½ pound unpeeled medium-
   size fresh shrimp
½ cup butter or margarine,
   softened
1 (3-ounce) package cream
   cheese, softened
½ cup crumbled blue cheese
1 tablespoon lemon juice

2 tablespoons minced onion
1½ teaspoons chopped fresh
   parsley
⅛ teaspoon pepper
4 (6-ounce) flounder fillets
¼ cup dry white wine
Garnishes: lemon twists, whole
   cooked shrimp, fresh parsley
   sprigs

Bring water to a boil; add ½ pound shrimp, and cook 3 to 5 minutes or until shrimp turn pink. Drain well; rinse with cold water. Chill. Peel shrimp, and devein, if desired. Chop shrimp.

Combine chopped shrimp, butter, and next 6 ingredients; mix well. Spread one-fourth of shrimp mixture evenly over each fillet; roll up fillets, and place, seam side down, in a lightly greased 8-inch baking dish. Pour wine over fillets. Bake at 375° for 20 minutes or until fish flakes easily when tested with a fork. Place stuffed fillets on individual serving plates. Spoon pan juices over fillets. Garnish, if desired. Yield: 4 servings.

Tina Post McAlister

Altus "Wine Capital of Arkansas" Cookbook
Altus Chamber of Commerce
Altus, Arkansas

Grouper with Tomato and Black Olive Vinaigrette

1 pound fresh snow pea pods
8 (4-ounce) grouper fillets
¼ teaspoon salt
¼ teaspoon freshly ground
   pepper
1 cup peeled, chopped tomato

½ cup chopped ripe olives
⅓ cup sliced green onions
1 clove garlic, minced
¼ cup plus 2 tablespoons olive
   oil
2 tablespoons rice vinegar

Wash snow peas; trim ends, remove strings, and set aside.

Sprinkle fillets with salt and pepper. Place fillets on a lightly greased rack; place rack in broiler pan. Broil 5½ inches from heat (with electric oven door partially opened) 5 minutes on each side or until fish flakes easily when tested with a fork. Transfer fillets to a serving dish; set aside, and keep warm.

Cook tomato and next 5 ingredients in a medium skillet over medium heat 2 minutes or until slightly thickened; remove from heat. Set aside, and keep warm.

Cook snow peas in boiling water to cover 1 minute, and drain immediately.

To serve, top fish with tomato mixture. Serve with snow peas. Yield: 8 servings.

Taste Without Waist
The Service League of Hickory, North Carolina

Grilled Honey-Macadamia Mahimahi

Mahimahi and macadamia nuts blend deliciously because they both hail from the tropics. But if you need a substitute for the mahimahi, any firm white fish will do.

2 (8-ounce) mahimahi fillets
½ teaspoon vegetable oil
¼ teaspoon salt
⅛ teaspoon pepper

3 tablespoons honey, divided
¼ cup macadamia nuts, finely chopped and toasted

Rub fillets with oil; sprinkle both sides of fillets with salt and pepper. Brush 1 side of fillets with 1½ tablespoons honey. Place fillets in a greased grilling basket, brushed side up. Cook, covered with grill lid, over medium-hot coals (350° to 400°) 7 minutes; turn basket. Baste fillets with remaining 1½ tablespoons honey, and sprinkle with nuts. Grill, covered, 3 to 4 additional minutes or until fish flakes easily when tested with a fork. Serve immediately. Yield: 2 servings.   Vicki Pate

It's Not as Good as Patty Makes It
The San Francisco School
San Francisco, California

Orange Roughy with Creole Sauce

4 (8-ounce) orange roughy
   fillets
1 tablespoon lemon juice
2 to 3 0teaspoons Cajun blackened seasoning for seafood
2½ cups chopped tomato
   (about 2 large)

½ cup chopped green onions
¼ cup chopped green pepper
¼ cup chopped celery
2 tablespoons butter or
   margarine, melted

Place fillets in a lightly greased 13- x 9- x 2-inch baking dish; brush fillets with lemon juice. Sprinkle blackened seasoning evenly over fillets. Bake at 350° for 15 minutes.

Cook tomato, green onions, green pepper, and celery in melted butter in a large skillet over medium-high heat, stirring constantly, 5 minutes or until vegetables are tender. Spoon vegetable mixture over fish, and bake 15 additional minutes or until fish flakes easily when tested with a fork. Yield: 4 servings.

The Roaring Fork
Gloria J. Deschamp Donation Fund
Grand Junction, Colorado

Crab-Stuffed Orange Roughy

Offer Crab-Stuffed Orange Roughy when you want an elegant entrée for company.

1 large egg, lightly beaten
⅔ cup fine, dry breadcrumbs
1 tablespoon finely chopped
   onion
2 teaspoons Old Bay seasoning
1½ teaspoons dry mustard
2 teaspoons finely chopped
   sweet red pepper
2 teaspoons chopped fresh
   parsley

2 teaspoons mayonnaise
1 teaspoon hot pepper sauce
1 pound fresh lump crabmeat,
   drained
8 (8-ounce) orange roughy
   fillets
2 tablespoons plus 2 teaspoons
   butter or margarine
2 tablespoons lemon juice
½ teaspoon paprika

Combine first 9 ingredients in a large bowl; stir well. Add crabmeat, and stir gently. Spoon ½ cup crabmeat mixture onto each fillet, and roll up to enclose filling. Place rolls, seam side down, in a lightly greased 13- x 9- x 2-inch baking dish. Place 1 teaspoon butter on each fillet; sprinkle with lemon juice and paprika.

Bake, uncovered, at 350° for 30 minutes or until fish flakes easily when tested with a fork. Yield: 8 servings. Lem Sentz

Sun Valley Celebrity & Local Heroes Cookbook
Advocates for Survivors of Domestic Violence
Hailey, Idaho

Savory Salmon Steaks

We recommend using a grilling basket for these flavorful salmon steaks. In testing we found they stuck when cooked directly on the grill rack, even though we used vegetable cooking spray.

4 (8-ounce) salmon steaks (1 inch thick)
3 tablespoons dark brown sugar
3 tablespoons prepared horseradish
3 tablespoons Dijon mustard
3 tablespoons vegetable oil
3 tablespoons low-sodium soy sauce

Place steaks in a large shallow dish. Combine brown sugar and next 4 ingredients; brush half of mixture over steaks, reserving remaining half of marinade. Cover and marinate in refrigerator up to 6 hours.

Remove steaks from dish; place in a greased grilling basket. Cook, covered with grill lid, over medium-hot coals (350° to 400°) 5 minutes on each side or until fish flakes easily when tested with a fork, basting often with reserved marinade. Yield: 4 servings. Joy Nelson

The Christ Church Cookbook
Christ Episcopal Church
Woodbury, Minnesota

Poached Salmon in Champagne with Rosemary Sauce

¼ cup sour cream
¼ cup whipping cream
2 tablespoons sugar
2 teaspoons Dijon mustard
1 teaspoon dried rosemary
¼ cup plus 2 tablespoons
　unsalted butter, melted

3 tablespoons lemon juice
3 tablespoons finely chopped
　green onions
½ cup champagne
2 pounds salmon fillets (1 inch
　thick), cut into 6 portions

Combine first 5 ingredients in a bowl; stir with a wire whisk until smooth. Cover and chill.

Combine butter and next 3 ingredients in a fish poacher or large skillet. Add salmon, and baste with butter mixture. Cover and cook over low heat 30 minutes or until fish flakes easily when tested with a fork. Remove salmon from poaching liquid; drain on paper towels. Serve with chilled sauce. Yield: 6 servings.　　　　Susan McDonald

Gatherings: A West Texas Collection of Recipes
Caprock Girl Scout Council
Lubbock, Texas

Salmon Corn Cakes

1 (7-ounce) can red salmon,
　drained
3 large eggs
2 tablespoons all-purpose flour
2 teaspoons lemon juice
½ to 1 teaspoon salt
½ teaspoon pepper
2 drops of hot sauce

1 (11-ounce) can whole kernel
　corn, drained
½ cup sour cream
¼ cup (1 ounce) shredded
　process American cheese
1 (2-ounce) jar diced pimiento,
　drained

Remove skin and bones from salmon; flake salmon, and set aside.

Combine eggs and next 5 ingredients in a bowl; beat at medium speed of an electric mixer until foamy. Stir in salmon and corn.

Spoon ¼ cup salmon mixture for each cake onto a hot, lightly greased griddle or skillet. Cook 3 minutes on each side or until golden. Set aside, and keep warm.

Combine sour cream, cheese, and pimiento in a small saucepan; cook over low heat, stirring constantly, until thoroughly heated. To serve, spoon sauce over cakes. Yield: 4 servings.

Classic Connecticut Cuisine
Connecticut Easter Seals
Uncasville, Connecticut

Spinach Sole with Pesto Sauce

2 **pounds sole fillets**
½ **teaspoon salt**
¼ **teaspoon freshly ground pepper**
1 **cup dry vermouth**
1 **tablespoon fresh lemon juice**
¼ **cup chopped onion**
1 **clove garlic, minced**
2 **tablespoons butter or margarine, melted**

1 **(10-ounce) package frozen chopped spinach, thawed and drained**
¾ **cup freshly grated Parmesan cheese, divided**
½ **teaspoon dried oregano**
1 **(8-ounce) carton sour cream**
¼ **cup commercial pesto sauce**

Place fish in a single layer in two lightly greased 13- x 9- x 2-inch baking dishes; sprinkle with salt and pepper. Pour vermouth over fish; sprinkle with lemon juice.

Cover and bake at 400° for 10 minutes; drain, reserving liquid. Place fillets in one 13- x 9- x 2-inch baking dish; cover and keep warm. Pour reserved liquid into a medium saucepan. Bring to a boil; cook, uncovered, 10 minutes or until reduced to ½ cup. Set aside.

Cook onion and garlic in butter in a large skillet over medium-high heat, stirring constantly, until tender. Remove from heat; stir in spinach, ¼ cup Parmesan cheese, and oregano. Spoon spinach mixture over fish.

Combine sour cream and pesto sauce. Stir in reduced liquid. Spoon over spinach mixture; top with remaining ½ cup cheese.

Bake, uncovered, at 350° for 10 minutes or until thoroughly heated. Broil 3 inches from heat (with electric oven door partially opened) 1 minute or until cheese melts. Yield: 4 servings.   Carole J. Williams

Silver Selections
Catawba School Alumni
Rock Hill, South Carolina

Swordfish Steaks with Basil Butter

If there's leftover Basil Butter, team it within three days with any fish or shellfish.

½ cup butter, softened
¼ cup loosely packed fresh
  basil leaves
¼ cup Dijon mustard
1½ teaspoons capers
8 (8-ounce) swordfish steaks
  (about 1 inch thick)

½ teaspoon salt
¼ teaspoon freshly ground
  pepper
Anchovy fillets (optional)
Garnishes: fresh parsley or
  watercress sprigs, lemon
  wedges

Position knife blade in food processor bowl; add first 4 ingredients. Process until blended, stopping once to scrape down sides. Cover and chill at least 2 hours.

Sprinkle steaks with salt and pepper. Cook steaks, covered with grill lid, over medium-hot coals (350° to 400°) about 8 minutes on each side or until fish flakes easily when tested with a fork.

Serve with Basil Butter. Top with anchovy fillets, if desired. Garnish, if desired. Yield: 8 servings.

Presentations
Friends of Lied, Lied Center for Performing Arts
Lincoln, Nebraska

Trout Louis

This recipe calls for dressed trout. Dressed fish has been gutted and scaled. Usually the head, fins, and tail have been removed also.

2 (6-ounce) cans crabmeat, drained
½ cup grated onion
½ teaspoon ground white pepper
¾ cup cracker meal, divided
2 large eggs, lightly beaten
½ teaspoon hot sauce
6 dressed freshwater trout (about 3 pounds)

¼ cup unsalted butter, melted
½ teaspoon salt
1 teaspoon dried dillweed, divided
⅛ teaspoon ground white pepper
Mustard Sauce
½ teaspoon garlic salt, divided
Garnish: lemon slices

Combine crabmeat, onion, ½ teaspoon pepper, ½ cup cracker meal, eggs, and hot sauce, stirring gently, set aside.

Brush trout cavities with butter; sprinkle with salt, ½ teaspoon dillweed, and ⅛ teaspoon pepper. Spoon crabmeat mixture evenly into cavities. Place trout in a greased 13- x 9- x 2-inch baking dish.

Spoon half of Mustard Sauce over fish. Sprinkle evenly with ¼ teaspoon dillweed, ¼ teaspoon garlic salt, and 2 tablespoons cracker meal. Turn fish; repeat procedure with remaining Mustard Sauce, dillweed, garlic salt, and cracker meal. Bake at 425° for 35 minutes or until fish flakes easily when tested with a fork. Garnish, if desired. Serve immediately. Yield: 6 servings.

Mustard Sauce

1 cup grated onion
½ cup unsalted butter, melted
¼ cup plus 2 tablespoons Dijon mustard
¼ cup all-purpose flour

1 tablespoon grated lemon rind
3 tablespoons fresh lemon juice
3 cloves garlic, pressed

Combine all ingredients in a medium bowl; stir well. Yield: about 2 cups.

Dona Webber

Ridgefield Cooks
Women's Committee of the Ridgefield Community Center
Ridgefield, Connecticut

Yellowfin Tuna with Green Peppercorn Sauce

The Green Peppercorn Sauce lends a robust flavor that enhances this tuna dish.

¼ cup Dijon mustard
¼ cup dry red wine
3 tablespoons green peppercorns
2 tablespoons teriyaki sauce
1 tablespoon butter or margarine
1 teaspoon dried thyme

1 teaspoon dried dillweed
¼ teaspoon pepper
1 tablespoon crushed garlic
3 tablespoons butter or margarine, melted
1 tablespoon fresh lemon juice
6 (8-ounce) yellowfin tuna steaks

Combine first 7 ingredients in a small saucepan, stirring well. Cook over low heat until thoroughly heated; keep warm.

Combine pepper, garlic, melted butter, and lemon juice in a small bowl. Brush butter mixture evenly over both sides of tuna steaks. Cook steaks, covered with grill lid, over medium-hot coals (350° to 400°) about 5 minutes on each side or until fish flakes easily when tested with a fork. Serve with warm Green Peppercorn Sauce. Yield: 6 servings.

A Slice of Paradise
The Hospital Service League of Naples Community Hospital
Naples, Florida

Pacific Rim Tuna Steaks

You can make the ginger marinade for these tuna steaks ahead and store it in the refrigerator up to a week. The recipe makes two cups—use one cup now and reserve the remaining one for another use.

6 (4-ounce) yellowfin tuna
  steaks (¾ inch thick)
1 cup soy sauce
½ cup dark sesame oil
½ cup lime juice
¼ cup mirin (rice wine)
2 tablespoons grated
  gingerroot

2 cloves garlic, minced
2 tablespoons dried crushed
  red pepper
Vegetable cooking spray
Garnish: fresh cilantro sprigs

Place tuna steaks in a heavy-duty, zip-top plastic bag. Combine soy sauce and next 6 ingredients. Pour 1 cup soy mixture over tuna in bag; reserve remaining soy mixture for another use. Seal bag, and shake until tuna is well coated. Marinate in refrigerator 30 minutes.

Remove tuna from marinade, discarding marinade. Coat a grill basket with cooking spray, and place steaks in basket. Cook steaks, covered with grill lid, over medium coals (300° to 350°) 5 minutes on each side or until fish flakes easily when tested with a fork. Remove steaks to a serving platter. Garnish, if desired. Yield: 6 servings.

Simply Classic
The Junior League of Seattle, Washington

Casserole of Baked Crab Imperial

¼ cup soft breadcrumbs
1 teaspoon butter or
   margarine, melted
¼ cup butter or margarine
¼ cup all-purpose flour
2 cups milk
1 teaspoon salt
½ teaspoon celery salt
⅛ teaspoon ground red pepper
⅛ teaspoon black pepper
1 egg yolk, beaten
2 tablespoons sherry
1 cup soft breadcrumbs
1 pound fresh lump crabmeat,
   drained
1 teaspoon minced fresh
   parsley
1 teaspoon minced onion
Paprika

Combine ¼ cup breadcrumbs and 1 teaspoon melted butter, stirring well. Place buttered crumbs on a baking sheet, and bake at 350° for 3 to 5 minutes or until golden. Set aside.

Melt ¼ cup butter in a heavy saucepan over low heat; add flour, stirring until smooth. Cook 1 minute, stirring constantly. Gradually add milk; cook over medium heat, stirring constantly, until thickened and bubbly. Stir in 1 teaspoon salt and next 3 ingredients. Stir about one-fourth of hot mixture into egg yolk; add to remaining hot mixture, stirring constantly. Remove from heat; add sherry and next 4 ingredients. Stir gently; spoon into a well-greased 1½-quart casserole. Top with buttered crumbs; sprinkle with paprika. Bake at 400° for 20 to 25 minutes or until bubbly. Yield: 6 servings.   Genevieve Hall Valliant

Queen Anne Goes to the Kitchen
The Episcopal Church Women of St. Paul's Parish
Centreville, Maryland

Mussels Steamed in Wine

6 dozen raw mussels in shells
½ cup plus 2 tablespoons
   butter, divided
1 large onion, chopped
2 shallots, chopped
2 cloves garlic, minced
2½ cups finely chopped fresh
   parsley
½ teaspoon freshly ground
   pepper
1½ cups dry white wine
½ cup fresh lemon juice

Scrub mussels with a brush, removing beards. Discard opened, cracked, or heavy mussels (they're filled with sand).

Melt ¼ cup plus 3 tablespoons butter in a large Dutch oven over medium-high heat. Add mussels, onion, and next 5 ingredients. Cover and cook 4 minutes or until mussels open, shaking pot several times. Transfer mussels to a serving dish with a slotted spoon, discarding any unopened mussels; set aside, and keep warm.

Pour remaining liquid in pan through a wire-mesh strainer into a heavy saucepan, discarding parsley mixture. Bring liquid to a boil over medium-high heat. Cook 30 minutes or until thickened. Remove from heat; whisk in remaining 3 tablespoons butter. Stir in lemon juice, and pour over mussels. Yield: 6 servings.

The Bountiful Arbor
The Junior League of Ann Arbor, Michigan

Oysters Fidalgo

Don't be intimidated by oysters in the shell. Look for shells that are tightly closed and unbroken, and follow our easy recipe for successful cooking.

½ cup butter or margarine
¼ cup dry white wine
1 clove garlic, crushed
½ teaspoon garlic pepper
½ to 1 teaspoon seasoned salt

2 dozen fresh oysters (in the shell)
½ cup grated Parmesan cheese
Hot sauce (optional)

Combine first 5 ingredients in a small saucepan; cook over medium heat until butter melts.

Scrub oysters with a stiff brush under cold running water. Cook oysters in shells, covered with grill lid, over medium-hot coals (350° to 400°) 10 minutes. Remove from grill, and open oysters; to open, insert an oyster knife into hinge of shell, and twist. Discard tops of shells. Scrape a knife between oyster and shell to free the meat from shell. Return oysters on half shell to grill.

Spoon butter sauce evenly onto oysters; sprinkle evenly with cheese. Sprinkle with hot sauce, if desired. Cook 3 to 5 minutes or until oyster edges curl and cheese melts. Yield: 8 servings.   Bob Fraser

It's Rainin' Recipes
Charles B. Hopkins Chapter, Telephone Pioneers of America
Seattle, Washington

Marinated Scallops

The larger sea scallops are more common than the smaller, more delicately flavored bay scallops. You can use either size in this recipe, but cooking times may vary.

¼ cup olive oil
2 tablespoons chopped fresh parsley
2 tablespoons lemon juice
1 tablespoon grated orange rind
½ teaspoon fennel seeds

1 clove garlic, minced
1 pound fresh sea scallops
1 medium zucchini, cut into ¼-inch-thick slices
1 medium-size purple onion, cut into 1-inch pieces

Combine first 6 ingredients in a medium bowl; add scallops, and toss well. Cover and marinate in refrigerator 2 hours.

Remove scallops from marinade, reserving marinade. Bring marinade to a boil in a small saucepan; set aside.

Brush zucchini and onion with boiled marinade. Alternate scallops and zucchini on four 12-inch skewers; place onion on a separate skewer. Place onion kabob on a rack; place rack in broiler pan.

Broil onion kabob 5½ inches from heat (with electric oven door partially opened) 5 minutes. Add scallop and zucchini kabobs alongside onion kabob; broil 5 additional minutes or until scallops are opaque. Serve immediately. Yield: 2 servings.   Al Giordano

Cooking in Alexander Valley: A Tradition of Excellence in Food, Wine and Education
Alexander Valley Parents Club
Healdsburg, California

Chipotle-Spiced Shrimp with a Salad of Fennel and Radicchio

1 pound unpeeled medium-size fresh shrimp
2 canned chipotle peppers in adobo sauce, drained
¼ cup olive oil
2 heads fennel (about 2 pounds)
1 purple onion, sliced
1 tablespoon olive oil
½ teaspoon salt
½ teaspoon pepper

2 medium-size sweet red peppers, cut into thin strips
1 head radicchio, cut into thin strips
⅓ cup commercial Italian salad dressing
2 tablespoons coarsely chopped fresh flat-leaf parsley
1 teaspoon honey

Peel and devein shrimp, leaving tails intact; set aside.

Position knife blade in food processor bowl; add chipotle peppers, and process until smooth.

Combine shrimp, pepper puree, and ¼ cup olive oil in a glass bowl; cover and marinate in refrigerator 1 hour.

Rinse fennel thoroughly. Trim and discard bulb bases. Trim stalks from the bulb; discard hard outside stalks, reserving leaves. Chop ¼ cup leaves, discarding remaining leaves; set aside. Cut bulbs into thin slices.

Combine sliced fennel, onion, 1 tablespoon olive oil, salt, and pepper; toss well. Place mixture on a large baking sheet. Bake at 350° for 40 to 50 minutes or until browned.

Combine fennel mixture, fennel leaves, red pepper strips, and next 4 ingredients in a large bowl; toss well.

Cook shrimp mixture in a large nonstick skillet over medium-high heat, stirring constantly, 5 minutes or until shrimp turn pink.

To serve, spoon salad mixture onto four individual serving plates; arrange shrimp on salad. Serve immediately. Yield: 4 servings.

Cooking Atlanta Style
Atlanta Community Food Bank
Marietta, Georgia

Garlic Shrimp with Pesto Sauce

8 ounces vermicelli, uncooked
1 pound unpeeled medium-size
   fresh shrimp
4 green onions, sliced
4 cloves garlic, minced
¼ cup plus 2 tablespoons
   butter, melted
1 cup ricotta cheese

½ cup grated Parmesan cheese
½ cup minced fresh parsley
½ cup pine nuts, toasted
1 teaspoon chopped fresh basil
2 cloves garlic, minced
¼ teaspoon salt
3 tablespoons olive oil
Freshly grated Parmesan cheese

Cook pasta according to package directions; drain. Set aside, and keep warm.

Peel shrimp, and devein, if desired.

Cook green onions and 4 cloves garlic in butter in a large skillet over medium-high heat, stirring constantly, until tender. Add shrimp; cook 3 minutes or until shrimp turn pink, stirring occasionally.

Place pasta on a serving platter; spoon shrimp mixture over pasta.

Combine ricotta cheese and next 6 ingredients in food processor; process until combined, stopping frequently to scrape down sides. Add oil with processor running; process until smooth. (Mixture will be thick.) Top shrimp with sauce, and sprinkle with Parmesan cheese. Yield: 4 servings.

Ann Dickens

Tell Me More
The Junior League of Lafayette, Louisiana

Camarones al Ajillo (Shrimp with Garlic)

Serve this saucy dish with French baguette slices to sop up the juice!

1½ pounds unpeeled large
   fresh shrimp
4 large cloves garlic, pressed
½ cup butter or margarine,
   melted

½ cup dry white wine
½ cup chopped fresh parsley,
   divided
½ cup chopped fresh cilantro,
   divided

Peel and devein shrimp, leaving tails intact; cut a slit almost through back of shrimp. Open shrimp, and flatten; set aside.

Cook garlic in melted butter in a large skillet 3 minutes, stirring constantly. Add wine, ¼ cup parsley, and ¼ cup cilantro; bring to a boil. Boil 1 minute. Add shrimp and remaining ¼ cup parsley and ¼ cup cilantro. Cook 3 minutes or until shrimp turn pink. Yield: 6 servings.   Pablo Elvira

Montana Celebrity Cookbook
Intermountain Children's Home
Helena, Montana

Lime Shrimp in Tortillas

1 **pound unpeeled medium-size fresh shrimp**
¼ **cup fresh lime juice**
2 **tablespoons canned ready-to-serve, fat-free chicken broth, undiluted**
1 **tablespoon olive oil**
1 **teaspoon garlic powder**
1 **teaspoon dried cilantro**
1 **teaspoon pepper**

¼ **teaspoon salt**
8 **(8-inch) flour tortillas**
1 **small onion, sliced into rings**
½ **medium-size green pepper, sliced**
2 **teaspoons olive oil**
Toppings: salsa, shredded Cheddar cheese, sour cream, lime wedges

Peel shrimp, and devein, if desired. Place shrimp in a heavy-duty, zip-top plastic bag. Combine lime juice and next 6 ingredients. Pour over shrimp; seal bag, and shake until shrimp are well coated. Marinate in refrigerator 30 minutes.

Heat tortillas according to package directions; keep warm.

Cook onion and green pepper in hot olive oil in a large skillet over medium-high heat, stirring constantly, 3 minutes or until tender. Remove shrimp from marinade, discarding marinade. Add shrimp to skillet, and cook 3 to 5 minutes or until shrimp turn pink.

Spoon mixture into warmed tortillas, using a slotted spoon. Serve with salsa, shredded cheese, sour cream, and lime wedges. Yield: 8 servings.   Cindy Stewart and Joan M. Surso

River Road Recipes III: A Healthy Collection
The Junior League of Baton Rouge, Louisiana

Valencian Paella

If you don't have a paella pan for this one-dish meal, use a deep skillet or Dutch oven that holds about 3½ quarts.

3 cups water
1 pound unpeeled medium-size fresh shrimp
3 cloves garlic, cut in half
¼ cup olive oil, divided
1 pound skinned and boned chicken breast halves, cut into 1-inch pieces
1 medium onion, chopped
3 medium tomatoes, chopped
3 small sweet red peppers, seeded and cut into thin strips
1 teaspoon paprika
2 cups long-grain rice, uncooked
1 teaspoon threads of saffron
4 cups chicken broth
1 cup frozen English peas, thawed
3½ ounces chorizo sausage, cut into 1-inch pieces
Lemon wedges (optional)

Bring water to a boil; add shrimp, and cook 3 to 5 minutes or until shrimp turn pink. Drain well; rinse with cold water. Chill.

Peel shrimp, and devein, if desired. Set aside.

Cook garlic in 3 tablespoons hot olive oil in a paella pan or deep skillet over medium-high heat, stirring constantly, until browned; discard garlic. Cook chicken in garlic-flavored oil over medium-high heat until browned, stirring occasionally. Add onion, tomato, and sliced red pepper; cook, stirring constantly, until vegetables are crisp-tender. Reduce heat; add paprika. Cook 5 additional minutes, stirring occasionally. Remove chicken mixture from pan; keep warm.

Cook rice in remaining 1 tablespoon oil in same pan over medium-high heat, stirring constantly, until rice is lightly browned. Add chicken mixture, saffron, and next 3 ingredients; bring to a boil. Reduce heat; cover and cook 15 minutes, stirring occasionally. Add shrimp; cover and cook 5 minutes. Serve with lemon wedges, if desired. Yield: 8 servings.

Creative Chef 2
Tourette Syndrome Association
Bayside, New York

Meats

Firehouse Burgers, page 190

Pot Roast Braised in Ginger-Plum Sauce

If you can't find plum wine to make this succulent pot roast recipe, substitute ¼ cup water and ¼ cup plum syrup that you drain from the canned plums.

1   (3½- to 4-pound) boneless
   chuck roast
2   tablespoons olive oil, divided
3   tablespoons finely chopped
   green onions
2   shallots, finely chopped
2   tablespoons grated
   gingerroot
2   cloves garlic, minced

2   (15-ounce) cans sweet whole
   purple plums in heavy syrup,
   drained, pitted, and coarsely
   chopped
1½ cups beef broth
½   cup plum wine
¼   cup teriyaki sauce
2   tablespoons cider vinegar

Brown roast in 1 tablespoon oil in a large skillet over medium-high heat. Add green onions; cook, stirring constantly, until lightly browned. Transfer to a roasting pan.

Cook shallot, gingerroot, and garlic in remaining 1 tablespoon oil in skillet over medium-high heat, stirring constantly, until tender. Add plums and next 4 ingredients; stir well. Pour over roast. Cover and bake at 350° for 3 to 3½ hours or until meat is tender. Serve roast with sauce. Yield: 10 servings.

Delicious Developments
Friends of Strong Memorial Hospital
Rochester, New York

Stuffed Beef Tenderloin

1 cup chopped onion
1 (4-ounce) can sliced
  mushrooms, drained
½ cup diced celery
¼ cup butter or margarine,
  melted
2 cups soft breadcrumbs
½ teaspoon salt

½ teaspoon dried basil
⅛ teaspoon dried parsley
  flakes
⅛ teaspoon pepper
1 (3-pound) beef tenderloin,
  trimmed
4 slices bacon

Cook first 3 ingredients in butter in a large skillet over medium-high heat, stirring constantly, until vegetables are tender. Remove from heat. Stir breadcrumbs and next 4 ingredients into vegetables, and set aside.

Slice tenderloin lengthwise to, but not through, the center, leaving 1 long side connected. Spoon stuffing mixture into opening of tenderloin. Fold top side over stuffing, and tie securely with heavy string at 2-inch intervals. Place tenderloin, seam side down, on a rack in a greased roasting pan. Insert meat thermometer into thickest part of tenderloin.

Arrange bacon slices in a crisscross pattern over tenderloin; secure at ends with wooden picks. Bake at 350° for 1 hour or until bacon is crisp and thermometer registers 145° (medium-rare) or 160° (medium). Remove wooden picks. Yield: 6 servings.   Kuality Katering

Coastal Cuisine, Texas Style
The Junior Service League of Brazosport
Lake Jackson, Texas

Jalapeño- and Beer-Baked Short Ribs

8 pounds beef short ribs
2 large onions, coarsely chopped
2¼ cups tomato sauce
¼ cup firmly packed brown sugar
¼ cup seeded and finely chopped jalapeño peppers
¼ cup red wine vinegar

4 large cloves garlic, minced
3 tablespoons chopped green pepper
1 tablespoon dry mustard
½ teaspoon ground red pepper
¼ teaspoon ground cinnamon
¼ teaspoon ground cloves
2 cups beer

Place ribs in a large roasting pan. Place onion around ribs.

Combine tomato sauce and next 9 ingredients in a large saucepan; stir well. Bring to a boil; reduce heat, and simmer, uncovered, 10 minutes or until slightly thickened. Stir in beer. Pour sauce over ribs and onion. Cover and bake at 425° for 2½ hours or until ribs are tender. Yield: 8 servings.   Linda Holmstrand

The Best of Wheeling
The Junior League of Wheeling, West Virginia

Peppered Herb Steaks

¾ cup olive oil
⅓ cup red wine vinegar
¼ cup chopped green onions
¼ cup Dijon mustard
4 cloves garlic, minced
1 tablespoon plus 1 teaspoon coarsely ground pepper
1 tablespoon minced fresh thyme

1 tablespoon minced fresh rosemary
1 teaspoon salt
2 (1½-pound) flank steaks
Garnishes: fresh thyme sprigs, fresh rosemary sprigs

Combine first 9 ingredients in a small bowl; stir well.

Place steaks in a large heavy-duty, zip-top plastic bag. Pour marinade over steaks; seal bag securely. Marinate in refrigerator 8 hours, turning occasionally.

Remove steaks from marinade, discarding marinade. Cook, covered with grill lid, over medium-hot coals (350° to 400°) 7 to 8 minutes on each side or to desired degree of doneness.

To serve, slice steaks diagonally across grain into thin slices. Garnish, if desired. Yield: 9 servings.

Simply Classic
The Junior League of Seattle, Washington

Spicy Steak and Corn Soft Tacos

Cumin, chili powder, and cilantro add the spice to this steak and corn taco filling. Serve it in a flour tortilla instead of the usual crunchy taco shell.

½ pound flank steak
1½ cups sliced purple onion
1 cup sliced sweet red pepper
2 tablespoons olive oil
¾ cup frozen whole kernel corn
½ teaspoon ground cumin
½ teaspoon chili powder

½ teaspoon salt
¼ teaspoon pepper
1½ tablespoons minced fresh cilantro
4 (10-inch) flour tortillas
Toppings: shredded Cheddar cheese, chopped tomato, sour cream

Slice steak diagonally across grain into thin strips. Cook onion and red pepper in hot oil in a large skillet over medium-high heat, stirring constantly, until tender. Remove vegetables; set aside. Cook steak in skillet over medium-high heat, stirring constantly, 3 minutes or until no longer pink.

Add onion mixture, corn, cumin, and chili powder to steak; cook until thoroughly heated. Remove from heat; stir in salt, pepper, and cilantro. Keep warm.

Heat tortillas according to package directions. Spoon steak mixture into tortillas; add desired toppings, and serve immediately. Yield: 2 servings.

Linda Burke

Cane River's Louisiana Living
The Service League of Natchitoches, Louisiana

Sukiyaki

For easy slicing, partially freeze the sirloin steak before slicing it across the grain into thin strips. An electric knife makes the job a snap.

½ cup boiling water
1 beef-flavored bouillon cube
⅓ cup soy sauce
1 teaspoon sugar
½ teaspoon ground ginger
1½ pounds boneless sirloin steak
2 tablespoons vegetable oil
1½ cups diagonally sliced celery
1 medium onion, sliced and quartered (about 1 cup)
1 cup chopped green pepper

½ cup shredded carrot
¼ pound fresh mushrooms, sliced (about 1½ cups)
1 cup fresh bean sprouts
3 green onions, cut into 1-inch pieces (about 1 cup)
1 (8-ounce) can bamboo shoots, drained
1 (8-ounce) can sliced water chestnuts, drained
4½ cups loosely packed torn fresh spinach
Hot cooked rice

Combine first 5 ingredients; stir well, and set aside.

Trim excess fat from steak; slice steak diagonally across grain into thin strips. Pour oil around top of a preheated wok or large skillet, coating sides; heat at medium-high (375°) for 2 minutes. Add steak strips, and stir-fry 4 to 5 minutes or until no longer pink.

Add bouillon mixture, celery, and next 3 ingredients; stir-fry 3 minutes or until vegetables are crisp-tender. Add mushrooms and next 4 ingredients; stir-fry 3 additional minutes. Add spinach; stir-fry just until spinach wilts. Serve over rice. Yield: 8 servings.   Ann Miller

888 Favorite Recipes
Boy Scout Troop 888
Maryville, Tennessee

Pepperpot Beef

Serve this beef and kidney bean dish over hot cooked rice for a hearty one-dish meal.

¼ cup all-purpose flour
1 teaspoon salt
½ teaspoon ground ginger
⅛ teaspoon pepper
2 pounds beef stew meat
3 tablespoons vegetable oil
8 ounces sliced fresh
   mushrooms
1 (8-ounce) can stewed
   tomatoes

2½ tablespoons brown sugar
2½ tablespoons red wine
   vinegar
1½ tablespoons Worcestershire
   sauce
1 teaspoon chili sauce
2 cloves garlic, crushed
1 bay leaf
1 (15-ounce) can red kidney
   beans, drained

Combine first 4 ingredients in a heavy-duty, zip-top plastic bag; add beef. Seal bag; shake until beef is coated. Brown beef in hot oil in a large ovenproof Dutch oven over medium-high heat. Drain and discard pan drippings.

Combine mushrooms and remaining ingredients except beans; pour over meat in Dutch oven. Cover and bake at 325° for 1½ hours. Add beans; bake 30 additional minutes or until meat is tender. Remove and discard bay leaf. Yield: 4 servings.   Nora Herren

Fanconi Anemia Family Cookbook
Fanconi Anemia Research Fund
Eugene, Oregon

Firehouse Burgers

You can minimize the heat by choosing a mild or medium salsa.

2 pounds ground round
1 onion, finely chopped
⅓ cup soft breadcrumbs
1 large egg, beaten
2 tablespoons hot salsa
2 teaspoons brown sugar
1 teaspoon salt

1 teaspoon prepared mustard
½ teaspoon pepper
8 hamburger buns with sesame
    seeds
Toppings: lettuce leaves,
    tomato slices, onion slices
Additional hot salsa

Combine first 9 ingredients in a bowl; shape into 8 patties.
Cook, covered with grill lid, over medium-hot coals (350° to 400°) 5 to 6 minutes on each side or until done. Place bottom half of each hamburger bun on a plate; top with a patty. Add desired toppings, and spoon additional salsa over toppings. Cover with bun tops. Yield: 8 servings.   Gary Barrows

Cookin' with Fire
Milford Fire Department
Milford, Massachusetts

Apricot Meat Loaf

2 pounds ground chuck
½ cup crushed corn flakes
    cereal
1 (6-ounce) package dried
    apricot halves, chopped

2 large eggs, lightly beaten
1½ teaspoons salt
⅛ teaspoon pepper
½ cup firmly packed brown
    sugar

Combine first 6 ingredients in a large bowl; stir well. Shape mixture into a loaf, and place in a lightly greased 9- x 5- x 3-inch loafpan. Bake, uncovered, at 350° for 1 hour. Sprinkle brown sugar over meat loaf, and bake 10 additional minutes. Remove to a serving platter. Yield: 8 servings.   Joann Stewart

Gatherings: A West Texas Collection of Recipes
Caprock Girl Scout Council
Lubbock, Texas

Sicilian Meat Roll

Roll this fancy meatloaf jellyroll fashion around thin slices of ham and mozzarella cheese.

2 **pounds ground chuck**
¾ **cup soft breadcrumbs**
½ **cup tomato juice**
2 **large eggs, beaten**
2 **tablespoons chopped fresh parsley**
½ **teaspoon dried oregano**

¼ **teaspoon salt**
¼ **teaspoon pepper**
6 **ounces thinly sliced cooked ham**
1 **(6-ounce) package sliced mozzarella cheese, divided**

Combine first 8 ingredients in a large bowl; stir well. Shape mixture into a 10- x 8- x 1-inch rectangle on wax paper. Arrange ham over meat mixture, leaving a 1-inch margin on all sides. Reserve 1 slice of cheese; tear remaining cheese slices into pieces, and place on ham.

Carefully roll meat, jellyroll fashion, starting at narrow end, using wax paper to support meat. Pinch ends and seam to seal. Remove from wax paper, and place roll, seam side down, on a rack in a greased shallow roasting pan.

Bake at 350° for 1 hour and 20 minutes. Cut remaining slice of cheese into 4 triangles. Arrange on top of meat roll. Bake 2 additional minutes or until cheese melts. Let stand 5 minutes before slicing. Yield: 8 servings.

Harriet Nevins

Madison County Cookbook
St. Joseph Church
Winterset, Iowa

Veal Chops with Mustard-Sage Butter

2 (1½-inch-thick) veal loin
  chops
3 tablespoons minced fresh
  sage, divided
1 large clove garlic, minced
¼ teaspoon freshly ground
  pepper

3 tablespoons butter, softened
2 teaspoons balsamic vinegar
1 tablespoon olive oil
2 teaspoons Dijon mustard
2 teaspoons minced fresh
  parsley
Vegetable cooking spray

Rub both sides of veal with 1½ tablespoons sage, garlic, and pepper. Cover and chill 2 hours.

Combine remaining 1½ tablespoons sage, butter, and next 4 ingredients; stirring until blended. Set aside.

Place veal on a rack coated with cooking spray; place rack in broiler pan. Broil 5½ inches from heat (with electric oven door partially opened) 10 minutes on each side or to desired degree of doneness.

Place a dollop of butter mixture on top of each chop; serve immediately. Yield: 2 servings.

From Generation to Generation
Sisterhood of Temple Emanu-El
Dallas, Texas

Veal Scallops with Fresh Tomato

1½ pounds veal cutlets
¼ cup all-purpose flour
1 tablespoon butter or
  margarine, melted
1 tablespoon olive oil
½ pound fresh mushrooms,
  thinly sliced
1½ tablespoons lemon juice
½ cup dry sherry
½ cup peeled, seeded, and
  diced tomato

2 tablespoons chopped fresh
  basil
2 tablespoons chopped fresh
  parsley
1 large clove garlic, minced
1 beef-flavored bouillon cube
2 tablespoons freshly grated
  Parmesan cheese
Hot cooked pasta

Place veal between two sheets of heavy-duty plastic wrap, and flatten to ⅛-inch thickness, using a meat mallet or rolling pin. Cut veal into 1-inch pieces; dredge in flour. Brown veal in butter and oil in a large skillet over medium heat. Remove veal, reserving drippings in skillet. Place veal in an ungreased 11- x 7- x 1½-inch baking dish.

Add mushrooms to drippings in skillet; sprinkle with lemon juice. Add sherry and next 5 ingredients; cook over medium-high heat, stirring constantly, until bouillon cube dissolves. Pour mushroom mixture over veal; sprinkle with cheese. Cover and bake at 350° for 15 minutes. Serve over pasta. Yield: 4 servings.

Taste the Good Life
The Assistance League of Omaha, Nebraska

Veal Shanks à la Grecque

3½ pounds (2-inch-thick) cross-cut veal shanks
½ teaspoon salt
½ teaspoon freshly ground pepper
½ cup all-purpose flour
¼ cup olive oil
1 cup finely chopped onion
1 cup finely chopped celery

1 teaspoon minced garlic
½ cup dry white wine
1 cup chopped canned tomatoes
2¼ cups chicken broth, divided
2 tablespoons chopped fresh dill
1 bay leaf
½ cup orzo, uncooked

Sprinkle veal with salt and pepper; dredge in flour. Heat olive oil in a large ovenproof Dutch oven; add veal, and brown in oil. Drain and discard pan drippings.

Add onion, celery, and garlic to veal in Dutch oven; cook until tender. Add wine, deglazing skillet by scraping particles that cling to bottom. Add tomatoes, ½ cup broth, dill, and bay leaf. Cover and bake at 375° for 1 hour. Add remaining 1¾ cups broth and orzo; stir well. Cover and bake 15 additional minutes. Remove and discard bay leaf. Yield: 4 servings.

Carmine Kline

Coe Hall Cooks!
Coe Hall
Oyster Bay, New York

Brazilian-Grilled Lamb and Black Beans

Be sure not to overcook this flavorful meat. Lamb should be juicy and slightly pink on the inside.

1 medium-size purple onion
1 (8-ounce) bottle red wine vinegar and oil salad dressing
2 cloves garlic, minced
2 (15-ounce) cans black beans, rinsed and drained
1 (3-pound) boneless leg of lamb, butterflied
1 teaspoon salt

½ teaspoon ground cumin
½ teaspoon ground red pepper
½ teaspoon dried thyme
½ teaspoon dried oregano
3 medium-size sweet red peppers, quartered
2 large oranges, peeled, cut in half lengthwise, and sliced crosswise

Slice onion in half crosswise; cut a thin slice from one half, and separate slice into rings. Reserve rings for garnish. Finely chop remaining onion.

Combine salad dressing and garlic. Combine ⅓ cup salad dressing mixture, chopped onion, and beans; cover and chill.

Trim fat from lamb. Brush lamb with another ⅓ cup salad dressing mixture; sprinkle lamb with salt and next 4 ingredients. Cook, covered with grill lid, over medium-hot coals (350° to 400°) 30 minutes; turn and insert meat thermometer into thickest part of meat. Place peppers on grill; cook lamb and peppers, covered, 15 minutes or to desired degree of doneness (150° medium-rare, 160° medium) and until peppers are roasted. Let stand 10 minutes.

To serve, place chilled bean mixture in center of a large serving platter; arrange peppers and oranges around beans. Slice lamb diagonally across grain into thin slices, and arrange over beans. Garnish with reserved onion rings, and drizzle with remaining salad dressing mixture. Yield: 8 servings.

Ellen Burr

A Quest for Good Eating
Cape Cod Questers
Yarmouth Port, Massachusetts

Charcoaled Bourbon-Marinated Lamb

1 (8-pound) leg of lamb, cut
   into ½-inch-thick steaks
1½ cups bourbon
¾ cup olive oil
¾ cup soy sauce
3 large onions, thinly sliced
3 large cloves garlic, minced
Garnishes: chutney, Dijon
   mustard, sliced green onions

Place steaks in two large heavy-duty, zip-top plastic bags. Combine bourbon and next 4 ingredients. Pour over steaks. Seal bags; marinate in refrigerator 8 to 24 hours, turning occasionally.

Remove steaks from marinade, discarding marinade. Cook in batches, covered with grill lid, over medium-hot coals (350° to 400°) 7 minutes on each side or until steaks are done. Garnish, if desired. Yield: 16 servings.

Martha Kipcak

Flavors of Fredericksburg
St. Barnabas Episcopal Church
Fredericksburg, Texas

Pinchitos (Spanish Kabobs)

8 cloves garlic, crushed
7 bay leaves
1 (7-ounce) jar diced
   pimiento, undrained
1 cup olive oil
½ cup red wine vinegar
⅓ cup fresh lemon juice
3½ tablespoons ground cumin
3 tablespoons dried thyme
3 tablespoons paprika
2 tablespoons dried crushed
   red pepper
1½ teaspoons salt
½ teaspoon ground red pepper
4 pounds boneless leg of lamb,
   cut into 1-inch cubes

Combine all ingredients in a large bowl. Cover and marinate in refrigerator 24 hours.

Thread lamb onto four 15-inch metal skewers, discarding marinade. Cook, covered with grill lid, over medium-hot coals (350° to 400°) 10 minutes or to desired degree of doneness, turning often. Yield: 10 servings.

Cecelia Thygeson

A Continual Feast
St. Mary's Guild of St. Clement's Episcopal Church
Berkeley, California

Spiced Apple Pork Roast

Apple and pork are perfect flavor partners. Applesauce forms the base of the basting mixture in this recipe.

1 cup applesauce
⅓ cup firmly packed brown
  sugar
2 teaspoons white vinegar
⅛ to ¼ teaspoon ground cloves
1 (4- to 5-pound) rolled
  boneless pork loin roast

1 clove garlic, thinly sliced
1 teaspoon prepared mustard
2 tablespoons all-purpose flour
1 teaspoon salt
½ teaspoon sugar
⅛ teaspoon pepper

Combine applesauce, brown sugar, vinegar, and cloves; stir well, and set aside. Remove strings from roast; trim fat. Cut ½-inch slits at 1-inch intervals on top of roast; insert garlic slices. Lightly rub surface of roast with mustard. Reroll roast, tying securely with heavy string at 2-inch intervals.

Combine flour and next 3 ingredients; sprinkle over roast. Place roast on a rack in a roasting pan. Bake, uncovered, at 325° for 2 hours and 20 minutes or until meat thermometer inserted in thickest part registers 160° (medium); brush generously with applesauce mixture during last 30 minutes of baking. Yield: 12 servings.   Celeste Pelc

Door County Cooking
Bay View Lutheran Church
Sturgeon Bay, Wisconsin

Four-Peppercorn Pork Roast

1 (4- to 5-pound) rolled
  boneless pork loin roast
½ teaspoon salt
¼ cup plus 2 tablespoons all-
  purpose flour, divided
3 tablespoons unsalted butter,
  softened
¼ cup multicolored
  peppercorns, crushed

Vegetable oil
1 (14½-ounce) can ready-to-
  serve chicken broth
1 cup water
2 tablespoons red wine vinegar
½ teaspoon salt
Garnish: fresh rosemary sprigs

Remove strings from roast; trim fat. Sprinkle roast with ½ teaspoon salt. Reroll roast, tying securely with heavy string at 2-inch intervals.

Combine 2 tablespoons flour and butter; spread on top of roast. Press crushed peppercorns into butter mixture. Place roast on a rack in a greased shallow roasting pan. Bake, uncovered, at 475° for 30 minutes. Reduce heat to 325°, and bake 1 additional hour or until meat thermometer inserted in thickest part registers 160° (medium).

Remove roast to a serving platter, reserving drippings in pan. Set roast aside, and keep warm.

Combine pan drippings and enough oil to make 3 tablespoons; heat in a heavy saucepan over low heat; add remaining ¼ cup flour, stirring until smooth. Cook 1 minute, stirring constantly. Gradually add chicken broth and water; cook over medium heat, stirring constantly, until mixture is thickened and bubbly. Stir in vinegar and ½ teaspoon salt. Serve roast with warm gravy. Garnish, if desired. Yield: 12 servings.

Another Taste of Aloha
The Junior League of Honolulu, Hawaii

Stuffed Pork with Apples and Prunes

Applejack has a high alcohol content, so it's important to ignite it and burn off the alcohol to make sure it doesn't "ignite itself" while in the oven. Light it carefully, using a long-handled match.

¾ cup applejack or other apple-flavored brandy, divided
½ cup dry white wine
1 medium-size Granny Smith apple, peeled, cored, and coarsely chopped
6 ounces dried pitted prunes, finely chopped
2 (2-pound) boneless pork loin roasts, cut with pockets

¼ cup plus 2 tablespoons butter or margarine, melted
2 tablespoons vegetable oil
¼ cup whipping cream
1 tablespoon minced fresh parsley
½ teaspoon salt
¼ teaspoon pepper

Bring ½ cup applejack and wine to a boil in a small saucepan; boil 2 minutes. Pour over apple and prunes; let stand 1 hour. Drain fruit, reserving applejack mixture.

Stuff ¼ cup fruit mixture into each roast pocket; tie securely with heavy string at 2-inch intervals. Brown roasts in butter and oil in a large Dutch oven over medium-high heat.

Place remaining ¼ cup applejack in a small, long-handled saucepan. Bring to a boil. Remove from heat and ignite; let flames die down. Pour over roasts. Bring to a boil; cover, reduce heat, and simmer 45 minutes or until meat thermometer inserted in thickest part registers 160° (medium). Transfer roasts to a serving platter, reserving drippings in Dutch oven. Cut strings, and remove from roasts. Set roasts aside, and keep warm.

Add reserved fruit and applejack mixture to drippings in Dutch oven. Bring to a boil, and cook 2 minutes, stirring constantly. Add whipping cream and next 3 ingredients. Reduce heat to medium, and cook, stirring constantly, 5 minutes or until mixture is thickened and bubbly. Serve roasts with sauce. Yield: 8 servings.   Gale Dahl

Holiday Sampler
Welcome Wagon Club of the Mid Ohio Valley
Vienna, West Virginia

Bourbon and Honey Smoke-Roasted Pork Tenderloins

3 (¾-pound) pork tenderloins
½ cup thinly sliced onion
1 cup olive oil
½ cup bourbon
½ cup lemon juice
¼ cup soy sauce
3 tablespoons honey
2 tablespoons coarsely chopped fresh sage
1½ tablespoons minced gingerroot
1 tablespoon minced garlic
2 teaspoons pepper
1 teaspoon salt
Applewood chips

Place tenderloins and onion in a large heavy-duty, zip-top plastic bag. Combine olive oil and next 9 ingredients in a bowl; stir well. Pour marinade over tenderloins and onion. Seal bag; marinate in refrigerator 8 to 24 hours, turning occasionally.

Soak applewood chips in water to cover at least 30 minutes; drain.

Remove tenderloins from marinade, discarding marinade. Pat tenderloins dry. Place applewood chips on coals. Cook, covered with grill lid, over medium-hot coals (350° to 400°) 25 minutes or until meat thermometer inserted in thickest part registers 160° (medium), turning occasionally. Yield: 6 servings.   Josie George

Champions: Favorite Foods of Indy Car Racing
Championship Auto Racing Auxiliary
Indianapolis, Indiana

Grilled Blue Cheese-Stuffed Chops

½ cup shredded carrot
¼ cup chopped pecans
¼ cup crumbled blue cheese
1 green onion, thinly sliced
1 teaspoon Worcestershire
  sauce
4 (1½-inch-thick) rib pork
  chops, trimmed and cut with
  pockets

1 tablespoon plus 1 teaspoon
  all-purpose flour
¼ cup plain low-fat yogurt
¾ cup milk
½ teaspoon chicken-flavored
  bouillon granules
⅛ teaspoon pepper
Crumbled blue cheese
  (optional)

Combine first 5 ingredients in a small bowl; stir well. Stuff carrot mixture into pockets of chops; secure openings with wooden picks. Cook, covered with grill lid, over medium-hot coals (350° to 400°) 20 to 25 minutes or until done, turning once. Combine flour and yogurt in a saucepan, stirring until smooth. Slowly stir in milk; add bouillon granules and pepper, and cook over medium heat, stirring constantly, until thickened and bubbly. Serve chops with sauce; top with crumbled blue cheese, if desired. Yield: 4 servings.

The Bess Collection
The Junior Service League of Independence, Missouri

Pork Meatballs with Cranberry Sauce

2 pounds ground pork
2 large eggs, lightly beaten
1 cup crushed corn flakes
  cereal
⅓ cup ketchup
2 tablespoons dried onion
  flakes
2 tablespoons soy sauce
1 tablespoon dried parsley
  flakes

1¼ teaspoons salt
¼ teaspoon pepper
1 (16-ounce) can jellied
  cranberry sauce
1 cup ketchup
3 tablespoons brown sugar
1 tablespoon lemon juice

Combine first 9 ingredients in a large bowl. Shape into 32 meatballs (about 1½-inch). Place in a greased 13- x 9- x 2-inch baking dish.

Combine cranberry sauce and next 3 ingredients in a medium saucepan; cook over medium heat until smooth, stirring occasionally.

Pour sauce over meatballs; bake, uncovered, at 350° for 1 hour or until done. Yield: 8 servings. Marsha Gloe

St. George Parish Cookbook
St. George Parish
Hermann, Missouri

Belgian Endive and Ham au Gratin

8 large heads Belgian endive
1 tablespoon lemon juice
1 teaspoon salt
2 tablespoons butter or
  margarine
2 tablespoons all-purpose flour
1¼ cups milk
½ cup (2 ounces) shredded
  Swiss cheese

1 egg yolk, beaten
¼ teaspoon salt
¼ teaspoon freshly ground
  pepper
8 (1-ounce) slices cooked ham
2 tablespoons grated Parmesan
  cheese

Rinse endive; pat dry, and trim ends.

Place endive in a Dutch oven. Add water to cover, lemon juice, and 1 teaspoon salt. Bring to a boil. Cover, reduce heat, and simmer 10 minutes or until endive is tender. Drain well, and set aside.

Melt butter in a heavy saucepan over low heat; add flour, stirring until smooth. Cook 1 minute, stirring constantly. Gradually add milk; cook over medium heat, stirring constantly, until mixture is thickened and bubbly. Add Swiss cheese, stirring until cheese melts. Gradually stir about ¼ cup cheese mixture into egg yolk; add to remaining cheese mixture, stirring constantly. Add ¼ teaspoon salt and pepper.

Place 1 endive on each slice of ham; roll up ham, jellyroll fashion. Place ham rolls, seam side down, in a greased 13- x 9- x 2-inch baking dish. Pour cheese mixture over top; sprinkle with Parmesan cheese. Bake at 375° for 17 to 20 minutes or until browned and bubbly. Yield: 4 servings.

Among the Lilies
Women in Missions, First Baptist Church of Atlanta, Georgia

Grilled Venison and Vegetables

1½ pounds boneless venison sirloin, cut into 1¼-inch cubes
½ cup red wine vinegar
¼ cup honey
¼ cup soy sauce
2 tablespoons ketchup
Dash of garlic powder
Dash of pepper

12 small round red potatoes
1 large onion, cut into 6 wedges
1 medium zucchini, cut into 1-inch pieces
1 medium-size green pepper, cut into 1½-inch pieces
12 fresh mushrooms
12 cherry tomatoes

Place venison in a heavy-duty, zip-top plastic bag. Combine vinegar and next 5 ingredients in a bowl; stir well. Set ¼ cup marinade aside. Pour remaining marinade over venison. Seal bag; marinate in refrigerator 4 hours, turning occasionally.

Cook potatoes in boiling water to cover 10 minutes; drain. One hour before grilling, combine potatoes, ¼ cup reserved marinade, onion, and next 4 ingredients; toss gently.

Remove venison from marinade, reserving marinade. Bring marinade to a boil in a small saucepan; set aside. Alternately thread venison and vegetables on six 15-inch metal skewers. Cook, covered with grill lid, over medium-hot coals (350° to 400°) 15 minutes or to desired degree of doneness, turning and basting occasionally with reserved marinade. Yield: 6 servings.   Shane Chandler

Living off the Land: Arkansas Style
Howard County 4-H Foundation
Nashville, Arkansas

Pasta, Rice & Grains

Monterey Coast Seafood Pasta, page 214

Black Bean Spaghetti

This recipe calls for angel hair pasta, which is a very thin spaghetti. But any type of spaghetti would work nicely.

1 (12-ounce) package angel hair pasta
1 (3½-ounce) jar capers, undrained
1 large onion, thinly sliced
1 small sweet red pepper, cut into thin strips
1 small sweet yellow pepper, cut into thin strips
½ pound fresh mushrooms, sliced
2 tablespoons olive oil
1 (16-ounce) can whole tomatoes, undrained and chopped
1 (15-ounce) can black beans, rinsed and drained
1 (15-ounce) can kidney beans, undrained
¼ cup sliced ripe olives
¼ teaspoon dried rosemary
¼ teaspoon dried basil
¼ teaspoon pepper
Freshly grated Parmesan cheese

Cook pasta according to package directions; drain well. Set aside, and keep warm. Drain capers, reserving 1½ tablespoons liquid; set aside.

Cook onion and next 3 ingredients in oil in a large saucepan over medium-high heat, stirring constantly, until vegetables are tender. Add reserved capers and liquid, tomatoes, and next 6 ingredients. Bring to a boil; reduce heat, and simmer, uncovered, 30 minutes, stirring mixture occasionally.

Remove pasta to a serving platter; spoon tomato mixture over pasta. Sprinkle with cheese. Yield: 6 servings.   Myrtle Ann Saxon

Cooking on the Coast
Mississippi Gulf Coast YMCA
Ocean Springs, Mississippi

Thai Noodles

Use your choice of creamy or crunchy peanut butter in this recipe. Either way, the flavor's the same, but the nuggets in the crunchy spread will hint at the flavor of the dish.

1 (8-ounce) package angel hair pasta
¼ cup soy sauce
¼ cup peanut butter
3 tablespoons sugar
3 tablespoons vegetable oil
3 tablespoons dark sesame oil
1 tablespoon minced garlic
1 teaspoon dried crushed red pepper
¼ teaspoon hot red chili oil
Toppings: chopped fresh cilantro, slivered carrot, sliced green onions, toasted sesame seeds, unsalted dry roasted peanuts

Cook pasta according to package directions; drain well. Set aside, and keep warm.

Combine soy sauce and next 7 ingredients in a small bowl; stir well with a wire whisk. Pour over pasta; toss gently. Add toppings, if desired. Yield: 4 servings.

Tasteful Treasures
Docent Guild, Bowers Museum of Cultural Art
Santa Ana, California

Fettuccine with Pesto Chicken

2 cups loosely packed torn
  fresh spinach
1 cup loosely packed fresh
  basil leaves
¾ cup chicken broth
3 tablespoons pine nuts
3 tablespoons grated Parmesan
  cheese
1 large clove garlic, minced
1 tablespoon olive oil

1 teaspoon grated lemon rind
Freshly ground pepper to taste
1 (8-ounce) package fettuccine
4 skinned and boned chicken
  breast halves, cut into thin
  strips
1 medium-size sweet red
  pepper, cut into thin strips
Salt to taste

Position knife blade in food processor bowl; add first 6 ingredients. Process until smooth, stopping once to scrape down sides. Pour olive oil through food chute with processor running, processing until combined; stir in lemon rind and freshly ground pepper to taste. Set aside.

Cook pasta according to package directions; drain well. Set aside, and keep warm.

Cook chicken in a large nonstick skillet over medium-high heat, stirring constantly, 5 minutes or until done. Remove chicken from skillet; set aside, and keep warm.

Add sweet red pepper strips to skillet, and cook over medium heat until crisp-tender, stirring occasionally. Add spinach mixture and chicken to skillet; cook over medium heat 2 minutes. Add pasta, tossing gently. Add salt to taste, and serve immediately. Yield: 4 servings.

By Special Request, Our Favorite Recipes
Piggly Wiggly Carolina Employees
Charleston, South Carolina

Fettuccine with Roquefort Sauce

If you have Roquefort cheese leftover, serve this strong-flavored cheese at the end of another meal accompanied by a fine red dessert wine.

½ cup pine nuts
1 tablespoon vegetable oil
1½ cups whipping cream
1 cup crumbled Roquefort
   cheese
1 (8-ounce) package cream
   cheese, cubed

1 (16-ounce) package fettuccine
1 (10-ounce) package torn fresh
   spinach
6 ounces thinly sliced prosciutto
¼ cup chopped fresh parsley
¼ teaspoon salt

Cook pine nuts in hot oil in a small skillet over medium-high heat, stirring constantly, 3 to 4 minutes or until lightly browned; set aside.

Combine whipping cream and cheeses in a heavy saucepan; cook over medium heat, stirring constantly, until smooth. Set sauce aside, and keep warm.

Cook pasta according to package directions; drain well. Set aside, and keep warm.

Slice spinach and prosciutto into thin strips. Combine spinach, prosciutto, parsley, and salt in a large bowl; add pasta, and toss gently. Pour cheese sauce over pasta mixture, and toss until coated. Spoon into a greased 13- x 9- x 2-inch baking dish. Bake, uncovered, at 375° for 15 minutes or until thoroughly heated. Sprinkle with toasted pine nuts. Yield: 8 servings.   Lynn Diestelkamp

Immacolata Cookbook
Immacolata Church Ladies Society
St. Louis, Missouri

Linguine with Spicy Tomato-Cream Sauce

If you prefer, you can substitute half-and-half for the whipping cream.

1 tablespoon minced onion
2 cloves garlic, crushed
¼ to ½ teaspoon dried crushed
   red pepper
2 tablespoons olive oil
1 (14½-ounce) can whole
   tomatoes, undrained

½ cup whipping cream
1 (16-ounce) package linguine
¼ cup chopped fresh basil
¼ teaspoon salt
¼ teaspoon freshly ground
   pepper
Freshly grated Romano cheese

Cook first 3 ingredients in oil in a large skillet over medium heat 3 minutes, stirring often. Add tomatoes, crushing with back of a spoon; cook over high heat 8 minutes or until thickened. Stir in whipping cream; bring to a boil, and cook 1 minute. Set aside, and keep warm.

Cook pasta according to package directions; drain well. Combine pasta, whipping cream mixture, basil, salt, and pepper; toss gently. Remove pasta mixture to a serving platter. Sprinkle with cheese, and serve immediately. Yield: 4 servings.   Sarah W. D'Addabbo

Simple Elegance
Our Lady of Perpetual Help Women's Guild
Germantown, Tennessee

Orzo with Dried Cherries

Looking for a new side dish for poultry? Try this unusual blend of orzo, saffron, and dried cherries.

6 cups water
1 cup orzo, uncooked
¼ teaspoon threads of saffron
1 tablespoon grated orange
   rind
2 tablespoons orange juice

3 tablespoons olive oil
⅓ cup dried cherries, chopped
3 tablespoons slivered
   almonds, toasted
2 green onions, thinly sliced
Salt and pepper to taste

Combine first 3 ingredients in a saucepan; bring to a boil. Cover, reduce heat, and simmer 8 minutes; drain. Set aside.

Combine orange rind, juice, and oil in a small bowl; stir with a wire whisk. Pour over orzo. Add cherries and remaining ingredients; toss gently. Yield: 4 servings.

Sterling Performances
The Guilds of the Orange County Performing Arts Center
Costa Mesa, California

Orzo Salad with Shrimp and Herbal Vinaigrette

¾ cup olive oil
½ cup vegetable oil
⅓ cup minced fresh dill
⅓ cup minced fresh parsley
1 tablespoon crushed garlic
1¾ teaspoons salt
1 teaspoon pepper
½ teaspoon dried basil
½ teaspoon dried oregano
2 cups orzo, uncooked
4½ cups water

1½ pounds unpeeled medium-size fresh shrimp
1 pound fresh asparagus
2 medium-size sweet red peppers, cut into thin strips
½ cup golden raisins
½ cup chopped purple onion
¼ cup capers, drained
½ teaspoon salt
¼ teaspoon pepper
Mixed salad greens

Combine first 9 ingredients; stir well, and set dressing aside.

Cook pasta according to package directions; drain and set aside.

Bring water to a boil; add shrimp, and cook 3 to 5 minutes or until shrimp turn pink. Drain well; rinse with cold water. Chill. Peel shrimp, and devein, if desired. Cut into thirds, if desired; set aside.

Snap off tough ends of asparagus. Remove scales from stalks with a vegetable peeler, if desired. Cut diagonally into ½-inch pieces. Blanch in boiling water to cover 3 minutes or until crisp-tender; drain. Plunge into ice water to stop the cooking process; drain.

Combine orzo, shrimp, asparagus, red pepper, and next 3 ingredients; toss. Add dressing, ½ teaspoon salt, and ¼ teaspoon pepper; toss. Serve warm or chilled on salad greens. Yield: 6 servings.

Cuisine for Connoisseurs: Food Among the Fine Arts
Boca Raton Museum of Art
Boca Raton, Florida

Penne with Artichokes, Sun-Dried Tomatoes, and Basil

Be sure to cook pasta in plenty of rapidly boiling water to prevent it from becoming gummy.

1 (14-ounce) can artichoke
  hearts, drained and halved
5 cloves garlic
¼ cup olive oil, divided
⅛ teaspoon salt
½ cup drained oil-packed
  sun-dried tomatoes

1 (16-ounce) package penne
  pasta
5 quarts water
1 teaspoon salt
1 cup chopped fresh basil
Salt and pepper to taste

Arrange artichoke hearts and whole garlic cloves in an ungreased 11- x 7- x 1½-inch baking dish. Drizzle with 2 tablespoons olive oil, and sprinkle with ⅛ teaspoon salt. Bake, uncovered, at 350° for 25 minutes or until garlic is golden. Remove garlic and artichoke hearts; set aside.

Position knife blade in food processor bowl; add garlic, remaining 2 tablespoons olive oil, and sun-dried tomatoes. Process until finely chopped, stopping once to scrape down sides.

Cook pasta in a large Dutch oven according to package directions, using 5 quarts water and 1 teaspoon salt; drain well, and place in a large bowl. Add artichoke hearts, tomato mixture, and chopped basil; toss gently. Add salt and pepper to taste. Serve immediately. Yield: 4 servings.   Mary Lawrence-Roberts

The East Hampton L.V.I.S. Centennial Cookbook
The Ladies' Village Improvement Society of East Hampton,
New York

Baked Rigatoni and Ham with Four Cheeses

This pasta dish is flavor-packed with cheese—mozzarella, provolone, fontina, and Parmesan.

3 tablespoons butter or
   margarine, divided
¼ cup fine, dry breadcrumbs
8 ounces rigatoni, uncooked
2 tablespoons all-purpose flour
2 cups milk
¼ teaspoon salt
¼ teaspoon pepper
4 ounces diced cooked ham

1 cup (4 ounces) shredded
   mozzarella cheese
½ cup (2 ounces) shredded
   provolone cheese
½ cup (2 ounces) shredded
   fontina cheese
¼ cup freshly grated Parmesan
   cheese

Melt 1 tablespoon butter in a small saucepan over low heat. Add breadcrumbs, and toss well. Set aside.

Cook pasta according to package directions; drain well. Set aside, and keep warm.

Melt remaining 2 tablespoons butter in a heavy saucepan over low heat; add flour, stirring until smooth. Cook 1 minute, stirring constantly. Gradually add milk; cook over medium heat, stirring constantly, until mixture is thickened and bubbly. Stir in salt and pepper. Add ham and cheeses, stirring until cheeses melt.

Add cooked pasta to cheese mixture; stir well. Pour into a buttered 2-quart baking dish. Cover and bake at 375° for 25 minutes or until bubbly. Uncover and sprinkle with breadcrumb mixture. Bake 7 additional minutes or until golden. Yield: 4 servings.   Mrs. Dan West

Simply Irresistible
The Junior Auxiliary of Conway, Arkansas

Pasta with Green Tomatoes

Tired of the same old tomato sauce on your spaghetti? Gather summer's harvest early, and enjoy the unique flavor of green tomatoes on your pasta.

2 medium onions, finely chopped
¼ cup vegetable oil
1 teaspoon minced garlic
4 large green tomatoes, coarsely chopped
3 tablespoons chopped fresh parsley, divided
¾ cup chicken broth

3 tablespoons coarsely chopped fresh basil
½ teaspoon salt
¼ teaspoon freshly ground pepper
1 (16-ounce) package rigatoni
¼ cup plus 3 tablespoons freshly grated Parmesan cheese

Cook onion in oil in a large skillet over medium-high heat, stirring constantly, until tender. Add garlic, and cook 1 minute.

Add tomato, 2 tablespoons parsley, and next 4 ingredients. Bring to a boil; cover, reduce heat, and simmer 30 to 35 minutes or until tomato is tender.

Cook pasta according to package directions; drain well. Add pasta to tomato mixture; toss gently. Sprinkle with remaining 1 tablespoon parsley and cheese. Yield: 6 servings.

The Maine Collection
Portland Museum of Art
Portland, Maine

Sesame-Crusted Salmon with Asian Noodles

Sesame seeds and sesame oil give this salmon a crunchy coating and nutty flavor.

1 (1½-pound) salmon fillet
1 tablespoon dark sesame oil
2 tablespoons sesame seeds, lightly toasted
8 ounces spaghettini, uncooked
Dressing

½ cup chopped green onions
½ cup plus 2 tablespoons chopped fresh cilantro, divided
½ medium cucumber, cut into thin strips

Brush salmon with oil, and sprinkle with sesame seeds; place salmon on a large square of heavy-duty aluminum foil. Place foil on grill rack. Cook, covered with grill lid, over medium-hot coals (350° to 400°) 18 minutes or until fish flakes easily when tested with a fork.

Cook pasta according to package directions; drain well, and place in a large bowl. Add Dressing, green onions, ½ cup cilantro, and cucumber; toss well.

Divide pasta evenly among four individual serving plates. Cut salmon into 4 portions, and place 1 portion over each serving of pasta. Sprinkle with remaining 2 tablespoons cilantro. Serve immediately. Yield: 4 servings.

Dressing

¼ cup peanut oil
3 tablespoons rice wine vinegar
2 tablespoons dark sesame oil
2 tablespoons fresh lime juice

1 tablespoon plus 1 teaspoon soy sauce
1 teaspoon hot red chili oil

Combine all ingredients in a small bowl; stir well with a wire whisk. Yield: ¾ cup.

Simply Classic
The Junior League of Seattle, Washington

Monterey Coast Seafood Pasta

Vermicelli is a pasta cut thinner than spaghetti, and thin vermicelli is even more delicate. Angel hair, the finest strands of all, makes a good substitute for thin vermicelli.

1 pound unpeeled medium-size fresh shrimp
1½ cups sliced fresh mushrooms
½ cup chopped carrot
⅓ cup chopped celery
1 medium onion, chopped
2 cloves garlic, minced
¼ cup olive oil
2 (14½-ounce) cans Italian-style tomatoes, undrained and chopped
1 (8-ounce) bottle clam juice
1 cup dry red wine

¼ cup chopped fresh parsley
1 teaspoon dried oregano
1 teaspoon dried basil
½ teaspoon salt
¼ teaspoon pepper
1 (16-ounce) package thin vermicelli
1 (10-ounce) can whole clams, undrained
1 pound halibut fillets, cut into 2-inch pieces
3 tablespoons butter
¼ teaspoon hot sauce

Peel shrimp, and devein, if desired. Set aside.

Cook mushrooms and next 4 ingredients in oil in a large skillet over medium-high heat, stirring constantly, until tender. Add tomatoes and next 7 ingredients; bring to a boil. Reduce heat, and simmer, uncovered, 30 minutes.

While mushroom mixture simmers, cook pasta according to package directions; drain well. Set aside, and keep warm.

Add shrimp, clams with liquid, and fish to mushroom mixture; bring to a boil. Cover, reduce heat, and simmer 10 minutes or until shrimp turn pink and fish flakes easily when tested with a fork. Add butter and hot sauce, stirring until butter melts. Serve immediately over pasta. Yield: 8 servings.

Kay Schenk

What's Cooking at Chico State
Staff Council/California State University
Chico, California

Ziti with Mozzarella and Tomato

This pasta dish tastes unbelievably fresh because the tomato mixture never cooks; it heats slightly when you toss it with the hot pasta.

1 (16-ounce) package ziti pasta
¼ cup plus 2 tablespoons
  vegetable oil
1 clove garlic, minced
1 tablespoon dried basil
2 tablespoons red wine vinegar
½ teaspoon salt
¼ teaspoon pepper
4 cups diced tomato
½ cup diced ripe olives
⅓ cup diced purple onion
8 ounces mozzarella cheese,
  diced
½ cup grated Parmesan cheese

    Cook pasta according to package directions; drain, and set aside.
    Combine oil and next 5 ingredients; stir well. Add tomato, olives, and onion; toss well. Add pasta and cheeses; toss gently. Serve immediately. Yield: 7 servings.   Linda Saraceni

Ridgefield Cooks
Women's Committee of the Ridgefield Community Center
Ridgefield, Connecticut

Celebrity Green Rice

2 cups chicken broth
1 cup long-grain rice, uncooked
½ teaspoon salt
⅛ teaspoon pepper
¾ cup chopped celery
¾ cup chopped green onions
¼ cup butter or margarine,
  melted
¼ cup chopped fresh parsley
1 (8-ounce) can sliced water
  chestnuts, drained and
  slivered

    Combine first 4 ingredients in a saucepan. Bring to a boil; cover, reduce heat, and simmer 20 minutes or until liquid is absorbed and rice is tender. Set aside, and keep warm.
    Cook celery and green onions in butter in a skillet over medium-high heat, stirring constantly, until tender. Stir in parsley, rice, and water chestnuts. Yield: 6 servings.   Debbie McCormick

Good to the Core
The Apple Corps of the Weller Center for Health Education
Easton, Pennsylvania

Rice Stroganoff

We recommend serving this creamy rice and mushroom combo as a side dish with beef or chicken. It also makes a great meatless meal for one paired with English peas, broccoli, or a tossed green salad.

1 cup sliced fresh mushrooms
¼ cup sliced green onions
1 clove garlic, minced
2 teaspoons butter or margarine, melted
¾ cup chicken broth
¼ cup dry white wine
1 tablespoon chopped fresh parsley
⅛ teaspoon salt
Dash of ground white pepper
½ cup long-grain rice, uncooked
¼ cup reduced-fat sour cream

Cook mushrooms, green onions, and garlic in butter in a medium saucepan over medium-high heat, stirring constantly, until vegetables are tender. Add chicken broth and next 4 ingredients; bring to a boil. Stir in rice; cover, reduce heat, and simmer 20 minutes or until liquid is absorbed and rice is tender. Stir in sour cream. Serve immediately. Yield: 2 servings.

Teri Larson

Our Best Home Cooking
Citizens of Zion Missionary Baptist Church Women's Ministry
Compton, California

Texas Rice

1 cup chopped cooked ham
1 cup chopped green onions
¼ cup butter or margarine, melted
3 cups cooked rice
1 (8-ounce) carton sour cream
1 cup (4 ounces) shredded sharp Cheddar cheese
½ cup small-curd cottage cheese
1 (4½-ounce) can chopped green chiles, undrained
½ teaspoon salt
⅛ teaspoon ground white pepper
⅛ teaspoon ground bay leaves
Garnishes: paprika, fresh parsley sprigs

Cook chopped ham and green onions in butter in a large skillet over medium-high heat, stirring constantly, until green onions are tender. Remove from heat. Stir in rice and next 7 ingredients. Spoon into a lightly greased 11- x 7- x 1½-inch baking dish. Bake, uncovered, at 375° for 20 minutes or until thoroughly heated. Garnish, if desired. Yield: 6 servings.

Tastes and Traditions: The Sam Houston Heritage Cookbook
The Study Club of Huntsville, Texas

Lentil Pilaf

Go vegetarian with this recipe by substituting vegetable broth for the chicken broth and omitting the chopped cooked chicken.

¾ cup chopped green onions
1¼ cups chopped celery
1 cup dried lentils
½ cup butter or margarine, melted
4 cups chicken broth
½ teaspoon dried thyme

1¼ cups long-grain rice, uncooked
1 cup chopped cooked chicken
¼ cup slivered almonds, toasted
½ teaspoon salt
¼ teaspoon pepper

Cook first 3 ingredients in butter in a large skillet over medium-high heat, stirring constantly, until vegetables are tender. Add chicken broth and thyme; bring to a boil. Cover, reduce heat, and simmer 25 minutes. Add rice and chicken; bring to a boil. Cover, reduce heat, and simmer 25 minutes or until liquid is absorbed and rice is tender. Stir in almonds, salt, and pepper. Serve immediately. Yield: 9 servings.

Sheridan School Brown Bag Cookbook
The Sheridan School
Houston, Texas

Risotto with Asparagus and Basil

Be sure to remove the dry, woody stems of the shiitake mushrooms before cooking.

1 cup dry white wine
½ ounce dried shiitake
  mushrooms, stemmed
1 pound fresh asparagus
5 cups chicken broth
1 cup finely chopped onion
2 cloves garlic, minced
¼ cup butter or margarine,
  melted

1½ cups Arborio or other
  short-grain rice, uncooked
⅓ cup freshly grated Parmesan
  cheese
⅓ cup minced fresh basil
Freshly grated Parmesan
  cheese
Freshly ground pepper

Bring wine to a boil in a small saucepan; add mushrooms. Remove from heat, and let stand 10 minutes. Drain mushrooms, reserving liquid; mince mushrooms, and set aside.

Snap off tough ends of asparagus. Remove scales from stalks with a vegetable peeler, if desired. Cut asparagus into 1-inch pieces; arrange in a steamer basket over boiling water. Cover and steam 5 minutes or until crisp-tender. Set aside.

Combine mushroom liquid and chicken broth in a large saucepan; bring to a boil. Reduce heat to low, and keep warm.

Cook mushrooms, onion, and garlic in butter in a large saucepan over medium-high heat, stirring constantly, until vegetables are tender. Add rice; stir well. Add 1 cup chicken broth mixture; cook over medium heat, stirring constantly, until most of the liquid is absorbed. Continue adding chicken broth mixture, ½ cup at a time, and cook, stirring constantly, until mixture is creamy and rice is tender. (The entire process should take 30 to 35 minutes.) Stir in asparagus, ⅓ cup cheese, and basil. Cover and let stand 2 to 3 minutes. Sprinkle with additional cheese and pepper. Serve immediately. Yield: 6 servings.

Presentations
Friends of Lied, Lied Center for Performing Arts
Lincoln, Nebraska

Pecan Wild Rice

Looking for a traditional menu partner for poultry? This test-kitchen favorite is sure to satisfy.

5½ cups chicken broth
1 cup wild rice, uncooked
4 green onions, thinly sliced
1 cup pecan halves, toasted
1 cup golden raisins
⅓ cup orange juice
¼ cup chopped fresh parsley
¼ cup olive oil
1 tablespoon grated orange rind
1½ teaspoons salt
¼ teaspoon freshly ground pepper

Combine broth and rice in a medium saucepan. Bring to a boil; reduce heat, and simmer, uncovered, 45 minutes. Drain and place in a medium bowl. Add green onions and remaining ingredients; toss gently. Serve immediately. Yield: 6 servings. Peggy Grossman

Sun Valley Celebrity & Local Heroes Cookbook
Advocates for Survivors of Domestic Violence
Hailey, Idaho

Pine Nut-Barley Bake

½ cup chopped green onions
¼ cup chopped celery
¼ cup sliced fresh mushrooms
¼ cup plus 1 tablespoon butter or margarine, melted
1 cup pearl barley, uncooked
2 cups chicken broth, divided
⅓ cup chopped fresh parsley
½ cup pine nuts, toasted
Salt and pepper to taste

Cook first 3 ingredients in butter in a large skillet over medium-high heat, stirring constantly, until vegetables are tender. Add barley; cook, stirring constantly, until barley is golden.

Combine barley mixture, 1 cup broth, and parsley in an ungreased 2-quart casserole. Cover and bake at 350° for 30 minutes. Stir in remaining 1 cup broth and pine nuts. Bake, uncovered, 30 additional minutes or until liquid is absorbed and barley is tender. Stir in salt and pepper to taste. Serve immediately. Yield: 4 servings.

The Bountiful Arbor
The Junior League of Ann Arbor, Michigan

Sweet Corn Polenta with Mushroom Sauce

2 cups chicken broth
1 cup yellow cornmeal
1 cup cold water
1 cup frozen whole kernel corn, thawed
½ cup grated Parmesan cheese, divided
1 medium onion, chopped
2 teaspoons olive oil
1 clove garlic, minced
1 teaspoon dried basil
½ teaspoon dried oregano

⅛ teaspoon dried crushed red pepper
½ pound fresh mushrooms, thinly sliced
½ cup dry white wine, divided
1 (16-ounce) can whole tomatoes, chopped
½ teaspoon salt
¼ teaspoon pepper
3 tablespoons chopped fresh parsley
1 tablespoon olive oil, divided

Bring broth to a boil in a saucepan. Combine cornmeal and water; stir with a wire whisk until smooth. Add cornmeal mixture to broth; cook over medium-high heat, stirring constantly, until thickened and bubbly. Add corn; cook over medium heat, stirring constantly, 15 minutes or until very thick. Stir in ¼ cup plus 1 tablespoon Parmesan cheese. Spoon mixture into a lightly greased 9-inch round cakepan, spreading evenly; let cool completely. Cover and chill 8 hours.

Cook onion in 2 teaspoons oil in a skillet over medium-high heat, stirring constantly, until tender. Add garlic and next 3 ingredients; cook 1 minute, stirring constantly. Add mushrooms; cook 2 minutes, stirring constantly. Add ¼ cup wine; cook 3 minutes or until wine is absorbed. Add remaining ¼ cup wine, tomatoes, salt, and pepper. Bring to a boil; reduce heat, and simmer 40 minutes or until mixture is reduced to 2¼ cups. Stir in parsley. Set aside, and keep warm.

Brush top of polenta in pan with 1 teaspoon olive oil. Invert polenta onto a baking sheet; brush with remaining 2 teaspoons oil. Cut polenta into 6 wedges. Broil 5½ inches from heat (with electric oven door partially opened) 5 minutes or until lightly browned.

Place polenta wedges on individual serving plates; spoon tomato mixture over polenta. Sprinkle evenly with remaining 3 tablespoons Parmesan cheese. Yield: 6 servings.   Louis Bertonazzi

Cookin' with Fire
Milford Fire Department
Milford, Massachusetts

Pies & Pastries

Black Russian Pie, page 230

Buttered Rum-Apple Pie

If you can't find Granny Smith apples, substitute another tart variety such as Jonathan or Northern Spy.

½ cup unsalted butter or
  margarine, divided
½ cup firmly packed brown
  sugar
7½ cups peeled, sliced Granny
  Smith apple (about 8
  medium)
1 teaspoon grated lemon rind

1 tablespoon fresh lemon juice
¼ teaspoon ground nutmeg
¼ cup light rum
1 tablespoon cornstarch
1 unbaked 9-inch pastry shell
½ cup all-purpose flour
½ cup sugar
¼ cup sliced almonds

Melt ¼ cup butter in a large skillet over medium-low heat; stir in brown sugar and next 4 ingredients. Cover, reduce heat, and simmer 10 minutes or until apple is tender, stirring occasionally. Combine rum and cornstarch, stirring until smooth. Stir into apple mixture; cook, stirring constantly, 1 minute or until thickened. Pour into pastry shell.

Combine flour and ½ cup sugar in a bowl; cut in remaining ¼ cup butter with pastry blender until mixture is crumbly. Stir in almonds. Sprinkle crumb mixture over apple mixture. Bake at 375° for 30 to 35 minutes or until golden. Let stand 15 minutes before serving. Yield: one 9-inch pie.   Pancho and Carla Carter

Champions: Favorite Foods of Indy Car Racing
Championship Auto Racing Auxiliary
Indianapolis, Indiana

Amaretto-Coconut Pie

This super-speedy pie is mixed in one bowl and makes its own crust.

¼ cup butter or margarine,
  softened
1 cup sugar
2 large eggs

¾ cup milk
¼ cup amaretto
¼ cup self-rising flour
⅔ cup flaked coconut

Beat butter and sugar at medium speed of an electric mixer until light and fluffy. Add eggs; beat well. Add milk, amaretto, and flour, beating well. Stir in coconut. Pour mixture into a lightly greased 9-inch pieplate. Bake at 350° for 35 minutes or until set. Cool completely on a wire rack. Yield: one 9-inch pie.

Specialties of Indianapolis, Volume 2
Home Economists' Guild of Indianapolis, Indiana

Cinnamon Custard Pie

Small- or large-curd cottage cheese will work equally well in this pie.

2 **cups cottage cheese**	1 **teaspoon vanilla extract**
¼ **cup milk**	⅛ **teaspoon salt**
1 **cup sugar**	1 **unbaked 9-inch pastry shell**
3 **large eggs, lightly beaten**	1 **teaspoon sugar**
1 **tablespoon all-purpose flour**	½ **teaspoon ground cinnamon**

Combine cottage cheese and milk in container of an electric blender; cover and process until smooth, stopping once to scrape down sides.

Combine cottage cheese mixture, 1 cup sugar, and next 4 ingredients in a medium bowl; stir well. Pour into pastry shell.

Combine 1 teaspoon sugar and cinnamon; stir well. Sprinkle over cottage cheese mixture. Bake at 450° for 5 minutes. Reduce oven temperature to 350°, and bake 25 additional minutes or until a knife inserted in center comes out clean. Serve warm or at room temperature. Yield: one 9-inch pie.

Joan E. Bashford

Reading, Writing, Recipes
Literacy Volunteers of Greater Syracuse, New York

Fudge Pie

Strong brewed coffee brings out the rich, fudgy flavor of this easy chocolate pie–it's a "must try." If you usually use instant coffee granules, use 2 teaspoons of the granules per 1 cup of water to make the strong coffee.

2 cups (12 ounces) semisweet chocolate morsels
¼ cup butter or margarine, softened
¾ cup firmly packed brown sugar
3 large eggs
2 teaspoons strong brewed coffee
1 teaspoon vanilla extract
1½ cups chopped pecans, divided
¼ cup all-purpose flour
1 unbaked 9-inch pastry shell
1 cup whipping cream, whipped

Place chocolate morsels in top of a double boiler; bring water to a boil. Reduce heat to low; cook until chocolate melts, stirring occasionally. Set aside, and let cool slightly.

Beat butter at medium speed of an electric mixer until creamy; gradually add sugar, beating well. Add eggs, one at a time, beating after each addition. Stir in melted chocolate, coffee, and vanilla. Gradually add 1 cup pecans and flour, stirring well. Spoon chocolate mixture into pastry shell; sprinkle with remaining ½ cup pecans. Bake at 375° for 30 minutes or until a knife inserted in center comes out almost clean. Cool completely on a wire rack. Serve with whipped cream. Yield: one 9-inch pie.

Almost Chefs, A Cookbook for Kids
Palm Beach Guild for the Children's Home Society
West Palm Beach, Florida

Cranberry Cream Pie

Be sure to use the whole-berry cranberry sauce rather than jellied for tangy bits of the fruit. If you're in a hurry, use 4 cups of thawed frozen whipped topping instead of whipping cream.

1 envelope unflavored gelatin
2 tablespoons orange juice
1 (16-ounce) can whole-berry cranberry sauce
¼ cup sugar
½ teaspoon grated orange rind
2 cups whipping cream, whipped and divided
1 (9-inch) graham cracker crust

Sprinkle gelatin over orange juice in a small bowl; stir well, and let stand 1 minute.

Combine cranberry sauce and sugar in a small saucepan; bring to a boil. Remove from heat; add gelatin mixture and orange rind, stirring until gelatin dissolves. Let cool to room temperature.

Gently fold in half of whipped cream. Pour cranberry sauce mixture into crust. Cover and chill 2 hours or until firm. Serve with remaining whipped cream. Yield: one 9-inch pie.   Tina Roy

Tell Me More
The Junior League of Lafayette, Louisiana

Fresh Strawberry Glacé Pie

Prepare this pie in early spring when strawberries are sweetest and juiciest.

1 quart fresh strawberries, hulled and halved
1¾ cups sugar, divided
2 cups milk
¼ cup plus 1 tablespoon all-purpose flour
¼ teaspoon salt
4 egg yolks, beaten
1 teaspoon vanilla extract

1 baked 9-inch pastry shell
Orange juice
2½ tablespoons cornstarch
1 tablespoon all-purpose flour
1 tablespoon butter or margarine
½ cup whipping cream, whipped

Combine strawberries and 1 cup sugar in a medium bowl; stir until strawberries are coated. Let stand at room temperature 1 hour.

Combine milk, remaining ¾ cup sugar, ¼ cup plus 1 tablespoon flour, and salt in a medium saucepan, stirring until smooth. Cook over medium heat, stirring constantly, 5 minutes or until thickened. Gradually stir about one-fourth of hot mixture into yolks; add to remaining hot mixture, stirring constantly. Cook, stirring constantly, until thickened and bubbly. Stir in vanilla. Pour custard into pastry shell. Let cool completely.

Drain strawberries, reserving juice. Set strawberries aside. Add enough orange juice to strawberry juice to equal 1½ cups. Pour juice mixture into a medium saucepan. Combine cornstarch and 1 tablespoon flour; add to juice mixture, stirring until smooth. Cook over medium heat, stirring constantly, until mixture thickens and boils. Remove from heat; add butter, stirring until butter melts. Add strawberries, stirring gently. Spoon strawberry mixture over custard. Cover and chill 8 hours or until firm. Serve with whipped cream. Yield: one 9-inch pie.

Dede Elmore

Lake Murray Presbyterian Preschool Cookbook
Lake Murray Presbyterian Preschool Parents Organization
Chapin, South Carolina

Glazed Strawberry Pie

If your fresh strawberries aren't very red, try adding a few drops of red food coloring to the reserved juice in this recipe to give the pie more intense color.

4 cups fresh strawberries, hulled and divided
¾ cup water
¾ cup sugar
3 tablespoons cornstarch
¼ teaspoon salt
1 baked 9-inch pastry shell
½ cup whipping cream
1 tablespoon sugar

Crush 1 cup strawberries, and place in a medium saucepan; add water. Bring to a boil; reduce heat, and simmer, uncovered, 3 minutes. Drain, reserving juice. Add enough water to juice to equal 1 cup. Set aside.

Combine ¾ cup sugar, cornstarch, and salt in a medium saucepan. Gradually stir juice into sugar mixture. Cook over medium heat, stirring constantly, until mixture thickens and boils. Boil 1 minute, stirring constantly. Remove from heat, and let glaze cool slightly.

Arrange remaining 3 cups strawberries, stem end down, in pastry shell. Pour glaze over strawberries; cover and chill.

Beat whipping cream until foamy; gradually add 1 tablespoon sugar, beating until soft peaks form. Serve pie with whipped cream. Yield: one 9-inch pie.   Meade Fasciano

Cooks by the Yard
Harvard Neighbors, Harvard University
Cambridge, Massachusetts

Butter Crunch-Chocolate Pie

1 cup all-purpose flour
¼ cup firmly packed brown
  sugar
½ cup butter or margarine
½ cup chopped walnuts
2 cups milk
1 cup sugar
⅓ cup all-purpose flour

1 tablespoon plus 1 teaspoon
  cocoa
¼ teaspoon salt
3 egg yolks, lightly beaten
¼ cup butter or margarine
1 teaspoon vanilla extract
1 cup whipping cream,
  whipped

Combine 1 cup flour and brown sugar in a medium bowl; cut in ½ cup butter with pastry blender until mixture is crumbly. Stir in walnuts. Firmly press mixture in bottom and up sides of a 10-inch pieplate. Bake at 375° for 10 minutes or until golden. Cool completely on a wire rack.

Combine milk and next 4 ingredients in a heavy saucepan; stir well. Cook over low heat, stirring constantly, 25 minutes or until mixture is thickened and bubbly.

Gradually add one-fourth of hot mixture to egg yolks. Add to remaining hot mixture, stirring constantly. Cook 5 minutes, stirring constantly. Remove from heat; add ¼ cup butter and vanilla, stirring until butter melts. Pour into prepared crust. Let cool 30 minutes; cover and chill until firm. Serve with whipped cream. Yield: one 10-inch pie.

A Slice of Paradise
The Hospital Service League of Naples Community Hospital
Naples, Florida

Chocolate-Caramel Pecan Pie

2 cups finely chopped pecans
¼ cup sugar
¼ cup butter or margarine,
  melted
1 (14-ounce) package caramels
¼ cup milk

1 cup chopped pecans
8 (1-ounce) squares semisweet
  chocolate
⅓ cup milk
¼ cup sifted powdered sugar
½ teaspoon vanilla extract

Combine first 3 ingredients in a small bowl; stir well. Firmly press mixture in bottom and up sides of a 9-inch pieplate. Bake at 350° for 12 minutes. Cool completely on a wire rack.

Unwrap caramels, and place in a medium saucepan. Add ¼ cup milk; cook over low heat until caramels melt, stirring often. Remove from heat, and pour over prepared crust. Sprinkle 1 cup chopped pecans over caramel mixture.

Combine chocolate, ⅓ cup milk, powdered sugar, and vanilla in top of a double boiler; bring water to a boil. Reduce heat to low; cook until chocolate melts, stirring occasionally. Spoon melted chocolate mixture evenly over pecans. Cover and chill at least 2 hours. Yield: one 9-inch pie. Chris Waters

BMC on Our Menu
Baptist Medical Center Auxiliary of Volunteers
Columbia, South Carolina

Marbled Chocolate-Mint Pie

Crème de menthe, a mint-flavored liqueur, is available in two colors—green and white. Use either in this recipe.

1 **(14-ounce) can sweetened**
  condensed milk, divided
¼ **cup chocolate syrup**
1 **cup whipping cream,**
  whipped and divided

1 **tablespoon crème de menthe**
1 **(6-ounce) chocolate-flavored**
  crumb crust
Garnish: chocolate curls

Combine 1 cup sweetened condensed milk and chocolate syrup in a large bowl; stir well. Gently fold in half of whipped cream.

Combine remaining condensed milk and crème de menthe, stirring well. Gently fold in remaining half of whipped cream. Spoon chocolate and crème de menthe mixtures into crust, and swirl gently with a knife. Cover and freeze 6 hours or until firm. Garnish, if desired. Yield: one 9-inch pie.

Classic Connecticut Cuisine
Connecticut Easter Seals
Uncasville, Connecticut

Black Russian Pie

*If you don't have the 8-inch pieplate this recipe calls for, use a
9-inch one. For the crust, just increase the number of cookies to 21 and
the melted butter to 3 tablespoons.*

14 cream-filled chocolate
   sandwich cookies, finely
   crushed
2 tablespoons butter or
   margarine, melted
24 large marshmallows
½ cup milk

⅛ teaspoon salt
⅓ cup Kahlúa or other coffee-
   flavored liqueur
1 cup whipping cream,
   whipped
Garnish: semisweet chocolate
   curls

Combine cookie crumbs and butter; stir well. Firmly press mixture
in bottom and up sides of an 8-inch pieplate. Freeze 30 minutes or
until firm.

Combine marshmallows, milk, and salt in top of a double boiler;
bring water to a boil. Reduce heat to low; cook until marshmallows
melt, stirring occasionally. Let cool 1 hour. Stir in Kahlúa. Gently fold
whipped cream into marshmallow mixture. Chill 30 minutes; spoon
into prepared crust. Cover and freeze 8 hours or until firm. Garnish,
if desired. Yield: one 8-inch pie.   Maureen Cash

Favorite Recipes
St. Isaac Jogues Senior Guild, St. Mary's of the Hills Catholic Church
Rochester Hills, Michigan

A Tart for All Seasons

To make ¼ cup ground almonds for the crust, grind ¼ cup slivered almonds in your food processor.

1½ cups all-purpose flour
½ cup sugar
½ cup butter or margarine, softened
¼ cup ground almonds
1 egg yolk
1 teaspoon vanilla extract
1 teaspoon almond extract
1 (8-ounce) package cream cheese, softened
3 tablespoons sugar

3 tablespoons orange juice
½ cup apricot preserves
1 tablespoon butter or margarine
1 tablespoon lemon juice
1 tablespoon amaretto
2 cups fresh raspberries
2 kiwifruit, peeled and sliced
1 (11-ounce) can mandarin oranges, drained
¼ cup sliced almonds, toasted

Combine first 4 ingredients in a mixing bowl; beat at medium speed of an electric mixer until blended. Add egg yolk and flavorings; mix just until dough holds together. Firmly press dough in bottom and up sides of an 11-inch tart pan with removable bottom. Bake at 375° for 15 minutes or until lightly browned. Cool completely on a wire rack.

Combine cream cheese, 3 tablespoons sugar, and orange juice; beat at medium speed of electric mixer until smooth. Spread mixture evenly over cooled crust. Cover and chill 30 minutes or until cream cheese mixture is firm. Combine preserves and next 3 ingredients in a small saucepan; cook over low heat, stirring constantly, until preserves and butter melt. Set glaze aside, and let cool.

Arrange raspberries, kiwifruit, and mandarin oranges on top of cream cheese mixture up to 2 hours before serving; brush fruit with glaze. Sprinkle with toasted almonds.

To serve, carefully remove sides of pan. Serve chilled or at room temperature. Yield: one 11-inch tart.   Sue Donovan

In the Serving Tradition
Durham Woman's Club
Durham, Connecticut

Pecan Tassies

½ cup butter or margarine, softened
1 (3-ounce) package cream cheese, softened
1 cup all-purpose flour
1½ cups firmly packed brown sugar

2 tablespoons butter or margarine, melted
2 large eggs, lightly beaten
1 teaspoon vanilla extract
⅔ cup chopped pecans

Beat softened butter and cream cheese at medium speed of an electric mixer until creamy. Gradually add flour, beating well. Cover and chill 2 hours.

Shape dough into 30 (1-inch) balls; press balls into lightly greased miniature (1¾-inch) muffin pans. Set aside.

Combine brown sugar and next 3 ingredients; stir well. Stir in pecans. Spoon 1 tablespoon pecan mixture into each pastry shell. Bake at 350° for 25 minutes. Remove from pans immediately, and let cool completely on wire racks. Yield: 2½ dozen.   Brenda Owen

Recipes on Parade
Calloway County Band Boosters
Murray, Kentucky

Apricot Strudel

After rolling up this strudel, slightly pinch the ends of the pastry and tuck them under to keep the filling in place during baking.

1 cup butter or margarine, softened
1 (8-ounce) package cream cheese, softened
2 tablespoons sugar
2 cups all-purpose flour
1 (12-ounce) jar apricot jam

1 cup flaked coconut
1 cup pecans, chopped
½ cup sugar
1½ teaspoons ground cinnamon
Sifted powdered sugar

Beat butter, cream cheese, and 2 tablespoons sugar in a large mixing bowl at medium speed of an electric mixer until creamy. Gradually add flour, beating at low speed just until blended. Shape pastry into 3 equal balls; cover and chill 8 hours.

Roll one portion of pastry into a 10- x 8-inch rectangle. Spread ⅓ cup jam over rectangle to within ½ inch of edges. Combine coconut and next 3 ingredients; stir well. Sprinkle one-third of pecan mixture over jam. Roll up pastry, starting at long side, slightly pinching and tucking under ends of pastry. Arrange pastry roll, seam side down, on a greased baking sheet. Repeat procedure twice with remaining pastry, jam, and pecan mixture.

Bake at 350° for 30 to 35 minutes or until lightly browned. Cut each roll crosswise into fourths; let cool completely on wire racks. Sprinkle with powdered sugar. Yield: 12 servings.   Jackie Tepper

Still Fiddling in the Kitchen
National Council of Jewish Women
Southfield, Michigan

Blackberry Cobbler

If fresh blackberries are out of season, you can substitute 1 (16-ounce) package frozen blackberries that have been thawed and drained.

3 cups fresh blackberries	2 large eggs, lightly beaten
1 cup sugar	1 cup all-purpose flour
2 tablespoons all-purpose flour	2 teaspoons baking powder
1 teaspoon lemon juice	½ teaspoon salt
2 tablespoons butter or margarine	Half-and-half or vanilla ice cream
¼ cup sugar	
¼ cup butter or margarine, melted	

Combine first 4 ingredients; toss gently. Spoon mixture into a greased 9-inch pieplate. Dot with 2 tablespoons butter.

Combine ¼ cup sugar, ¼ cup melted butter, and eggs; stir well. Combine 1 cup flour, baking powder, and salt; gradually add to butter mixture, stirring well. Spoon over blackberry mixture, and spread evenly. Bake at 375° for 30 minutes or until golden. Serve warm with half-and-half or ice cream. Yield: 6 servings.   Ruthel M. Harper

What's Cooking at Cathedral Plaza
Cathedral Plaza
Denver, Colorado

Blueberry Cobbler with Cookie Dough Topping

Picture rotund fresh blueberries and tender sugar cookies. Add a sprinkling of cinnamon and a scoop of vanilla ice cream to the image and you have this recipe's number.

4 cups fresh blueberries
¼ cup plus 1 tablespoon sugar
¾ cup orange juice
1 cup butter or margarine, softened
1 cup sugar
1 large egg
½ teaspoon vanilla extract
1 cup all-purpose flour
½ teaspoon baking powder
⅛ teaspoon salt
½ teaspoon ground cinnamon
Vanilla ice cream

Combine first 3 ingredients, stirring gently. Spoon into a lightly greased 13- x 9- x 2-inch baking dish.

Beat butter at medium speed of an electric mixer until creamy; gradually add 1 cup sugar, beating well. Add egg and vanilla; beat well.

Combine flour, baking powder, and salt; add to butter mixture, beating well. Drop batter by tablespoonfuls over blueberry mixture. Sprinkle with cinnamon. Bake at 375° for 35 minutes or until lightly browned and bubbly. Serve warm or at room temperature with ice cream. Yield: 8 servings.

Steven E. Keip

Picnic in the Park
Atwood Community Center
Madison, Wisconsin

Cherry Crisp

1 cup all-purpose flour
½ cup firmly packed brown
  sugar
¼ teaspoon salt
½ cup butter or margarine
4 (14½-ounce) cans tart red
  cherries in water, undrained
1 cup sugar
¼ cup cornstarch

Red liquid food coloring
  (optional)
1½ cups quick-cooking oats,
  uncooked
½ cup firmly packed brown
  sugar
¼ cup all-purpose flour
¼ cup plus 1 tablespoon butter
  or margarine

Combine first 3 ingredients; cut in ½ cup butter with pastry blender until mixture is crumbly. Press in bottom of a greased 11- x 7- x 1½-inch baking dish. Bake at 350° for 15 minutes. Let cool.

Drain cherries, reserving 4 cups cherries and 1 cup juice. Reserve remaining cherries and juice for another use.

Combine 1 cup sugar, cornstarch, and reserved 1 cup juice in a medium saucepan; stir well. Cook over medium heat, stirring constantly, until mixture is thickened and bubbly. Remove from heat; add reserved 4 cups cherries and food coloring, if desired, stirring gently. Pour over crust.

Combine oats, ½ cup brown sugar, and ¼ cup flour in a small bowl; cut in ¼ cup plus 1 tablespoon butter with pastry blender until mixture is crumbly. Sprinkle oat mixture evenly over cherry mixture. Bake at 350° for 20 to 25 minutes or until bubbly. Serve warm. Yield: 6 servings.   Ann Conard

Feeding the Flock
Holy Family Parish
Davenport, Iowa

Warm Cream Cheese Strudel

Keep the thawed phyllo pastry supple by covering it with a slightly damp towel when you're not working with it.

4 (3-ounce) packages cream cheese, softened	4 sheets frozen phyllo pastry, thawed in refrigerator
½ cup sugar	⅓ cup butter or margarine, melted
3 egg yolks	
½ cup golden raisins	⅓ cup fine, dry breadcrumbs
2 teaspoons grated lemon rind	Sifted powdered sugar

Beat cream cheese in a large mixing bowl at medium speed of an electric mixer until creamy; gradually add ½ cup sugar, beating well. Add egg yolks; beat well. Stir in raisins and lemon rind. Cover and chill 30 minutes.

(Work with 1 sheet of phyllo at a time, keeping remaining sheets covered with a slightly damp towel.) Layer sheets of phyllo on wax paper, brushing each with butter and sprinkling each with one-fourth of breadcrumbs. Gently spread cream cheese mixture down one short side of phyllo stack to within 1 inch of sides. Fold sides over mixture. Roll up phyllo, starting at short side.

Place roll, seam side down, on a large greased baking sheet. Brush strudel with any remaining melted butter. Bake at 375° for 40 to 45 minutes or until golden. Cool on a wire rack 30 minutes. Sprinkle with powdered sugar. Serve warm. Yield: 6 servings.

The Elegant Cook
Friends of the Eastern Christian School Association
North Haledon, New Jersey

Poultry

Turkey and Stuffing, page 254

Roasted Chicken with Lemon Cream Sauce

Roasting chickens are larger than broiler-fryers; roasters have a higher fat content as well as more flavor than smaller birds.

1 (6-pound) roasting chicken
¼ teaspoon salt
¼ teaspoon pepper
½ cup mixed fresh basil, oregano, and thyme sprigs

Lemon Cream Sauce
½ cup freshly grated Parmesan cheese

Remove giblets, and rinse chicken with cold water; pat dry. Sprinkle cavity with salt and pepper. Place herbs in cavity. Tie ends of legs together with string. Lift wingtips up and over back, and tuck under bird. Place chicken on a rack in a shallow roasting pan, breast side up. Insert meat thermometer into meaty portion of thigh, making sure it does not touch bone.

Bake, uncovered, at 350° for 2 hours or until thermometer registers 180°. Remove chicken from roasting pan, discarding drippings. Cut chicken into serving pieces, and return to roasting pan. Pour Lemon Cream Sauce over chicken; sprinkle evenly with cheese. Broil 5½ inches from heat (with electric oven door partially opened) 3 to 4 minutes or until cheese melts. Serve immediately. Yield: 8 servings.

Lemon Cream Sauce

½ cup butter or margarine
2 tablespoons dry sherry
2 tablespoons dry white wine
1 tablespoon grated orange rind

1 tablespoon grated lemon rind
3 tablespoons lemon juice
¼ teaspoon salt
¼ teaspoon pepper
1 cup whipping cream

Melt butter in a large skillet over medium heat. Add sherry and next 6 ingredients; bring to a boil. Gradually stir in whipping cream; cook 1 minute. Yield: 1¼ cups.

Holy Cow, Chicago's Cooking!
Church of the Holy Comforter
Kenilworth, Illinois

Southwestern Roast Chicken

This chicken is seasoned with three ingredients often found in southwestern cooking—chili powder, jalapeño pepper, and sage.

½ cup peanut oil
3 tablespoons chili powder
½ teaspoon jalapeño pepper, chopped
2 cloves garlic
2 (3½-pound) broiler-fryers
½ cup dried sage, divided
2 cloves garlic, halved and divided

2 teaspoons red wine vinegar
1 teaspoon chopped purple onion
1 teaspoon prepared mustard
¼ teaspoon salt
¼ teaspoon pepper

Combine first 4 ingredients in container of an electric blender; cover and process until smooth, stopping once to scrape down sides.

Remove giblets, and rinse chickens with cold water; pat dry. Place ¼ cup sage and 1 halved garlic clove in cavity of each chicken. Tie ends of legs together with string. Lift wingtips up and over back, and tuck under bird. Place chickens on a lightly greased rack in a shallow roasting pan, breast side up. Insert meat thermometer into meaty portion of thigh of 1 chicken, making sure it does not touch bone.

Brush chickens with oil mixture. Bake, uncovered, at 500° for 10 minutes. Reduce oven temperature to 350°, and bake 55 additional minutes or until meat thermometer registers 180°. Remove sage and garlic from chicken cavities; set aside. Remove chickens to a serving platter; set aside, and keep warm. Skim fat from pan drippings; reserve pan drippings.

Combine reserved sage, garlic, vinegar, and next 4 ingredients in container of an electric blender; cover and process until smooth, stopping once to scrape down sides. Add reserved pan drippings; process until smooth, stopping once to scrape down sides. Serve chicken with sauce. Yield: 8 servings.

Tastes and Traditions: The Sam Houston Heritage Cookbook
The Study Club of Huntsville, Texas

Baked Chicken with Orzo

Orzo is a type of pasta that looks like rice, but is slightly larger.

1 (3- to 3½-pound) broiler-
   fryer, quartered
½ teaspoon salt
¼ teaspoon pepper
⅓ cup water
1 tablespoon butter or
   margarine
8 cups water
1¾ cups orzo, uncooked

½ teaspoon vegetable oil
1 cup water
1 cup chicken broth
1 (6-ounce) can tomato paste
1 teaspoon salt
¼ teaspoon pepper
½ cup freshly grated Parmesan
   cheese
Plain yogurt (optional)

Sprinkle chicken with ½ teaspoon salt and ¼ teaspoon pepper. Place chicken, skin side up, in a lightly greased 13- x 9- x 2-inch pan. Add ⅓ cup water to pan; dot chicken with butter. Bake, uncovered, at 350° for 40 minutes.

Bring 8 cups water to a boil; stir in orzo and oil. Reduce heat to medium, and cook 8 minutes. Drain well, and set aside.

Remove chicken, reserving drippings in pan. Set chicken aside, and keep warm. Add 1 cup water and chicken broth to drippings; stir well. Add orzo, tomato paste, 1 teaspoon salt, and ¼ teaspoon pepper, stirring well. Place chicken on top of orzo mixture. Bake, uncovered, 40 additional minutes or until liquid is absorbed. Sprinkle with cheese. Dollop with yogurt, if desired. Yield: 4 servings.　　　　Clara Doman

Town Hill Playground Cookbook
Town Hill Playground Committee
Whitingham, Vermont

Moroccan Chicken with Vegetables

Morocco is a country in northwest Africa where cinnamon, red pepper, coriander, ginger, and turmeric commonly spice the native cuisine.

1 tablespoon butter or margarine
1 (3- to 3½-pound) broiler-fryer, cut up
2 medium onions, sliced
1 (3-inch) stick cinnamon
½ dried red chile pepper
1½ teaspoons salt
¾ teaspoon ground coriander
¾ teaspoon ground ginger
¾ teaspoon ground turmeric
¼ teaspoon coarsely ground pepper
2 cups chicken broth

4 fresh parsley sprigs
2 tablespoons honey
1 (15-ounce) can garbanzo beans, drained
1 medium-size sweet potato, peeled and cut into 1-inch pieces
2 carrots, scraped and cut into 1-inch pieces
2 medium zucchini, cut into 1-inch pieces
2 tablespoons raisins
Hot cooked rice

Melt butter in a Dutch oven over low heat. Add chicken and next 8 ingredients; cover and cook 10 minutes, stirring occasionally. Add broth and parsley to pan; bring to a boil. Cover, reduce heat, and simmer 40 minutes or until chicken is done.

Remove chicken to an 11- x 7- x 1½-inch baking dish, reserving broth mixture in Dutch oven. Brush chicken with honey; bake, uncovered, at 300° for 12 minutes. Remove cinnamon stick, dried chile, and parsley from broth mixture. Bring broth mixture to a boil; add garbanzo beans and next 4 ingredients. Reduce heat, and simmer, uncovered, 15 to 20 minutes or until vegetables are tender. Serve chicken and vegetables over rice. Yield: 4 servings.   Alison Elizalde

The East Hampton L.V.I.S. Centennial Cookbook
Ladies' Village Improvement Society
East Hampton, New York

Plum-Glazed Chicken

1 medium onion, chopped
2 tablespoons butter or
  margarine, melted
1 (15-ounce) can purple plums
  in heavy syrup, undrained
⅓ cup firmly packed brown
  sugar
¼ cup chili sauce

2 tablespoons soy sauce
1 teaspoon ground ginger
2 teaspoons lemon juice
1 (3-pound) broiler-fryer,
  cut up
½ teaspoon salt
¼ teaspoon pepper

Cook onion in butter in a skillet over medium-high heat, stirring constantly, until tender. Remove from heat.

Drain plums, reserving syrup; remove and discard pits from plums. Place plums and syrup in container of an electric blender; cover and process until smooth, stopping once to scrape down sides. Add plum puree, brown sugar, and next 4 ingredients to onion in skillet. Cook, uncovered, over medium heat 15 minutes or until slightly thickened, stirring frequently.

Sprinkle chicken with salt and pepper. Place chicken, meaty side down, in a lightly greased 13- x 9- x 2-inch baking dish. Pour plum sauce evenly over chicken. Bake, uncovered, at 350° for 30 minutes, basting after 15 minutes. Turn chicken, meaty side up; bake 30 additional minutes or until chicken is done, basting occasionally. Yield: 4 servings.

More Than Delicious
Erie Art Museum
Erie, Pennsylvania

Drunken Chicken Kabobs

These kabobs are under the influence of bourbon. But in reality, their condition is not as dire as the name of the dish suggests—the alcohol in the bourbon evaporates during cooking.

1½ pounds chicken thighs, boned and cut into 1-inch pieces
¼ cup bourbon
¼ cup soy sauce
¼ cup Dijon mustard
½ cup chopped onion
¼ cup firmly packed brown sugar
½ teaspoon pepper
Dash of Worcestershire sauce

1 medium-size green pepper, cut into 1-inch pieces
1 medium-size sweet red pepper, cut into 1-inch pieces
2 medium onions, cut into 1-inch pieces
16 fresh pineapple chunks
8 small fresh mushrooms
8 cherry tomatoes

Place chicken in a large heavy-duty, zip-top plastic bag. Combine bourbon and next 6 ingredients; pour over chicken. Seal bag securely; marinate in refrigerator 8 hours, turning bag occasionally.

Remove chicken from marinade, reserving marinade. Bring marinade to a boil in a small saucepan; set aside.

Alternately thread chicken, green pepper, red pepper, onion, pineapple, and mushrooms onto eight 10-inch skewers. Place skewers on a lightly greased rack in a broiler pan. Broil 5½ inches from heat (with electric oven door partially opened) 10 minutes, turning and basting occasionally with marinade. Add tomatoes to end of skewers. Broil 3 additional minutes. Yield: 8 servings.

Another Taste of Aloha
The Junior League of Honolulu, Hawaii

Jerk Chicken

Jerking is the Jamaican equivalent of barbecuing. The Jamaicans traditionally have a heavy hand when they rub on their seasoning blend, so let your taste buds be your guide—the more seasoning you rub on the chicken, the spicier it will be.

1½ teaspoons coriander seeds
1½ teaspoons cumin seeds
1 teaspoon black peppercorns
½ teaspoon dried crushed red pepper
1 clove garlic
¼ cup chopped fresh parsley
1 tablespoon ground allspice
3 tablespoons minced green onions
2½ tablespoons ketchup

2 tablespoons soy sauce
2 tablespoons vegetable oil
1 tablespoon rum
2½ teaspoons minced gingerroot
½ teaspoon salt
⅛ teaspoon ground cinnamon
⅛ teaspoon ground nutmeg
8 chicken breast halves
Lemon wedges (optional)

Combine first 5 ingredients in a small skillet. Cook over high heat, stirring constantly, until seasonings become aromatic and are lightly browned.

Position knife blade in food processor bowl; add toasted seasonings, parsley, and next 10 ingredients. Process until smooth, stopping twice to scrape down sides.

Rub seasoning blend on both sides of chicken breasts. Cook, covered with grill lid, over medium-hot coals (350° to 400°) 15 minutes on each side or until chicken is done. Serve with lemon wedges, if desired. Yield: 8 servings.

Creative Chef 2
Tourette Syndrome Association
Bayside, New York

Grilled Ginger-Orange Chicken

If you like, you can use any kind of fruit marmalade instead of orange marmalade.

½ cup butter or margarine, softened

½ to ¾ teaspoon grated orange rind

¼ to ½ teaspoon ground ginger

¼ cup orange marmalade

¼ cup Dijon mustard

2 tablespoons orange juice

2 green onions, finely chopped

6 skinned and boned chicken breast halves

Garnishes: green onions, orange rind curls, orange wedges

Combine butter, grated orange rind, and ginger; stir well. Cover and chill until firm.

Combine marmalade and next 3 ingredients in a small bowl; stir well. Spread marmalade mixture on both sides of chicken. Cook, without grill lid, over medium-hot coals (350° to 400°) 9 to 10 minutes on each side or until chicken is done. Serve with chilled butter mixture. Garnish, if desired. Yield: 6 servings. Irene Exum

Cooking with Class
Park Maitland School
Maitland, Florida

Cajun Chicken with Melon Picante

For a mild picante, seed the jalapeño pepper before mincing.

2 tablespoons black pepper
2 tablespoons ground red pepper
1 tablespoon paprika
1 teaspoon all-purpose flour
1 teaspoon onion powder
½ teaspoon salt
6 skinned and boned chicken breast halves
¼ cup butter or margarine, melted
Melon Picante

Combine first 6 ingredients; dredge chicken in pepper mixture. Cook chicken in butter in a large skillet over medium heat 5 to 7 minutes on each side or until done. Remove chicken to a serving platter. Serve with Melon Picante. Yield: 6 servings.

Melon Picante

¼ cup chopped cantaloupe
¼ cup chopped honeydew
¼ cup chopped fresh pineapple
¼ cup chopped sweet yellow pepper
¼ cup chopped sweet red pepper
3 tablespoons chopped fresh cilantro
2 tablespoons minced purple onion
1 tablespoon lime juice
1 tablespoon lemon juice
1 small jalapeño pepper, minced
2 teaspoons taco seasoning

Combine all ingredients in a small bowl. Cover and chill thoroughly. Yield: 1¼ cups.   Tracy Schroen

Women Cook for a Cause
Women's Resource Center of Schoolcraft College
Livonia, Michigan

Chicken in Cranberry Cream Sauce

Tart dried cranberries add a burst of flavor to the buttery cream sauce.

½ cup dried cranberries
3 tablespoons Cognac
2 tablespoons Grand Marnier
  or other orange-flavored
  liqueur
4 skinned and boned chicken
  breast halves
½ cup all-purpose flour

2 tablespoons olive oil
2 tablespoons unsalted butter,
  melted
⅔ cup raspberry vinegar
2 shallots, minced
1½ cups chicken broth
1½ cups whipping cream
Garnish: fresh parsley sprigs

Combine first 3 ingredients in a small bowl; cover and let stand 30 minutes.

Dredge chicken in flour. Cook chicken in oil and butter in a large skillet over medium-high heat 5 minutes on each side or until done. Remove chicken to a serving platter, reserving drippings in skillet. Set chicken aside, and keep warm.

Add vinegar to drippings in skillet, deglazing skillet by scraping particles that cling to bottom. Add cranberry mixture and shallot; bring to a boil. Reduce heat, and simmer, uncovered, 5 minutes. Add chicken broth; bring to a boil. Reduce heat, and simmer, uncovered, 12 minutes. Gradually add whipping cream; cook over medium heat, stirring constantly, 6 minutes or until mixture is thickened and bubbly. Spoon sauce over chicken. Garnish, if desired. Serve immediately. Yield: 4 servings.

Jane Elizabeth Seaman

American Buffet
General Federation of Women's Clubs
Washington, DC

Chicken Breasts on Eggplant with Tomatoes

For more flavor, substitute basil- and tomato-flavored feta cheese for regular feta cheese.

¼ cup all-purpose flour
¼ teaspoon salt
¼ teaspoon black pepper
4 (¾-inch-thick) slices peeled eggplant
¼ cup olive oil
4 skinned and boned chicken breast halves
½ teaspoon salt

¼ teaspoon pepper
2 tablespoons vegetable oil
1 teaspoon minced garlic
1½ cups canned crushed tomatoes
1 teaspoon dried oregano
¼ teaspoon dried crushed red pepper
½ cup crumbled feta cheese

Combine flour, ¼ teaspoon salt, and ¼ teaspoon pepper; dredge eggplant slices in flour mixture, shaking off excess flour.

Cook eggplant in olive oil in a large skillet over medium-high heat 2 to 3 minutes on each side or until golden. Drain on paper towels. Arrange in a single layer in an ungreased 13- x 9- x 2-inch baking dish.

Sprinkle chicken with ½ teaspoon salt and ¼ teaspoon pepper. Brown chicken in vegetable oil in a large skillet over medium-high heat 5 minutes on each side. Remove chicken, reserving drippings in skillet. Place 1 chicken breast half on top of each eggplant slice.

Cook garlic in drippings in skillet over medium-high heat 1 minute, stirring constantly. Add tomato, oregano, and red pepper; cook 5 minutes, stirring often. Spoon over chicken; sprinkle with cheese. Bake, uncovered, at 425° for 10 minutes. Serve immediately. Yield: 4 servings.

Bill Sabanos

Favorite Recipes
St. Isaac Jogues Senior Guild, St. Mary's of the Hills Catholic Church
Rochester Hills, Michigan

Chicken Mango-Coconut

This chicken tastes like the tropics with its fresh mango, flaked coconut, and coconut milk.

4 skinned and boned chicken breast halves
4 (½-inch-thick) slices fresh mango
1 large egg, beaten
1 cup flaked coconut
½ cup butter or margarine, melted
¼ cup minced shallot
1 tablespoon minced garlic
3 tablespoons butter or margarine, melted
2 cups cubed fresh mango, divided
¾ cup chicken broth
½ cup dry white wine
½ teaspoon curry powder
¼ cup coconut milk
½ teaspoon salt
¼ teaspoon pepper

Cut a pocket in each chicken breast half, cutting to, but not through, remaining side. Place a mango slice in each pocket, and secure with wooden picks. Dip chicken in egg; dredge in coconut. Brown chicken in ½ cup butter in a large skillet. Remove chicken to an ungreased 11- x 7- x 1½-inch baking dish. Bake, uncovered, at 350° for 25 minutes or until chicken is done. Remove and discard wooden picks. Remove chicken to a serving platter. Set aside, and keep warm.

Cook shallot and garlic in 3 tablespoons butter in a saucepan over medium-high heat, stirring constantly, until tender. Add 1 cup cubed mango, broth, wine, and curry powder; bring to a boil. Reduce heat, and simmer, uncovered, 10 minutes. Add coconut milk, salt, and pepper; cook 2 additional minutes.

Pour mango mixture into container of an electric blender or food processor; cover and process until smooth, stopping once to scrape down sides. Pour mixture into a serving bowl. Stir in remaining 1 cup mango cubes. Serve mango mixture with chicken. Yield: 4 servings.

Historic Spanish Point: Cooking Then and Now
Gulf Coast Heritage Association
Osprey, Florida

Chicken Tandoori

This dish isn't cooked in traditional Indian style in a brick and clay (tandoor) oven, but it remains true to custom with its spices—curry, coriander, cumin, turmeric, and cinnamon.

6 skinned and boned chicken
   breast halves
¼ cup butter or margarine,
   melted
1 cup chopped onion
1 cup chopped tomato
¾ cup chopped green pepper
1 clove garlic, minced
1 teaspoon salt
1½ teaspoons curry powder

1½ teaspoons ground coriander
1½ teaspoons ground cumin
½ teaspoon ground turmeric
½ teaspoon pepper
¼ teaspoon ground cinnamon
1 cup chicken broth
Hot cooked rice
Chutney (optional)
Roasted peanuts (optional)

Place chicken in a greased 13- x 9- x 2-inch baking dish; drizzle with butter. Combine onion and next 10 ingredients; sprinkle over chicken. Pour broth over chicken mixture. Cover and bake at 350° for 1 hour or until chicken is done. Serve over rice. If desired, serve with chutney and peanuts. Yield: 6 servings.

Gloria Williford

An Apple a Day
Knoxville Academy of Medicine Alliance
Knoxville, Tennessee

Lemon Chicken Stir-Fry

2 tablespoons soy sauce
1 tablespoon cornstarch
1 pound skinned and boned
   chicken breast halves, cut
   into strips
2 to 4 tablespoons lemon juice
2 tablespoons wine vinegar
1 tablespoon plus 1 teaspoon
   sugar

1 teaspoon grated lemon rind
3 tablespoons vegetable oil,
   divided
3 green onions, sliced
1 carrot, scraped and sliced
1 cup green pepper strips
1 teaspoon minced garlic
Hot cooked rice

Combine soy sauce and cornstarch in a large bowl; stir until smooth. Add chicken, and toss well. Set aside.

Combine lemon juice and next 3 ingredients; stir well, and set aside.

Heat 1 tablespoon oil in a large skillet over medium heat until hot. Add green onions, carrot, green pepper, and garlic; cover and cook 2 minutes. Remove vegetable mixture from skillet; set aside, and keep warm. Add remaining 2 tablespoons oil to skillet; place over medium heat until hot. Add chicken mixture, and stir-fry 4 minutes or until done. Stir in lemon juice mixture. Cover, reduce heat, and simmer 2 minutes. Stir in vegetable mixture, and cook just until heated. Serve over rice. Yield: 4 servings.   Robin Mitchell

A Place Called Hope
The Junior Auxiliary of Hope, Arkansas

Chicken Liver Sauté

Chicken livers are an inexpensive source of protein, iron, and vitamin A. Our Test Kitchens gave this recipe a very high rating.

1 pound chicken livers	1 (14½-ounce) can whole
3 tablespoons butter or	tomatoes, chopped and
margarine, melted	drained
½ pound fresh mushrooms,	¼ cup chopped fresh parsley
sliced	½ teaspoon dried thyme
1¼ cups chopped onion	¼ to ½ teaspoon dried
1 clove garlic, minced	rosemary
1 tablespoon all-purpose flour	¼ teaspoon salt
½ cup dry white wine	Hot cooked rice

Cook livers in butter in a skillet over medium-high heat 7 to 9 minutes, stirring constantly. Remove livers, reserving drippings in skillet. Set livers aside; keep warm. Add mushrooms, onion, and garlic to drippings. Cook, stirring constantly, 5 minutes or until tender. Reduce heat to low. Stir in flour; cook 1 minute, stirring constantly. Stir in wine and next 5 ingredients. Bring to a boil; reduce heat, and simmer, uncovered, 5 minutes. Stir in livers; cook until heated, stirring occasionally. Serve over rice. Yield: 4 servings.   Lauralyn Pierce

Sweet Home Alabama Cooking
The 44th National Square Dancing Convention
Montgomery, Alabama

Lime- and Sesame-Roasted Cornish Hens

You may want to toast the sesame seeds in your microwave oven since they're such a small amount. Just place them in a shallow bowl and microwave, uncovered, at HIGH for 2 to 3 minutes or until toasted.

2 (1½-pound) Cornish hens, split
⅓ cup soy sauce
¼ cup vegetable oil
3 cloves garlic, sliced
2 tablespoons sesame seeds, lightly toasted

1 tablespoon brown sugar
2 teaspoons ground ginger
3 tablespoons lime juice
Garnishes: toasted sesame seeds, lime wedges

Place hens, breast side down, in a large shallow dish. Combine soy sauce and next 6 ingredients in container of an electric blender; cover and process until smooth, stopping once to scrape down sides. Pour marinade mixture over hens. Cover and marinate in refrigerator 8 hours, turning occasionally.

Remove hens from marinade, reserving marinade. Bring marinade to a boil in a small saucepan; set aside.

Place hens in a lightly greased 13- x 9- x 2-inch baking dish, breast side up. Bake, uncovered, at 400° for 45 minutes or until done, basting occasionally with marinade. Garnish, if desired. Yield: 4 servings.

Back Home Again
The Junior League of Indianapolis, Indiana

Orange-Glazed Roast Duck with Apple Stuffing

1 (5-pound) dressed duckling
1 teaspoon caraway seeds
1 small onion, chopped
¼ cup plus 2 tablespoons
  butter or margarine, melted
4 cups peeled, chopped
  cooking apple
3 cups soft breadcrumbs
1 cup chopped celery
¼ cup raisins
2 tablespoons minced fresh
  parsley
1 teaspoon salt
½ teaspoon pepper
½ teaspoon paprika
¼ teaspoon ground cloves
1 cup water
½ cup firmly packed brown
  sugar
2½ tablespoons sugar
1 tablespoon cornstarch
1 tablespoon grated orange
  rind
1 cup orange juice
1 drop of hot sauce

Remove giblets and neck from duckling; reserve for other uses. Rinse duckling with cold water, and pat dry. Sprinkle cavity with caraway seeds.

Cook onion in butter in a large skillet over medium-high heat, stirring constantly, until tender. Combine onion, apple, and next 9 ingredients; stir well.

Spoon stuffing mixture into cavity of duckling; close cavity with skewers. Tie ends of legs together with string. Lift wingtips up and over back, and tuck under bird. Place duckling on a rack in a shallow roasting pan, breast side up. Insert meat thermometer into meaty portion of thigh, making sure it does not touch bone. Bake, uncovered, at 350° for 1½ hours.

Combine brown sugar and next 5 ingredients in a small saucepan; bring to a boil. Reduce heat, and cook, uncovered, 5 minutes, stirring occasionally.

Bake duckling 30 additional minutes or until meat thermometer registers 180°, basting frequently with orange juice mixture. Remove duckling to a serving platter; let stand 10 minutes before carving. Yield: 4 servings.

Catherine Boyd

Cooking Up a Storm, Florida Style
Brookwood Guild
St. Petersburg, Florida

Turkey and Stuffing

Our Test Kitchens agreed that this is the best bread stuffing they've ever tasted. It's drier than some cornbread stuffings, so if you prefer a moist stuffing, add more half-and-half.

1 **pound fresh chestnuts**
1 **cup pistachio nuts in shells (about ½ cup shelled)**
1½ **pounds ground pork sausage**
1 **cup chopped onion**
½ **cup chopped celery**
1 **clove garlic, minced**
8 **cups cubed French bread**
¼ **cup chopped fresh parsley**
1½ **teaspoons poultry seasoning**
½ **teaspoon dried thyme**
¼ **teaspoon pepper**
Dash of salt
¾ **cup plus 2 tablespoons half-and-half**
1 **(12-pound) turkey**
3 **tablespoons butter or margarine, melted**
Garnishes: green leaf lettuce, red grapes, orange slices, fresh parsley sprigs

Cut a slit in each chestnut. Place chestnuts on an ungreased baking sheet, and bake at 400° for 15 minutes; let cool completely. Remove and discard shells; coarsely chop chestnuts, and set aside.

Remove and discard shells from pistachios; set pistachios aside.

Brown sausage in a large skillet, stirring until it crumbles. Drain and pat dry on paper towels, reserving 1 tablespoon drippings in skillet. Cook onion, celery, and garlic in drippings in skillet over medium-high heat, stirring constantly, until vegetables are tender. Remove from heat.

Place bread cubes in a large bowl. Stir in chestnuts, pistachios, sausage, onion mixture, parsley, and next 4 ingredients. Pour half-and-half over stuffing, stirring gently. Reserve 6½ cups stuffing to stuff turkey. Place remaining stuffing in a lightly greased 11- x 7- x 1½-inch baking dish; cover and chill. Uncover and bake at 325° last 35 to 45 minutes that turkey bakes.

Remove giblets and neck, and rinse turkey thoroughly with cold water; pat dry. Lightly pack 1½ cups stuffing mixture into neck cavity of turkey. Lightly pack remaining 5 cups stuffing into body cavity. Tie ends of legs together with string. Lift wingtips up and over back, and tuck under bird.

Place turkey on a lightly greased rack in a shallow roasting pan, breast side up; brush entire bird with melted butter. Insert meat thermometer into meaty portion of thigh, making sure it does not touch bone. Bake at 325° until meat thermometer registers 180° (about 3 to

3½ hours), basting turkey frequently with pan juices. If turkey starts to brown too much, cover loosely with aluminum foil.

Remove turkey to a platter. Let stand 15 minutes before carving. Garnish, if desired. Yield: 12 servings.   Karen Johnson

St. Catherine of Siena Celebration Cookbook
St. Catherine of Siena Church
DuBois, Pennsylvania

Herbed Turkey

1 (12-pound) turkey
2 tablespoons salt
1 tablespoon grated gingerroot
1 teaspoon cumin seeds
½ cup butter, melted
1 bay leaf
1½ teaspoons chopped fresh
  tarragon
1½ teaspoons chopped fresh
  rosemary
1½ teaspoons chopped fresh
  dill
½ cup dry sherry
1 tablespoon steak sauce
1 tablespoon honey
Vegetable cooking spray

Remove giblets and neck, and rinse turkey with cold water; pat dry.

Combine salt, gingerroot, and cumin seeds; crush until pulverized, using a mortar and pestle. Rub cavity and skin of turkey with salt mixture. Wrap turkey with plastic wrap, and chill 8 hours.

Combine butter and next 4 ingredients; cover and chill 8 hours. Let butter mixture stand at room temperature until softened.

Loosen skin from turkey breast and thighs without totally detaching skin. Spread butter mixture under skin on breast and thighs.

Combine sherry, steak sauce, and honey; set aside.

Soak hickory chunks in water 10 minutes; drain. Wrap chips in heavy-duty aluminum foil, and make several holes in foil. Light gas grill on one side; place foil-wrapped chips directly on hot coals. Coat grill rack on opposite side with cooking spray. Place rack over cool lava rocks; let grill preheat 10 to 15 minutes. Place turkey on rack opposite hot coals; cover and cook, basting occasionally with sherry mixture, 3 hours or until meat thermometer registers 180° when inserted into meaty portion of thigh, making sure it does not touch bone. Let stand 15 minutes before carving. Yield: 12 servings.

The Bess Collection
The Junior Service League of Independence, Missouri

Parmesan-Walnut Turkey Slices

½ cup grated Parmesan cheese
½ cup all-purpose flour
⅓ cup walnut pieces
1¼ pounds turkey tenderloins
½ teaspoon salt

¼ teaspoon pepper
½ cup milk
3 tablespoons olive oil
¼ cup finely chopped fresh
   parsley

Position knife blade in food processor bowl; add first 3 ingredients. Process until walnuts are finely chopped. Set aside.

Cut each turkey tenderloin in half lengthwise along tendon; remove tendons. Cut tenderloins in half crosswise.

Place turkey between two sheets of heavy-duty plastic wrap; flatten to ¼-inch thickness, using a meat mallet or rolling pin. Sprinkle with salt and pepper. Dredge turkey in cheese mixture. Dip in milk, and dredge in cheese mixture again, coating well.

Heat oil in a large nonstick skillet over medium-high heat until hot; add turkey, and cook 5 to 8 minutes or until lightly browned, turning occasionally. Sprinkle with parsley. Yield: 4 servings.

The Bountiful Arbor
The Junior League of Ann Arbor, Michigan

Salads

Traditional Greek Salad, page 261

Frozen Island Salads

1 (3-ounce) package cream
  cheese, softened
1 (8-ounce) carton strawberry
  low-fat yogurt
¼ cup sugar
1 (8¾-ounce) can crushed
  pineapple, drained

¼ cup chopped pecans, toasted
Lettuce leaves (optional)
1 pint fresh strawberries,
  hulled and halved
3 oranges, peeled and
  sectioned

Beat cream cheese at medium speed of an electric mixer until smooth. Add yogurt and sugar; beat well. Gently stir in pineapple and pecans. Spoon evenly into paper-lined muffin pans, filling each three-fourths full. Cover and freeze 3 hours or until firm. Unmold onto lettuce leaves, if desired. Serve immediately with strawberries and orange sections. Yield: 6 servings.

Cooking with Love
Standsfield Circle
Indianapolis, Indiana

Heavenly Honeydew Salad with Marshmallow Dressing

A splash of cider vinegar and a dash of red pepper balance the sweetness of this fruit salad's creamy marshmallow dressing.

4 egg yolks
¼ cup cider vinegar
1 tablespoon sugar
1 tablespoon butter or
  margarine
½ teaspoon salt
Dash of ground red pepper
12 large marshmallows
½ cup whipping cream,
  whipped

½ honeydew melon, peeled
  and sliced
½ large fresh pineapple,
  peeled and cut into chunks
2 kiwifruit, peeled and sliced
1 cup fresh raspberries
2 peaches, peeled and sliced
4 Bibb lettuce leaves
1 cup walnut pieces

Combine first 6 ingredients in a saucepan. Cook over medium heat, stirring constantly, until thickened and smooth. Add marshmallows, stirring until smooth. Remove from heat, and let cool completely. Fold whipped cream into marshmallow mixture.

Arrange fruit on lettuce-lined salad plates; pour dressing evenly over fruit. Sprinkle with walnuts. Yield: 4 servings.

Among the Lilies
Women in Missions, First Baptist Church of Atlanta, Georgia

Citrus Salad with Lime Vinaigrette

Four lettuces—Boston, Bibb, red leaf, and romaine—team up to add flavor, texture, and color to this refreshing citrus salad.

2 tablespoons lime juice
2 teaspoons rice vinegar
2 tcaspoons honey
2 teaspoons vegetable oil
½ teaspoon salt
¼ teaspoon ground ginger
⅛ teaspoon ground red pepper
1 cup loosely packed torn Boston lettuce
1 cup loosely packed torn Bibb lettuce

1 cup loosely packed torn red leaf lettuce
1 cup loosely packed torn romaine lettuce
1 orange, peeled and sectioned
1 grapefruit, peeled and sectioned
1 small purple onion, thinly sliced and separated into rings

Combine first 7 ingredients in a jar. Cover tightly, and shake vigorously. Cover and chill thoroughly.

Combine lettuces in a large bowl; toss gently.

Arrange 1 cup mixed salad greens on individual salad plates. Top evenly with orange sections, grapefruit sections, and onion rings. Drizzle evenly with chilled dressing. Yield: 4 servings.   Hali Exley

The Best of Wheeling
The Junior League of Wheeling, West Virginia

Spinach-Apple Salad

You can turn this side salad into a hearty main dish by adding 2 cups of chopped cooked chicken, turkey, or pork to the fresh spinach and apple mixture.

⅔ cup vegetable oil
½ cup white vinegar
1 tablespoon chutney
1 teaspoon salt
1 teaspoon curry powder
1 teaspoon dry mustard
9 cups tightly packed torn
   fresh spinach

3 cups diced Red Delicious
   apple
⅔ cup salted dry roasted
   peanuts
½ cup raisins
⅓ cup sliced green onions
2 tablespoons sesame seeds,
   toasted

Combine first 6 ingredients in a small bowl; stir well with a wire whisk until blended. Cover dressing, and let stand at room temperature 2 hours.

Combine spinach, apple, peanuts, raisins, green onions, and sesame seeds in a bowl; toss well. Pour dressing over spinach mixture, and toss gently. Serve immediately. Yield: 6 servings.   Sandy Lessenberry

A Place Called Hope
The Junior Auxiliary of Hope, Arkansas

Winter Salad with Raspberry Vinaigrette

½ pound fresh spinach,
   washed, trimmed, and
   torn
1 head Bibb lettuce, torn
2 oranges, peeled and
   sectioned
2 Red Delicious apples, thinly
   sliced

1 kiwifruit, peeled and thinly
   sliced
½ cup chopped walnuts,
   toasted
Raspberry Vinaigrette

Combine spinach, lettuce, orange, apple, kiwifruit, and walnuts in a large bowl; toss gently. Pour Raspberry Vinaigrette over spinach mixture just before serving; toss gently. Yield: 8 servings.

Raspberry Vinaigrette

½ cup vegetable oil
¼ cup raspberry vinegar
1 tablespoon honey

½ teaspoon grated orange rind
¼ teaspoon salt
⅛ teaspoon pepper

Combine all ingredients in a jar; cover tightly, and shake vigorously. Cover and chill thoroughly. Yield: about 1 cup.

The Bess Collection
The Junior Service League of Independence, Missouri

Traditional Greek Salad

For variety, substitute wine vinegar for the lemon juice and mint for the oregano.

1 clove garlic, halved
6 cups tightly packed torn
  mixed salad greens
1 medium tomato, cut into
  wedges
1 medium-size green pepper,
  thinly sliced into rings
1 small cucumber, thinly sliced
4 radishes, thinly sliced
3 green onions, thinly sliced

½ cup crumbled feta cheese
¼ cup large pitted ripe olives
1 (2-ounce) can anchovy fillets,
  drained
½ cup olive oil
¼ cup lemon juice
½ teaspoon salt
¼ teaspoon dried oregano
¼ teaspoon freshly ground
  pepper

Rub the inside of a large wooden salad bowl with cut sides of garlic. Discard garlic.

Add salad greens and next 8 ingredients to bowl; toss well. Combine olive oil and next 4 ingredients; stir well. Pour dressing over salad, and toss gently. Serve immediately. Yield: 6 servings.   Despina T. Saffo

A Greek Feast: A Book of Greek Recipes
The Daughters of Penelope
Wilmington, North Carolina

Gingered Cucumber Salad

Fresh gingerroot spices up these crispy cucumber slices. Store unpeeled gingerroot tightly wrapped in the refrigerator up to a week or in the freezer up to two months.

¾ **pound fresh snow pea pods**	½ **cup vegetable oil**
4 **pounds cucumbers**	¼ **cup rice vinegar**
2 **(8-ounce) cans sliced water**	¾ **teaspoon salt**
chestnuts, drained	½ **teaspoon ground white**
1 **cup chopped green onions**	**pepper**
3 **tablespoons minced**	**Lettuce leaves (optional)**
gingerroot	

Wash snow peas; trim ends, and remove strings. Cook in boiling water to cover 30 seconds. Plunge snow peas into ice water to stop the cooking process; drain and set aside.

Peel and seed cucumbers. Cut into ¼-inch-thick slices.

Combine snow peas, cucumber, water chestnuts, green onions, and gingerroot in a large bowl. Combine oil, vinegar, salt, and pepper; stir with a wire whisk. Pour oil mixture over cucumber mixture; toss gently. Serve immediately, or cover and chill. Serve on lettuce leaves, if desired. Yield: 15 servings.

Feast of Eden
The Junior League of Monterey County, California

Fireworks Salad

You can prepare this colorful vegetable salad up to 8 hours ahead.

¾ **pound fresh snow pea pods**	⅓ **cup olive oil**
1 **large sweet red pepper, cut**	2 **tablespoons lemon juice**
into very thin strips	2 **teaspoons grated gingerroot**
1 **large sweet yellow pepper, cut**	½ **teaspoon salt**
into very thin strips	¼ **teaspoon pepper**
1 **cup radishes, cut into very**	
thin strips	

Wash snow peas; trim ends, and remove strings. Cook in boiling water to cover 30 seconds. Plunge snow peas into ice water to stop the cooking process; drain. Cut diagonally into thin strips. Combine snow peas, pepper strips, and radishes in a large bowl; toss gently.

Combine olive oil and next 4 ingredients in a jar. Cover tightly, and shake vigorously. Pour over salad, and toss well. Cover and chill up to 8 hours. Yield: 7 servings.

Pass It On . . . A Treasury of Tastes and Traditions
Delta Delta Delta National Fraternity
Arlington, Texas

Italian Potato Salad

3½ pounds large baking potatoes, unpeeled and cut into 2-inch pieces
¾ cup olive oil, divided
2 teaspoons pepper
½ teaspoon salt
1 medium-size green pepper, cut into strips
1 medium-size sweet red pepper, cut into strips
1 small purple onion, cut into strips
1 cup canned, drained artichoke hearts, quartered
2 tablespoons chopped fresh basil
½ teaspoon minced garlic

Place potato pieces on a large baking sheet; drizzle with ¼ cup oil. Sprinkle with 2 teaspoons pepper and salt; toss well. Bake at 425° for 35 minutes or until potato pieces are tender.

Cook pepper strips and onion in ¼ cup oil in a large skillet over medium-high heat, stirring constantly, until vegetables are tender.

Combine potato pieces, pepper mixture, and artichoke in a bowl. Add remaining ¼ cup oil, basil, and garlic; toss. Serve warm or at room temperature. Yield: 10 servings.   Kathleen Brian

Women Cook for a Cause
The Women's Resource Center of Schoolcraft College
Livonia, Michigan

Marinated Brie and Tomato Salad

Turn this salad into a wonderful appetizer by serving it on French baguette slices instead of lettuce leaves.

1 (15-ounce) Brie
4 or 5 large ripe tomatoes, seeded and cubed
1 cup lightly packed fresh basil leaves, cut into thin strips
3 cloves garlic, minced
⅔ cup olive oil
1 teaspoon salt
½ teaspoon freshly ground pepper
Green leaf lettuce (optional)

Remove and discard rind from cheese, using a vegetable peeler; coarsely chop cheese. Combine cheese, tomato, and next 5 ingredients in a large bowl. Cover and let stand 2 hours at room temperature. Serve over lettuce leaves, if desired. Yield: 8 servings.   Debi Rahal

Champions: Favorite Foods of Indy Car Racing
Championship Auto Racing Auxiliary
Indianapolis, Indiana

Confetti Rice Salad

2 cups cooked rice
2 cups chopped tomato
1¼ cups chopped celery
½ cup chopped onion
½ cup chopped green pepper
½ cup pimiento-stuffed olives, chopped
½ cup mayonnaise or salad dressing
¼ cup Italian or Caesar salad dressing
½ teaspoon dried basil
½ teaspoon dried oregano
½ teaspoon dried parsley flakes
½ teaspoon dried tarragon

Combine first 6 ingredients in a large bowl; stir well. Combine mayonnaise and next 5 ingredients in a small bowl; stir with a wire whisk. Pour dressing over rice mixture, and toss gently. Cover and chill. Yield: 6 servings.   Beverly Close

Trinity and Friends Finest
Women of Holy Trinity
Churchville, Maryland

Couscous and Chick-Pea Salad

For a fun serving variation, roll up scoops of this salad in a lettuce leaf, and enjoy!

1½ cups water
½ teaspoon salt
1 cup couscous, uncooked
1 (15-ounce) can garbanzo
   beans (chick-peas), drained
1¼ cups diced sweet red
   pepper

⅔ cup sliced green onions
½ cup chopped carrot
½ cup kalamata olives, pitted
Mint Vinaigrette
6 ounces crumbled feta cheese
Romaine lettuce leaves (optional)

Combine water and ½ teaspoon salt in a medium saucepan; bring to a boil. Stir in couscous. Cover, remove from heat, and let stand 5 minutes or until liquid is absorbed.

Combine couscous, garbanzo beans, and next 4 ingredients in a large bowl; toss gently. Pour Mint Vinaigrette over couscous mixture; add feta cheese, and toss gently. Serve immediately, or cover and chill. Serve in a lettuce-lined salad bowl, if desired. Yield: 8 servings.

Mint Vinaigrette

¾ cup fresh mint sprigs
3 tablespoons white wine
   vinegar
2 cloves garlic
1 teaspoon Dijon mustard

¼ teaspoon sugar
¼ teaspoon salt
⅛ teaspoon pepper
⅔ cup olive oil

Position knife blade in food processor bowl; add first 7 ingredients. Process until mint and garlic are finely chopped. Pour olive oil through food chute with processor running; process until blended. Yield: about 1 cup.   Tom Bowman

Sun Valley Celebrity & Local Heroes Cookbook
Advocates for Survivors of Domestic Violence
Hailey, Idaho

Basil-Fettuccine Salad

You can easily shave a wedge of fresh Parmesan cheese, using a vegetable peeler.

1 pound fresh green beans
1 (8-ounce) package fettuccine
Red Wine-Basil Vinaigrette
6 plum tomatoes
2 cups pitted ripe olives
1½ cups loosely packed,
  julienne-sliced fresh basil
  leaves

2 tablespoons chopped fresh
  parsley
4 ounces Parmesan cheese,
  shaved

Wash beans and remove strings. Arrange beans in a steamer basket over boiling water. Cover and steam 4 minutes or until tender. Rinse beans with cold water; drain and set aside.

Cook pasta according to package directions. Drain and place in a large bowl. Toss with ½ cup Red Wine-Basil Vinaigrette; set aside.

Cut each tomato into 8 wedges. Add tomato, green beans, olives, basil, and parsley to pasta mixture; toss gently. Pour remaining Red Wine-Basil Vinaigrette over pasta mixture; toss gently. Sprinkle with cheese. Yield: 8 servings.

Red Wine-Basil Vinaigrette

½ cup red wine vinegar
2 cloves garlic, crushed
2 tablespoons Dijon mustard
1 teaspoon freshly ground
  pepper

1 cup light olive oil
½ cup loosely packed, julienne-
  sliced fresh basil leaves
½ cup chopped fresh parsley

Combine first 4 ingredients in a small bowl. Add oil in a slow, steady stream, beating with a wire whisk until blended. Stir in basil and parsley. Yield: 2 cups.   Lois Wroten Boatwright

Homecoming: Special Foods, Special Memories
Baylor University Alumni Association
Waco, Texas

Oriental Pasta Salad

You may find napa cabbage at your local market under another name. It's also called Chinese celery cabbage, wong bok, and Peking cabbage.

1 (16-ounce) package bow tie pasta
4 cups coarsely chopped napa cabbage
½ cup diced sweet red pepper
½ cup thinly sliced green onions
½ cup creamy peanut butter
¼ cup water
¼ cup rice wine vinegar
3 tablespoons soy sauce
2 tablespoons honey
2 tablespoons dark sesame oil
½ to ¾ teaspoon hot red chili oil
¾ cup unsalted dry roasted peanuts, coarsely chopped

Cook pasta according to package directions. Drain; rinse with cold water, and drain again.

Combine pasta, cabbage, pepper, and green onions in a large bowl. Combine peanut butter and next 6 ingredients in a small bowl; beat with a wire whisk until blended.

Pour peanut butter mixture over pasta mixture; add peanuts, and toss gently. Serve salad at room temperature, or cover and chill. Yield: 6 servings.

Cathy Kiley

Good to the Core
The Apple Corps of the Weller Center for Health Education
Easton, Pennsylvania

Greek-Style Tuna Salad

Tuna salad goes Greek with the addition of feta cheese, olives, and oregano.

1 cup orzo, uncooked
1 (6⅛-ounce) can solid white
   tuna, drained and flaked
2 cups chopped tomato
½ cup crumbled feta cheese
¼ cup chopped purple onion
3 tablespoons sliced ripe olives

½ cup red wine vinegar
2 tablespoons water
2 tablespoons olive oil
1 clove garlic, minced
½ teaspoon dried basil
½ teaspoon dried oregano
Green leaf lettuce (optional)

Cook orzo according to package directions; drain, rinse with cold water, and drain again.

Combine orzo, tuna, and next 4 ingredients in a large bowl; toss gently.

Combine vinegar and next 5 ingredients in container of an electric blender; cover and process until smooth, stopping once to scrape down sides. Pour vinegar mixture over pasta mixture, and toss gently. Cover and chill thoroughly. Serve on lettuce leaves, if desired. Yield: 6 servings.

Beth Smith

Briarwood Recipes to Crown Your Table
Women's Ministries of Briarwood Presbyterian Church
Birmingham, Alabama

Warm Salad of Grilled Shrimp, Scallops, and Endive

Grilled seafood makes this warm main-dish salad something you won't soon forget.

1 pound unpeeled large fresh shrimp
¼ cup plus 2 tablespoons extra virgin olive oil, divided
¼ cup plus 1 tablespoon lemon juice, divided
3 cloves garlic, minced and divided
½ teaspoon fennel seeds, crushed
½ teaspoon salt
½ teaspoon freshly ground pepper
1 pound fresh sea scallops
8 ounces Belgian endive
½ teaspoon Dijon mustard
⅓ cup coarsely chopped flat-leaf parsley

Peel shrimp, and devein, if desired; set aside.

Combine 2 tablespoons olive oil, 3 tablespoons lemon juice, 2 cloves minced garlic, fennel seeds, salt, and pepper in a large heavy-duty, zip-top plastic bag. Add shrimp and scallops; seal bag securely, and shake until seafood is coated. Marinate in refrigerator 1 hour, turning bag occasionally.

Cut endive in half lengthwise; brush with 1 tablespoon olive oil. Cook, without grill lid, over medium-hot coals (350° to 400°) 3 minutes or until edges are slightly browned, turning occasionally. Coarsely chop endive; place in a large bowl, and set aside.

Remove shrimp and scallops from marinade, discarding marinade; thread seafood alternately on four 12-inch skewers. Cook, covered with grill lid, over medium-hot coals (350° to 400°) 3 minutes on each side or until done. Remove seafood from skewers; add to endive, and toss gently.

Combine remaining 3 tablespoons olive oil, 2 tablespoons lemon juice, 1 clove minced garlic, and mustard; stir well. Pour dressing over seafood mixture; toss gently. Sprinkle with parsley. Serve immediately. Yield: 4 servings.

Karren Hecht

Paws and Refresh
Virginia Living Museum
Newport News, Virginia

Chicken and Tortellini Salad

Honey lends a distinctive sweetness to this chicken and cheese-filled pasta salad.

1½ pounds skinned and boned chicken breast halves
2 cloves garlic, minced
2 tablespoons olive oil
¾ cup cider vinegar
¾ cup vegetable oil
¼ cup honey
3 tablespoons chopped fresh parsley
1 tablespoon chopped fresh basil
1 teaspoon dry mustard
2 teaspoons Dijon mustard
1 (9-ounce) package refrigerated cheese-filled tortellini
1 medium-size sweet red pepper, chopped
1 medium-size green pepper, chopped
1 medium-size purple onion, chopped
½ cup sliced celery
¼ teaspoon salt
¼ teaspoon pepper

Place chicken in a large saucepan; add water to cover. Bring to a boil over medium heat; reduce heat, and simmer, uncovered, 15 minutes or until done. Drain chicken, and let cool. Cut chicken into strips, and set aside.

Cook garlic in oil in a large skillet over medium-high heat, stirring constantly, until golden. Add chicken, and cook 1 minute, stirring constantly. Remove garlic and chicken from skillet, and place in a large bowl; set aside.

Combine vinegar and next 6 ingredients in a jar. Cover tightly, and shake vigorously. Pour dressing mixture over chicken mixture. Cover and chill 2 hours.

Cook tortellini according to package directions; drain well. Add tortellini, chopped red peppers, and next 5 ingredients to chicken mixture; toss gently. Cover and chill thoroughly. Yield: 6 servings.

Back Home Again
The Junior League of Indianapolis, Indiana

Maple-Bacon Dressing for Garden Salad

Serve this bacon dressing warm or chilled. We loved it on a salad of fresh spinach, Bibb lettuce, grape halves, and shredded Cheddar cheese.

2 cups vegetable oil	5 slices bacon, cooked and crumbled
¼ cup cider vinegar	
⅓ cup firmly packed brown sugar	1 small onion, coarsely chopped
½ cup maple syrup	1 teaspoon dry mustard

Position knife blade in food processor bowl; add all ingredients. Cover and process until blended, stopping once to scrape down sides. Store in an airtight container in refrigerator. Serve over salad greens. Yield: 3½ cups.   Kay Hall

Traditions
First United Methodist Church/United Methodist Women
Tallassee, Alabama

Fresh Ginger Salad Dressing

¼ cup plus 2 tablespoons olive oil	¾ teaspoon sugar
1 teaspoon grated lime rind	½ to ¾ teaspoon salt
¼ cup plus 2 tablespoons lime juice	½ to ¾ teaspoon garlic salt
1 tablespoon plus ½ teaspoon grated gingerroot	1½ teaspoons chopped fresh basil
	1½ teaspoons soy sauce
	1½ teaspoons red wine vinegar

Combine all ingredients in a jar. Cover tightly, and shake vigorously. Serve dressing over salad greens. Yield: 1 cup.

Good Food, Good Company
The Junior Service League of Thomasville, Georgia

Orange Vinaigrette

½ cup vegetable oil
1 tablespoon sugar
2 tablespoons orange juice
2 tablespoons cider vinegar
½ teaspoon salt
¼ teaspoon pepper
¼ teaspoon dry mustard

Combine all ingredients in a jar. Cover tightly, and shake vigorously. Shake well just before serving. Serve dressing over salad greens. Yield: about ¾ cup.

Savory Secrets: A Collection of St. Louis Recipes
The Greater St. Louis Alumni Chapter of Sigma Sigma Sigma
Godfrey, Illinois

Ripe Olive Dressing

This chunky dressing's so full of flavor and texture that it's perfect to spoon generously over salad greens alone. If the recipe makes more than you need, it's easy to halve.

2 cups mayonnaise
½ cup ketchup
¼ cup cider vinegar
2 teaspoons paprika
4 large hard-cooked eggs, diced
1 cup chopped celery
1 cup chopped ripe olives
1 cup sliced almonds
2 tablespoons minced onion

Combine first 4 ingredients in a bowl; stir with a wire whisk until smooth. Gently stir in eggs and remaining ingredients. Store in an airtight container in refrigerator. Serve dressing over salad greens. Yield: about 6 cups.

June Dean

Candlelight and Wisteria
Lee-Scott Academy
Auburn, Alabama

Sauces & Condiments

Honey-Chocolate Sauce, page 274

Amaretto Sauce

For a healthier version of this recipe, substitute lower fat varieties of ricotta and cream cheese, and skim milk for the cream.

1 cup ricotta cheese	½ cup sugar
1 (8-ounce) package cream cheese, softened	¼ cup amaretto
	2 tablespoons whipping cream

Position knife blade in food processor bowl; add ricotta and cream cheese. Process until smooth, stopping once to scrape down sides. Add sugar and remaining ingredients; process until blended, stopping once to scrape down sides. Cover and chill. Serve over fresh fruit or pound cake. Yield: 2½ cups.

Heard in the Kitchen
The Heard Museum Guild
Phoenix, Arizona

Honey-Chocolate Sauce

Serve this honey-kissed sauce over scoops of your favorite ice cream or frozen yogurt.

½ cup whipping cream	1 tablespoon grated orange rind
¼ cup honey	
1 (1-ounce) square unsweetened chocolate	2 tablespoons light rum
1 (1-ounce) square semisweet chocolate	

Combine first 4 ingredients in a heavy saucepan. Cook over low heat until chocolate melts, stirring often. Bring just to a boil; reduce heat, and simmer 3 minutes, stirring constantly. Stir in orange rind. Remove from heat, and let cool. Stir in rum. Serve at room temperature. Cover and store in refrigerator. Yield: 1 cup.

The Elegant Cook
Friends of the Eastern Christian School Association
North Haledon, New Jersey

Lemon Crème Fruit Sauce

2 large eggs
1 cup sugar, divided
⅓ cup lemon juice
1 tablespoon cornstarch

½ cup water
1 teaspoon vanilla extract
1 cup whipping cream

Beat eggs, ½ cup sugar, and lemon juice in a large mixing bowl at medium speed of an electric mixer 1 minute or until foamy. Set aside.

Combine remaining ½ cup sugar and cornstarch in a medium saucepan. Gradually add water, stirring until smooth. Cook over medium heat, stirring constantly, until mixture thickens and comes to a boil. Boil 1 minute, stirring constantly. Remove from heat.

Gradually stir about one-fourth of hot mixture into egg mixture; add to remaining hot mixture, stirring constantly. Cook over low heat, stirring constantly, until thickened. Let cool completely. Stir in vanilla and whipping cream. Cover and chill at least 2 hours. Serve over fruit salad. Yield: 2¼ cups.

Emory Seasons, Entertaining Atlanta Style
Emory University Woman's Club
Atlanta, Georgia

Melba Sauce

1 (10-ounce) container frozen
   raspberries in light syrup,
   thawed and drained
½ cup red currant jelly

¼ cup sugar
2 tablespoons kirsch or other
   cherry-flavored liqueur

Place raspberries in container of an electric blender; cover and process until smooth. Pour through a wire-mesh strainer into a bowl, pressing raspberries against sides of strainer with back of a spoon to squeeze out juice. Discard pulp and seeds. Combine juice, jelly, and sugar in a saucepan. Cook over medium heat, stirring constantly, until mixture comes to a boil. Boil 1 minute, stirring constantly. Remove from heat; stir in kirsch. Cover and chill. Yield: ¾ cup.

Ridgefield Cooks
Women's Committee of the Ridgefield Community Center
Ridgefield, Connecticut

Asian Barbecue Sauce

Check an Asian market for chili puree with garlic. Add more or less of the puree according to the degree of heat you want in the sauce.

1 cup ketchup
2 tablespoons brown sugar
2 tablespoons red wine vinegar
1 teaspoon dry hot mustard

1 large clove garlic, minced
2 teaspoons chili puree with garlic

Combine first 5 ingredients in a small saucepan. Bring to a boil; remove from heat. Stir in chili puree. Use as a basting sauce for chicken, beef, or pork. Yield: 1⅓ cups.   Sarah Emily Newton

What's Cooking at Chico State
Staff Council/California State University
Chico, California

Puttanesca Sauce for Garlic Lovers

Spoon this easy, high-flavored tomato sauce over mounds of your favorite hot cooked pasta.

1 cup pitted, halved ripe olives
½ cup sun-dried tomatoes, cut into thin strips
¼ cup olive oil
1 (3½-ounce) jar capers, drained
8 large cloves garlic, chopped

6 anchovy fillets, mashed
3 cups quartered plum tomatoes
¼ cup pesto
1 teaspoon dried crushed red pepper

Combine first 6 ingredients in a large saucepan; bring to a boil. Add tomato, pesto, and red pepper; bring to a boil. Reduce heat, and simmer, uncovered, 10 minutes, stirring occasionally. Serve over pasta. Yield: 4 cups.   Carolyn Hughes

Collard Greens, Watermelons, and "Miss" Charlotte's Pie
Swansboro United Methodist Women
Swansboro, North Carolina

Hollandaise Sauce

It's easy to turn this classic hollandaise sauce into a béarnaise sauce—just stir in 1 teaspoon chopped fresh parsley, 1 teaspoon chopped fresh tarragon, and ⅛ teaspoon paprika at the end of the preparation.

3 egg yolks, lightly beaten
¼ teaspoon salt
⅛ teaspoon ground red pepper
1 tablespoon lemon juice

½ cup unsalted butter or
   margarine, divided
3 tablespoons hot water

Combine first 3 ingredients in top of a double boiler; place over hot (not boiling) water. Gradually add lemon juice, stirring constantly. Add butter, 2 tablespoons at a time, stirring constantly after each addition until butter melts. Add 3 tablespoons hot water; cook, stirring constantly, until temperature reaches 160° (about 10 to 15 minutes). Yield: ⅔ cup.   Susan Blumin

Signature Cuisine
Miami Country Day School Parents' Association
Miami, Florida

French Tartar Sauce

Dijon mustard gives traditional tartar sauce a flavor makeover.

3 tablespoons mayonnaise
1 tablespoon lemon juice
1 teaspoon minced onion
1 teaspoon sweet pickle relish
½ teaspoon garlic powder
½ teaspoon dry mustard
½ teaspoon Dijon mustard

½ teaspoon prepared mustard
¼ teaspoon salt
¼ teaspoon pepper
¼ teaspoon paprika
2 or 3 drops of hot sauce
   (optional)

Combine all ingredients in a small bowl; stir well. Serve with fish or shrimp. Yield: ⅓ cup.   Justin B. O'Keefe

Cooking on the Coast
Mississippi Gulf Coast YMCA
Ocean Springs, Mississippi

Chatni Annanaas (Sweet Pineapple Chutney)

1 medium-size fresh pineapple
1½ cups sugar
2 tablespoons lemon juice
1½ teaspoons ground
   cumin
1 teaspoon salt

1 teaspoon fennel seeds,
   crushed
¼ teaspoon ground cinnamon
¼ teaspoon ground coriander
¼ teaspoon ground red pepper
¼ teaspoon black pepper

Peel pineapple; remove and discard core. Finely chop pineapple.
   Combine chopped pineapple, sugar, and remaining ingredients in a nonaluminum saucepan; stir well. Bring to a boil; reduce heat, and simmer, uncovered, 35 to 40 minutes or until thickened, stirring often. Spoon chutney quickly into hot jars, filling to ½ inch from top. Remove air bubbles; wipe jar rims. Cover at once with metal lids, and screw on bands. Process in boiling-water bath 15 minutes. Store in refrigerator after opening. Yield: 2 half pints.

Global Feast Cookbook
Mystic Seaport Museum Stores
Mystic, Connecticut

Cranberry-Cherry Relish

1 (16-ounce) can whole-berry
   cranberry sauce
1 cup fresh or frozen pitted
   dark cherries
½ cup raisins
¼ cup minced onion

¼ cup firmly packed brown
   sugar
2 tablespoons balsamic vinegar
1 tablespoon minced
   gingerroot

Combine all ingredients in a heavy nonaluminum saucepan. Bring to a boil; reduce heat, and simmer, uncovered, 20 minutes or until thickened. Store in refrigerator. Yield: 2½ cups.   Meryl Olsen Dun

The Educated Palate: The Hamlin School Cookbook
The Hamlin School
San Francisco, California

Dixie Relish

We're not just whistling Dixie when we tell you this tangy relish received a high rating from our Test Kitchens staff. Try it on your next hot dog.

4 cups chopped cabbage
2 cups chopped onion
2 cups chopped green pepper
2 cups chopped sweet red
   pepper
½ cup salt
2 quarts water

1 quart cider vinegar (5% acidity)
1 cup water
2 tablespoons mustard seeds
2 tablespoons celery seeds
½ teaspoon dried crushed red pepper

Combine first 4 ingredients in a large nonmetal container; toss well. Sprinkle with salt. Add 2 quarts water; cover and let stand 1 hour. Drain well. Rinse with cold water, and drain again.

Place vegetables in a large Dutch oven; add vinegar and remaining ingredients. Bring to a boil; reduce heat, and simmer, uncovered, 20 minutes, stirring occasionally.

Spoon relish quickly into hot jars, filling to ½ inch from top. Remove air bubbles; wipe jar rims. Cover at once with metal lids, and screw on bands. Process in boiling-water bath 15 minutes. Store in refrigerator after opening. Yield: 9 half pints.   Hoyt Lewis

Georgia Hospitality
Georgia Elks Aidmore Auxiliary
Conyers, Georgia

Red Pepper Relish

Orange marmalade, chili powder, and hot sauce cleverly complement the flavor of the sweet red peppers in this relish. Serve it with fish or chicken.

10 sweet red peppers, cut into 1-inch pieces cubed
1 teaspoon salt
2 cups sugar
2 cups white vinegar

2 tablespoons orange marmalade
1½ teaspoons chili powder
½ teaspoon hot sauce

Position knife blade in food processor bowl; add pepper in batches, and pulse 8 or 10 times or until finely chopped. Transfer chopped pepper to a large bowl. Sprinkle with salt; cover and chill 8 hours. Drain well.

Combine pepper, sugar, and vinegar. Bring to a boil; reduce heat, and simmer, uncovered, 40 to 45 minutes. Remove from heat; add marmalade and remaining ingredients, stirring well. Spoon relish into jars; cover and store in refrigerator. Yield: 8 cups.   Betty Boyd

Soroptimist Cooks
Soroptimist International of Dixon, California

Wildfire

This fiery relish can double as a dip for corn chips.

1 pound jalapeño peppers
2 large carrots, scraped and quartered
1 medium onion, quartered

2 or 3 cloves garlic
⅓ cup vegetable oil
⅓ cup cider vinegar
1 teaspoon salt

Remove stems from peppers. Position knife blade in food processor bowl; add peppers, carrot, onion, and garlic. Process until chopped, stopping once to scrape down sides. Combine vegetable mixture, oil, vinegar, and salt; stir well. Cover and chill. Serve with grilled chicken, beef, or pork. Yield: 4½ cups.

Cafe Oklahoma
The Junior Service League of Midwest City, Oklahoma

Apple Butter

6 pounds cooking apples, peeled, cored, and coarsely chopped
1 cup water
4 cups sugar
½ cup white vinegar
2 teaspoons ground cinnamon
½ teaspoon ground allspice
½ teaspoon ground cloves

Combine apple and water in a large Dutch oven; bring to a boil. Cover, reduce heat, and simmer 20 to 25 minutes or until apple is tender. Mash apple. Stir in sugar and vinegar; bring to a boil. Reduce heat, and simmer, uncovered, 2½ hours or until mixture is very thick. Stir in cinnamon, allspice, and cloves. Store in refrigerator up to 1 month. Yield: 8 cups.   Shirley Lowe

Treasured Gems
Hiddenite Center Family
Hiddenite, North Carolina

Basil Butter

If you're in a creative mood, shape this flavored butter in small, flexible molds or roll it into balls.

1½ cups loosely packed fresh basil leaves
1½ cups butter, softened
1½ teaspoons ground white pepper
1 teaspoon salt
1½ teaspoons lemon juice

Position knife blade in food processor bowl; add fresh basil leaves, and process until finely chopped. Add butter and remaining ingredients; process until smooth, stopping once to scrape down sides. Store butter mixture in refrigerator. Serve on chicken, fish, or vegetables. Yield: 1⅔ cups.   Rose Marie McWilliams

What's Cooking at Cathedral Plaza
Cathedral Plaza
Denver, Colorado

Dried Apricot and Pineapple Jam

2½ cups water
2 cups dried apricots
4 cups sugar

2 cups undrained canned
   crushed pineapple
½ lemon, thinly sliced

Combine water and apricots in a large saucepan; bring to a boil. Reduce heat, and simmer, uncovered, 10 minutes or until apricots are tender. Mash apricots. Add sugar and remaining ingredients; bring to a boil. Reduce heat, and simmer, uncovered, 30 minutes.

Pour jam quickly into hot sterilized jars, filling to ¼ inch from top. Remove air bubbles; wipe jar rims. Cover at once with metal lids, and screw on bands. Process in boiling-water bath 5 minutes. Yield: 4 pints.

Dorothy Olson

Door County Cooking
Bay View Lutheran Church
Sturgeon Bay, Wisconsin

Rhubarb Jam

Stalks of fresh rhubarb will keep tightly wrapped in the refrigerator up to 3 days.

5 cups chopped fresh rhubarb
3 cups sugar
1 (3-ounce) package strawberry-
   flavored gelatin

2 tablespoons butter or
   margarine

Combine rhubarb and sugar in a large bowl; stir well. Cover and chill at least 8 hours. Place rhubarb mixture in a large saucepan; bring to a boil. Reduce heat, and simmer, uncovered, 12 minutes, stirring occasionally. Remove from heat; add gelatin and butter, stirring until gelatin dissolves and butter melts.

Spoon jam quickly into hot sterilized jars, filling to ¼ inch from top; wipe jar rims. Cover at once with metal lids; screw on bands. Process in boiling-water bath 5 minutes. Yield: 4 half pints.

M. Butz

Cookbook 1893-1993
Friends of North Tonawanda Public Library
North Tonawanda, New York

Vidalia Onion Jelly

Serve this sweet onion jelly on biscuits with slivers of roast beef or ham.

2 pounds Vidalia onions or
  other sweet onions, thinly
  sliced (about 9 cups)
2 cups water
1 (1¾-ounce) package
  powdered fruit pectin

¾ cup white vinegar (5%
  acidity)
5½ cups sugar

Combine onion and water in a large Dutch oven. Bring to a boil. Remove from heat, and let cool. Press onion through a jelly bag or cheesecloth to extract juice. If necessary, add water to juice to measure 3 cups. Discard onion pulp.

Combine onion liquid, pectin, and vinegar in a large saucepan; stir well. Bring to a boil, stirring constantly. Stir in sugar; return to a boil. Boil 1 minute, stirring constantly. Remove from heat; skim off foam.

Pour onion jelly quickly into hot sterilized jars, filling to ¼ inch from top. Remove air bubbles; wipe jar rims. Cover at once with metal lids, and screw on bands. Process in boiling-water bath 5 minutes. Yield: 6 half pints.

Lillian Huber

Ribbon Winning Recipes
South Carolina State Fair
Columbia, South Carolina

Chilled Marinated Peppers

3 large sweet red peppers
3 large sweet orange peppers
2 large sweet yellow peppers
3 tablespoons vegetable oil
1 tablespoon olive oil
2 cloves garlic, minced

1 tablespoon tarragon wine
  vinegar
½ teaspoon dried basil
¼ teaspoon dried rosemary
¼ teaspoon dried oregano

Wash and dry peppers; place on an aluminum foil-lined baking sheet. Broil peppers 5½ inches from heat (with electric oven door partially opened) 5 minutes or until peppers look blistered. Place in a heavy-duty, zip-top plastic bag; close bag, and let stand 10 minutes. Peel peppers; remove core and seeds. Cut peppers into ½-inch strips.

Combine vegetable oil and next 6 ingredients in a bowl. Add peppers; toss. Cover and marinate in refrigerator at least 8 hours. Serve with grilled beef or chicken. Yield: 3 cups.

Holy Cow, Chicago's Cooking!
Church of the Holy Comforter
Kenilworth, Illinois

Roasted Red Peppers

Roasted Red Peppers add a splash of color to salads and sandwiches.

8 medium-size sweet red
  peppers
½ cup olive oil
2 tablespoons balsamic vinegar

1 tablespoon fresh lemon juice
1 clove garlic, minced
1 teaspoon pickling salt
¼ teaspoon pepper

Wash and dry peppers; place on an aluminum foil-lined baking sheet. Broil 5½ inches from heat (with electric oven door partially opened) 5 minutes or until peppers look blistered. Place peppers in a heavy-duty, zip-top plastic bag; close bag, and let stand 10 minutes. Peel peppers; remove core and seeds. Cut peppers into ½-inch strips.

Combine peppers, oil, and remaining ingredients in a large bowl. Cover and let stand 30 minutes. Store in refrigerator. Yield: 2½ cups.

Sensational Seasons: A Taste & Tour of Arkansas
The Junior League of Fort Smith, Arkansas

Soups & Stews

Caldeirada, page 299

Cold Fruit Soup

A splash of sweet white wine enhances the fresh fruit flavors of this cold soup.

1 pound Granny Smith apples, peeled, cored, and coarsely chopped
1 pound ripe pears, peeled, cored, and coarsely chopped
1 pound plums, unpeeled, pitted, and coarsely chopped
2 cups water
½ cup soft breadcrumbs
1 tablespoon grated lemon rind
1 tablespoon lemon juice
½ teaspoon ground cinnamon
1 cup cranberry juice drink
¾ cup sweet white wine
½ cup sugar
¼ cup seedless raspberry jam

Combine first 8 ingredients in a large Dutch oven; bring mixture to a boil. Cover, reduce heat, and simmer 20 to 25 minutes or until fruit is tender.

Place one-third of mixture in container of an electric blender; cover and process until smooth, stopping once to scrape down sides. Repeat procedure twice with remaining fruit mixture. Add cranberry juice and remaining ingredients, stirring until jam melts. Cover and chill thoroughly. Yield: 8½ cups.   Alice Yatsko

A Ukrainian-American Potpourri
St. Stephen Ukrainian Catholic Church
Dover Township, New Jersey

Summer Pea Soup

4 cloves garlic
2 (10-ounce) packages frozen English peas, thawed and divided
2 cups plain yogurt
½ cup olive oil
½ cup lime juice
1 tablespoon chili powder
2 cups chicken broth
1 teaspoon salt
½ cup chopped tomato
½ cup chopped sweet red pepper
3 tablespoons chopped fresh cilantro
2 teaspoons minced jalapeño pepper

Position knife blade in food processor bowl. Drop garlic through food chute with processor running; process until garlic is minced.

Reserve ½ cup peas; add remaining peas, yogurt, and next 3 ingredients to processor bowl. Process until smooth, stopping once to scrape down sides. Pour pea mixture into a large bowl. Add chicken broth and salt; stir well. Cover and chill thoroughly.

Combine reserved ½ cup peas, tomato, and next 3 ingredients in a small bowl; toss gently. Cover and chill thoroughly.

To serve, ladle soup into individual soup bowls. Top each serving with tomato mixture. Yield: 7 cups. Nina DuPont Curran

Queen Anne Goes to the Kitchen
Episcopal Church Women of St. Paul's Parish
Centreville, Maryland

Blue Satin Soup

If the title doesn't tell, the flavor will—blue cheese distinguishes this creamy, ivory-colored soup.

¼ cup minced green onions
¼ cup minced green pepper
¼ cup finely chopped celery
¼ cup butter or margarine, melted
½ cup all-purpose flour
1 (14½-ounce) can ready-to-serve chicken broth
1 cup half-and-half
1 cup milk
4 ounces blue cheese, crumbled
¼ cup dry sherry
¼ teaspoon freshly ground pepper
Garnishes: sour cream, chopped fresh chives, croutons

Cook first 3 ingredients in butter in a saucepan over medium heat, stirring constantly, until vegetables are tender. Reduce heat to low; add flour, stirring well. Cook 1 minute, stirring constantly. Gradually add chicken broth, stirring until blended. Cook over medium heat 2 minutes, stirring constantly. Add half-and-half, milk, and cheese; cook over medium heat, stirring constantly, just until mixture is thickened and thoroughly heated (do not boil). Add sherry and pepper; stir well.

To serve, ladle soup into individual soup bowls. Garnish, if desired. Yield: 5 cups. Ian Lindridge

The Christ Church Cookbook
Christ Episcopal Church
Woodbury, Minnesota

Hungarian Mushroom Soup

You can use 12 ounces of fresh mushrooms instead of the more unusual shiitake and portabello varieties.

2 cups chopped onion
1 tablespoon plus 1 teaspoon
    butter or margarine, melted
1 tablespoon all-purpose flour
7 ounces fresh shiitake mush-
    rooms
1 (6-ounce) package presliced
    fresh portabello mushrooms
2 cups beef broth, divided
1 teaspoon sweet Hungarian
    paprika

1 teaspoon dried dillweed
2 teaspoons lemon juice
1 teaspoon soy sauce
¼ teaspoon salt
¼ teaspoon pepper
1 cup milk
¼ cup chopped fresh parsley
Garnishes: plain yogurt, sour
    cream, fresh dill sprigs

Cook onion in butter in a large Dutch oven over medium-high heat, stirring constantly, until tender. Add flour, stirring well. Cook 1 minute, stirring constantly. Add mushrooms, ½ cup beef broth, and next 6 ingredients. Bring to a boil; cover, reduce heat, and simmer 15 minutes. Gradually stir in remaining 1½ cups beef broth, milk, and parsley. Cook over medium heat, stirring constantly, until mixture is thickened and bubbly.

To serve, ladle soup into individual soup bowls. Garnish, if desired. Yield: 6 cups.   Joann Clements

Women Cook for a Cause
Women's Resource Center of Schoolcraft College
Livonia, Michigan

Cream of Vidalia Onion Soup

Vidalia onions are renowned for their sweetness and juiciness. They're usually available in the spring and early summer.

1 (16-ounce) loaf Italian bread
1 cup butter or margarine, melted and divided
¼ cup dried fines herbes
5 Vidalia onions, thinly sliced
1 tablespoon all-purpose flour
¾ cup dry white wine
8 cups chicken broth
8 cups half-and-half
½ teaspoon pepper

Cut bread into 1-inch cubes; set aside. Combine ½ cup butter and fines herbes in a large bowl; stir well. Add bread cubes; toss gently to coat. Arrange bread cubes in a single layer in an ungreased 15- x 10- x 1-inch jellyroll pan. Bake, uncovered, at 375° for 15 minutes or until golden, stirring once. Remove from oven. Set croutons aside, and let cool completely.

Cook sliced onion in remaining ½ cup butter in a Dutch oven over medium-low heat 20 to 25 minutes or until tender, stirring occasionally. Reduce heat to low. Add flour, stirring until smooth. Cook 1 minute, stirring constantly. Gradually add wine; cook over medium heat 15 minutes or until liquid evaporates, stirring often. Reduce heat to low; stir in chicken broth, half-and-half, and pepper. Cook over low heat 1 hour, stirring often (do not boil).

To serve, ladle soup into individual soup bowls. Top each serving with croutons. Yield: 18 cups.   Michelle Mitchell

Family Favorites
Optimist Clubs of Alabama/Mississippi District
Montgomery, Alabama

Jalapeño Soup

Love jalapeños? Then try this soup. For a spicy-hot version, don't seed the peppers.

1 medium onion, minced	3 tablespoons butter or margarine, melted
1 medium carrot, scraped and chopped	3 tablespoons all-purpose flour
1 medium-size sweet red pepper, chopped	3 cups chicken broth
1 medium-size sweet yellow pepper, chopped	2 cups whipping cream
3 jalapeño peppers, seeded and minced	1 cup (4 ounces) shredded Cheddar cheese

Cook first 5 ingredients in butter in a large saucepan over medium-high heat until vegetables are tender, stirring often. Reduce heat to low. Add flour, stirring until blended. Cook 1 minute, stirring constantly. Gradually add chicken broth; bring to a boil. Reduce heat to medium, and simmer, uncovered, 5 minutes. Stir in cream; cook just until thoroughly heated (do not boil). Add cheese, and cook, stirring constantly, just until cheese melts. Yield: 7 cups. Carolyn Ross

Recipes from the End of the Road
Homer Special Olympics
Homer, Alaska

Red Pepper-Corn Cream Soup

If you prefer, substitute a teaspoon of chopped fresh jalapeño pepper for the pickled variety.

2 cups frozen whole kernel corn

2 medium-size sweet red peppers

2½ cups chopped onion

1 (16-ounce) can whole tomatoes, drained and chopped

¼ cup unsalted butter or margarine, melted

1 teaspoon chopped pickled jalapeño pepper

3 cups chicken broth

1 tablespoon all-purpose flour

1 (8-ounce) carton sour cream

1 cup (4 ounces) shredded Monterey Jack cheese

Cook corn according to package directions; drain, and set aside.

Wash and dry red peppers; place on an aluminum foil-lined baking sheet. Broil peppers 5½ inches from heat (with electric oven door partially opened) about 5 minutes on each side or until peppers look blistered. Place in a heavy-duty, zip-top plastic bag; close, and let stand 10 minutes. Peel peppers; remove and discard core and seeds.

Cook red pepper, onion, and tomato in butter in a Dutch oven over medium-high heat 5 minutes, stirring constantly. Add corn, jalapeño pepper, and chicken broth; stir well. Place one-third of pepper mixture in container of an electric blender; cover and process until smooth, stopping once to scrape down sides. Repeat procedure twice with remaining pepper mixture. Return pureed mixture to pan; bring to a boil. Reduce heat, and simmer, uncovered, 10 minutes.

Combine flour and sour cream in a small bowl, stirring until smooth. Remove soup from heat; add sour cream mixture, stirring constantly with a wire whisk.

To serve, ladle soup into individual soup bowls. Top each serving evenly with cheese. Yield: 8 cups.   Barbara Pomfret

Cooking with Love
Standsfield Circle
Indianapolis, Indiana

Swiss Potato Soup with Gruyère

6 slices bacon, chopped
1 cup chopped onion
1 cup chopped cabbage
1 large leek, chopped
3½ cups chopped baking
   potato (about 1 pound)
3 cups chicken broth

¼ teaspoon salt
½ teaspoon pepper
1 cup (4 ounces) shredded
   Gruyère cheese
½ cup half-and-half
Garnish: chopped fresh dill

Cook bacon in a large saucepan over medium heat 4 minutes, stirring often. Add onion, cabbage, and leek; cook 5 minutes, stirring occasionally. Add potato and next 3 ingredients; bring to a boil. Cover, reduce heat, and simmer 40 minutes.

Transfer potato mixture in batches to container of an electric blender; cover and process until smooth, stopping once to scrape down sides. Return mixture to pan; add cheese, cook, stirring constantly, until cheese melts (do not boil). Stir in half-and-half.

To serve, ladle soup into individual soup bowls. Garnish, if desired. Yield: 8 cups.

Savory Secrets: A Collection of St. Louis Recipes
The Greater St. Louis Alumni Chapter of Sigma Sigma Sigma
Godfrey, Illinois

Butternut Squash Soup with Ginger and Lime

½ cup chopped onion
1½ tablespoons minced
   gingerroot
3 tablespoons butter or
   margarine, melted
4 cups peeled, seeded, and
   thinly sliced butternut
   squash
2 cups chicken broth

2 cups water
3 cloves garlic, minced
2 tablespoons lime juice
½ teaspoon salt
¼ teaspoon pepper
3 tablespoons julienne-sliced
   gingerroot
⅓ cup vegetable oil
4 thinly sliced lime slices

Cook onion and minced gingerroot in butter in a large saucepan over medium-high heat, stirring constantly, until onion is tender. Add squash and next 3 ingredients; bring to a boil. Cover, reduce heat, and simmer 15 minutes. Let cool slightly. Transfer in batches to container of an electric blender; cover and process until smooth, stopping once to scrape down sides. Return pureed mixture to pan. Stir in lime juice, salt, and pepper; cook until thoroughly heated.

Cook sliced gingerroot in oil in a skillet over medium heat, stirring constantly, until golden. Drain on paper towels. To serve, ladle soup into individual soup bowls. Top each serving with a lime slice; sprinkle with gingerroot slices. Yield: 6 cups.   Jody and Larry Carlson

The East Hampton L.V.I.S. Centennial Cookbook
Ladies' Village Improvement Society
East Hampton, New York

Minnesota Wild Rice Soup

Chervil is a mild, anise-flavored herb that tastes similar to parsley.

1 **cup finely chopped onion**
1 **teaspoon salt**
1 **teaspoon dried chervil**
1 **teaspoon curry powder**
½ **teaspoon dry mustard**
½ **teaspoon ground white pepper**
¼ **cup butter, melted**
½ **pound fresh mushrooms, sliced**

½ **cup thinly sliced celery**
½ **cup all-purpose flour**
6 **cups chicken broth**
2 **cups cooked wild rice**
2 **cups half-and-half**
⅔ **cup dry sherry**
Garnishes: chopped fresh parsley, chopped fresh chives

Cook first 6 ingredients in butter in a large Dutch oven over medium-high heat, stirring constantly, until onion is tender. Add mushrooms and celery; cook, stirring constantly, until mushrooms are tender. Reduce heat to low. Add flour, stirring until blended. Cook 1 minute, stirring constantly. Gradually add chicken broth; cook over medium heat, stirring constantly, until slightly thickened. Stir in rice, half-and-half, and sherry; cook until thoroughly heated. To serve, ladle soup into individual soup bowls. Garnish, if desired. Yield: 12 cups.

The Global Gourmet
Concordia Language Villages
Moorhead, Minnesota

Lentil and Sausage Soup

3 cups diced cooked ham
½ pound Polish sausage, cut into ½-inch pieces
4 cups chopped onion
2 cups chopped celery
1 large clove garlic, crushed
¼ cup vegetable oil
1 pound dried lentils, uncooked
5 cups water
1 large tomato, peeled and cut into ½-inch wedges
1½ teaspoons salt
½ teaspoon hot sauce
1 (10-ounce) package frozen chopped spinach, thawed and drained

Cook first 5 ingredients in oil in a Dutch oven over medium-high heat, stirring constantly, until vegetables are tender. Add lentils and next 4 ingredients; bring to a boil. Cover, reduce heat, and simmer 2 hours. Add spinach; bring to a boil. Cover, reduce heat, and simmer 10 minutes. Yield: 13 cups.

Eddis Harrison

The Richmond Museum of History Cookbook
Richmond Museum of History
Richmond, California

Famous Fish Chowder

Take the chill off a winter evening by serving generous bowlfuls of this chunky chowder.

2 pounds haddock fillets, skinned and cut into 1-inch pieces
4 cups peeled, cubed baking potato
3 cups chopped onion
2 cups boiling water
1 cup frozen whole kernel corn, thawed
½ cup butter or margarine, melted
¼ cup chopped celery
1 bay leaf
2½ teaspoons salt
½ teaspoon chili powder
¼ teaspoon ground red pepper
¼ teaspoon dried dillweed
¼ teaspoon ground white pepper
2 cups half-and-half
¼ cup chopped fresh parsley

Combine first 13 ingredients in an ungreased 3-quart baking dish. Cover and bake at 375° for 1 hour or until potato is tender.

Place half-and-half in a saucepan. Bring to a boil over medium-high heat, stirring constantly. Add half-and-half to fish mixture, stirring well. Remove and discard bay leaf.

To serve, ladle chowder into individual soup bowls. Sprinkle each serving evenly with parsley. Yield: 10 cups.

Moveable Feasts
Mystic Seaport Museum Stores
Mystic, Connecticut

Creole Beef Stew

This beef stew becomes a one-dish meal when you serve it over hot cooked rice or squares of cornbread.

3 tablespoons all-purpose
   flour
1 teaspoon salt
½ teaspoon ground ginger
½ teaspoon celery salt
¼ teaspoon garlic salt
¼ teaspoon pepper
3 pounds chuck roast, cut into
   2-inch cubes
2 tablespoons vegetable oil

1 (16-ounce) can whole
   tomatoes, undrained and
   chopped
3 medium onions, sliced
½ cup molasses
⅓ cup red wine vinegar
6 medium carrots, scraped and
   cut diagonally into 1-inch
   pieces
½ cup raisins

Combine first 6 ingredients in a large heavy-duty, zip-top plastic bag; add meat. Seal bag securely, and shake until meat is coated.

Brown meat in oil in a large Dutch oven over medium-high heat. Add tomato and next 3 ingredients; bring to a boil. Cover, reduce heat, and simmer 2 hours, stirring occasionally. Add carrot and raisins; bring to a boil. Cover, reduce heat, and simmer 30 minutes or until carrot is tender. Yield: 8 cups.

Heard in the Kitchen
The Heard Museum Guild
Phoenix, Arizona

Spicy Greek Lamb Stew

2 pounds boneless lamb
  shoulder
¼ cup plus 2 tablespoons
  unsalted butter or margarine,
  melted and divided
2 cups chopped onion
2 cloves garlic, minced
1 tablespoon olive oil
1 (16-ounce) can whole
  tomatoes, undrained and
  chopped
1 cup dry white wine
3 whole cloves

2 bay leaves
1 (3-inch) stick cinnamon,
  broken
½ teaspoon salt
½ teaspoon dried rosemary
¼ teaspoon freshly ground
  pepper
1 cup water (optional)
12 ounces penne pasta,
  uncooked
1 cup crumbled feta cheese,
  divided

Trim fat from lamb; cut lamb into 1-inch cubes. Brown lamb in 2 tablespoons butter in a Dutch oven over medium-high heat. Remove meat from pan, reserving drippings in pan. Set lamb aside.

Add 2 tablespoons butter, onion, garlic, and oil to drippings in pan; cook, stirring constantly, until onion is tender. Return meat to pan; add tomatoes and next 7 ingredients. Bring to a boil; cover, reduce heat, and simmer 1 hour and 10 minutes or until meat is tender, adding 1 cup water, if necessary. Remove and discard cloves, bay leaves, and cinnamon stick.

Cook pasta according to package directions; drain well. Combine pasta, remaining 2 tablespoons butter, and ¾ cup cheese; toss gently. Serve stew over pasta; sprinkle evenly with remaining ¼ cup cheese. Yield: 8 servings.

George Morfogen

As You Like It
Williamstown Theatre Festival Guild
Williamstown, Massachusetts

Hunter's Stew

This hearty stew makes good use of venison, but if you prefer, you can substitute an equal amount of lean beef stew meat.

1½ pounds boneless venison, cut into ½-inch pieces
½ pound smoked sausage, cut into ½-inch slices
2 tablespoons vegetable oil
½ cup chopped onion
½ cup chopped celery
2 (28-ounce) cans whole tomatoes, undrained and chopped
1 (12-ounce) can beer

1 teaspoon salt
1 teaspoon sugar
½ teaspoon dried rosemary, crushed
½ teaspoon dried basil
½ teaspoon freshly ground pepper
2 medium baking potatoes, peeled and cubed
½ cup diced carrot

Brown venison and sausage in oil in a large Dutch oven over medium heat. Add onion and celery; cook, stirring constantly, 5 minutes or until tender. Add tomato and next 6 ingredients. Bring to a boil; cover, reduce heat, and simmer 30 minutes, stirring occasionally. Add potato and carrot; bring to a boil. Cover, reduce heat, and simmer 30 minutes, stirring occasionally. Uncover and cook 30 additional minutes or until potato and carrot are tender. Yield: 10 cups.

A Flock of Good Recipes
Shepherd of the Bay Lutheran Church
Ellison Bay, Wisconsin

Sausage and Tasso Jambalaya

Tasso is a Cajun sausage generously seasoned with red pepper, garlic, gumbo filé, and other herbs and spices. Outside of Louisiana, tasso is available in gourmet food stores and through mail order.

1 pound pork tasso	2 cups long-grain rice,
1 pound ground pork sausage	uncooked
¼ cup vegetable oil	1 tablespoon plus 1 teaspoon
½ cup diced onion	salt
½ cup diced celery	2 teaspoons pepper
¼ cup diced green pepper	¼ cup chopped green onions
4 cups water, divided	¼ cup chopped fresh parsley

Place tasso in a medium saucepan, and cover with water. Bring to a boil; reduce heat, and simmer, uncovered, 15 minutes. Drain tasso, and cut into small pieces.

Brown tasso and sausage in oil in a large Dutch oven over medium-high heat 5 minutes, stirring occasionally. Add onion, celery, and green pepper; cook, stirring constantly, 5 minutes or until vegetables are tender.

Add 2 cups water; bring to a boil. Stir in remaining 2 cups water, rice, salt, and pepper; bring to a boil. Stir in green onions and parsley. Cover, reduce heat, and simmer 35 to 40 minutes or until rice is tender. Yield: 10 cups.

Tina Guillory

Tell Me More
The Junior League of Lafayette, Louisiana

Caldeirada

Next time you're hungry for seafood, try Caldeirada, a hearty seafood stew that's popular in Portugal. This version contains shrimp, haddock, scallops, and mussels.

1 pound unpeeled medium-size fresh shrimp
4 medium leeks
¼ cup olive oil
3 cloves garlic, minced
3 tablespoons chopped fresh cilantro
1 teaspoon coriander seeds, crushed
1 teaspoon to 1 tablespoon ground saffron
3 (28-ounce) cans Italian-style tomatoes, undrained and chopped
1 cup dry white wine
1 cup clam juice
1 bay leaf
1 teaspoon dried oregano
¼ teaspoon freshly ground pepper
1 pound mussels
1 pound haddock fillets, cut into 2-inch pieces
1 pound bay scallops

Peel shrimp, and devein, if desired.

Remove and discard roots, tough outer leaves, and tops of leeks to where dark green becomes pale. Chop leeks into ½-inch pieces. Cook leeks in oil in a Dutch oven over medium-high heat, stirring constantly, until tender. Add garlic and next 3 ingredients; cook 3 minutes, stirring constantly. Add tomato and next 5 ingredients; bring to a boil. Reduce heat, and simmer, uncovered, 30 minutes. Remove and discard bay leaf.

Scrub mussel shells with a brush, removing beards. Discard any opened or cracked mussels.

Add mussels and haddock to pan; simmer 5 minutes. Add shrimp and scallops; simmer 3 minutes or until shrimp turn pink. Discard any unopened mussels. Yield: 20 cups.

Sailing Through Dinner
Three Squares Press
Stonington, Connecticut

Iowa Chili

2 pounds ground beef
1 pound ground pork
1 large clove garlic, crushed
¼ cup olive oil
4 cups water
2 (16-ounce) cans whole
   tomatoes, undrained and
   chopped
1 (15-ounce) can tomato sauce
1 (12-ounce) can tomato paste
2 cups chopped green pepper
1 large onion, chopped
2 jalapeño peppers, seeded
   and chopped

2 bay leaves
2 sprigs fresh parsley
½ cup chili powder
1 tablespoon salt
2 tablespoons brown sugar
2 tablespoons hot barbecue
   sauce
1 teaspoon pepper
½ teaspoon hot sauce
¼ teaspoon dried basil
½ cup vermouth

Cook beef, pork, and garlic in olive oil in a large Dutch oven over medium heat until meat is browned, stirring until meat crumbles; drain well. Add water and remaining ingredients except vermouth; bring to a boil. Reduce heat, and cook, uncovered, 1 hour and 45 minutes. Add vermouth, and cook, uncovered, 15 additional minutes. Remove and discard bay leaves. Yield: 18 cups.   Paul Gartner

Feeding the Flock
Holy Family Parish
Davenport, Iowa

Vegetables

Cold Ginger Asparagus, page 302

Cold Ginger Asparagus

¾ cup rice vinegar
1½ tablespoons minced
  gingerroot
2 tablespoons sugar
1 pound fresh asparagus

3 tablespoons vegetable oil
2 tablespoons dark sesame oil
1 clove garlic, minced
1 teaspoon soy sauce
½ teaspoon salt

Combine vinegar and gingerroot in a small saucepan; bring to a boil. Boil 7 minutes or until liquid is reduced by half. Remove from heat, and stir in sugar. Set aside.

Snap off tough ends of asparagus. Remove scales from stalks with a knife or vegetable peeler, if desired. Place asparagus in a large skillet; add cold water to cover. Bring to a boil; remove from heat. Plunge asparagus into cold water to stop the cooking process; drain. Arrange asparagus on a serving platter.

Combine vegetable oil and next 4 ingredients, stirring well; drizzle over asparagus. Cover and chill. Drizzle vinegar mixture over asparagus; cover and chill 1 hour. Yield: 4 servings. Patty Dunn

The Kinderhaus Cookbook
Kinderhaus Children's Center
Williston, Vermont

Asparagus Custard

Here is a trick for crushing the crackers without creating a mess. Place the crackers in a heavy-duty, zip-top bag. Seal the bag securely, and crush the crackers with a rolling pin.

1 pound fresh asparagus
1 cup (4 ounces) shredded
  Cheddar cheese
1 cup milk
¾ cup saltine cracker crumbs
3 large eggs, lightly beaten

1 tablespoon diced pimiento
1 teaspoon salt
¼ teaspoon pepper
2 to 3 tablespoons butter or
  margarine, melted

Snap off tough ends of asparagus. Remove scales with a vegetable peeler, if desired. Arrange asparagus in a steamer basket over boiling water; cover and steam 6 to 8 minutes or until crisp-tender. Cut into 1-inch pieces.

Combine asparagus, cheese, and next 6 ingredients in a large bowl; stir well. Pour mixture into a buttered 1½-quart casserole. Drizzle with melted butter. Bake, uncovered, at 350° for 30 minutes or just until set. Yield: 6 servings.   Crista G. Martin

The East Hampton L.V.I.S. Centennial Cookbook
Ladies' Village Improvement Society
East Hampton, New York

Roasted Beets with Warm Dijon Vinaigrette

3 **pounds medium beets with greens**
½ **teaspoon salt**
⅓ **cup sliced green onions**
2 **tablespoons balsamic vinegar**
2 **tablespoons Dijon mustard**

⅓ **cup olive oil**
½ **teaspoon salt**
½ **teaspoon freshly ground pepper**
2 to 3 **tablespoons minced fresh dill**

Leave root and 1 inch stem on beets; reserve greens. Scrub beets with a vegetable brush; wrap in aluminum foil. Bake at 400° for 1 hour and 30 minutes or until tender. Unwrap beets; pour cold water over beets, and drain. Trim off roots and stems, and rub off skins. Cut cooked beets into ¼-inch slices. Set aside, and keep warm.

Wash greens thoroughly; pat dry with paper towels. Cut greens into thin strips. Place greens in a large saucepan; cover with water, and add ½ teaspoon salt. Bring to a boil; reduce heat, and simmer, uncovered, 10 minutes or until tender. Drain well. Set aside, and keep warm.

Position knife blade in food processor bowl; add green onions, vinegar, and mustard. Process until smooth, stopping once to scrape down sides. Pour olive oil through food chute with processor running, processing until smooth. Place vinegar mixture in a small saucepan; cook over medium heat until thoroughly heated, stirring occasionally.

Place greens and beets on individual serving plates; top evenly with vinegar mixture. Sprinkle with ½ teaspoon salt, pepper, and dill. Yield: 6 servings.

Presentations
Friends of Lied, Lied Center for Performing Arts
Lincoln, Nebraska

Herb Garden Green Beans

Let the flavors of this green bean dish inspire you to plant parsley, basil, and rosemary in an herb garden of your own.

1 pound fresh green beans
⅓ cup chopped onion
¼ cup finely chopped celery
¼ cup butter or margarine, melted
¼ cup minced fresh parsley
¼ cup tightly packed fresh basil, cut into thin strips
1 teaspoon minced fresh rosemary
1 clove garlic, minced
½ teaspoon salt

Wash beans; trim ends, and remove strings. Cook in boiling water to cover 4 minutes or until crisp-tender; drain. Rinse with cold water, and drain well.

Cook onion and celery in butter in a large skillet over medium heat, stirring constantly, 3 minutes or until vegetables are tender. Add parsley and remaining 4 ingredients, and cook 3 minutes, stirring constantly. Add beans, and cook 3 minutes or until thoroughly heated. Yield: 4 servings.

Simply Classic
The Junior League of Seattle, Washington

Vegetarian Black Beans

¾ cup chopped onion
½ cup chopped green pepper
½ cup chopped celery
½ cup chopped green onions
4 cloves garlic, crushed
1 tablespoon vegetable oil
3 tablespoons tomato paste
3 (15-ounce) cans black beans, drained
1 (14½-ounce) can ready-to-serve chicken broth
1 bay leaf
½ teaspoon dried basil
½ teaspoon dried oregano
½ teaspoon dried marjoram
½ teaspoon ground cumin
½ teaspoon paprika
¼ to ½ teaspoon dried thyme
¼ teaspoon ground red pepper
¼ teaspoon black pepper

Cook first 5 ingredients in oil in a skillet over medium heat, stirring constantly, until vegetables are tender. Add tomato paste, and cook 2 minutes, stirring constantly. Add beans and remaining ingredients;

bring to a boil. Reduce heat, and simmer, uncovered, 30 minutes or until thickened. Remove and discard bay leaf. Yield: 6 servings.

Canticle of Cookery
St. Irenaeus Church Music Ministry
Cypress, California

Savory Lima Bean Pot

A baked bean side dish such as this one adds variety to a casual buffet.

4 cups dried lima beans
2 medium onions, chopped
½ cup chopped green pepper
¼ cup plus 1 tablespoon butter
  or margarine, divided
½ cup ketchup
½ cup molasses
2 tablespoons white vinegar

2 teaspoons dry mustard
½ teaspoon hot sauce
1 teaspoon salt
½ teaspoon pepper
1 (14½-ounce) can sliced
  carrots, drained
2 cups diced cooked ham

Sort and wash beans; place beans in a large Dutch oven. Cover with water 2 inches above beans. Bring to a boil; remove from heat, cover, and let stand 1 hour. Drain beans, reserving 1 cup liquid. Set beans and liquid aside.

Cook onion and green pepper in 2 tablespoons butter in a large skillet over medium-high heat, stirring constantly, until vegetables are tender. Set aside.

Combine reserved liquid, ketchup, and next 6 ingredients in a medium bowl. Add carrot, stirring well.

Spread half of beans in bottom of a lightly greased 4-quart casserole; top with half of onion mixture and ham. Repeat procedure with remaining beans and onion mixture. Top with ketchup mixture; dot with remaining 3 tablespoons butter. Bake, uncovered, at 350° for 1 hour or until beans are tender. Yield: 14 servings.

Tastes and Traditions: The Sam Houston Heritage Cookbook
The Study Club of Huntsville, Texas

John's Famous Beans

To turn these baked beans into a hearty main dish, stir in cooked ground beef before serving.

1 pound dried pinto beans
10 cups water
2 teaspoons vegetable oil
1 medium onion, diced
4 cloves garlic, crushed
1 (16-ounce) can stewed tomatoes, undrained and chopped
¼ cup Worcestershire sauce

2 tablespoons mild picante sauce
1 teaspoon chopped fresh cilantro
1 teaspoon salt
1 teaspoon ground cumin
¼ teaspoon chili powder
1 cup (4 ounces) shredded sharp Cheddar cheese

Sort and wash beans; place in a large Dutch oven. Cover with water 2 inches above beans; let soak at least 8 hours. Drain. Add 10 cups water and vegetable oil to beans; bring to a boil. Reduce heat, and simmer, uncovered, 1½ hours.

Add onion and next 8 ingredients; bring to a boil. Reduce heat, and simmer, uncovered, 1½ hours.

To serve, ladle beans into individual serving bowls. Top evenly with cheese. Yield: 7 servings. Cynthia Lancaster

Coastal Cuisine, Texas Style
The Junior Service League of Brazosport
Lake Jackson, Texas

Broccoli with Garlic Butter and Cashews

1½ pounds fresh broccoli
⅓ cup butter or margarine
1 tablespoon brown sugar
3 tablespoons soy sauce

2 teaspoons white vinegar
¼ teaspoon pepper
¼ teaspoon minced garlic
⅓ cup salted roasted cashews

Remove and discard broccoli leaves and tough ends of stalks; cut into spears. Cook broccoli in a small amount of boiling water 8 minutes or until crisp-tender. Drain well. Arrange broccoli on a serving platter. Set aside, and keep warm.

Melt butter in a small skillet over medium heat; add brown sugar and next 4 ingredients. Bring to a boil; remove from heat. Stir in cashews. Pour sauce over broccoli, and serve immediately. Yield: 4 servings.   Jean Harbison

Saxony Sampler
GFWC Saxonburg District Woman's Club
Saxonburg, Pennsylvania

Broccoli in Olive-Nut Sauce

3 pounds fresh broccoli
1 teaspoon lemon-pepper seasoning
¼ cup sliced ripe olives
2 cloves garlic, crushed
3 tablespoons lemon juice
½ cup butter or margarine, melted
½ cup slivered almonds, toasted

Remove and discard broccoli leaves and tough ends of stalks; cut into flowerets. Arrange broccoli in a steamer basket over boiling water. Cover and steam 5 minutes or until crisp-tender. Arrange broccoli on a serving platter; sprinkle with lemon-pepper seasoning. Set aside, and keep warm.

Cook olives, garlic, and lemon juice in butter in a small skillet over medium-high heat 3 minutes, stirring constantly. Stir in almonds. Spoon sauce over broccoli. Serve immediately. Yield: 8 servings.

Dining by Fireflies: Unexpected Pleasures of the New South
The Junior League of Charlotte, North Carolina

Sesame-Ginger Brussels Sprouts

1½ pounds fresh brussels
   sprouts
¾ cup water
2 tablespoons dry vermouth
2 teaspoons honey
½ teaspoon salt

1 tablespoon plus 1 teaspoon
   minced gingerroot
2 teaspoons vegetable oil
2 teaspoons sesame seeds,
   toasted

Wash brussels sprouts thoroughly; remove discolored leaves. Cut off stem ends, and slash bottom of each sprout with a shallow X.

Combine brussels sprouts and water in a large saucepan; bring to a boil over medium-high heat. Cover, reduce heat, and simmer 10 minutes or until tender. Drain well, and set aside.

Combine vermouth, honey, and salt; stir well, and set aside.

Cook gingerroot in oil in a large skillet over medium-high heat 2 minutes, stirring constantly. Add brussels sprouts and vermouth mixture; cook, stirring constantly, 1 minute or until mixture is thoroughly heated. Sprinkle with toasted sesame seeds. Serve immediately. Yield: 4 servings.

Chet Marden

Favorite Recipes
Trinity United Methodist Women
North Myrtle Beach, South Carolina

Cabbage with Apples and Walnuts

Braised cabbage is at its best in this colorful, sweet-and-sour side dish.

6 slices bacon
½ cup firmly packed brown
   sugar
½ cup water
⅓ cup cider vinegar
½ medium cabbage, shredded
½ medium-size red cabbage,
   shredded

2 medium cooking apples,
   peeled, cored, and thinly
   sliced
⅓ cup chopped walnuts,
   toasted

Cook bacon in a large Dutch oven over medium heat until crisp; remove bacon, reserving 3 tablespoons drippings in pan. Crumble bacon, and set aside.

Add sugar, water, and vinegar to drippings; cook over medium-high heat 3 to 4 minutes or until liquid is reduced to ¾ cup. Add cabbage; cook, stirring constantly, 4 minutes or until cabbage wilts. Remove from heat. Add apple; toss gently. Sprinkle with bacon and walnuts. Serve immediately. Yield: 6 servings.

The Bountiful Arbor
The Junior League of Ann Arbor, Michigan

Cabbage Casserole

1 medium cabbage, cut into thin wedges	½ teaspoon pepper
½ cup water	⅔ cup (2.6 ounces) shredded Cheddar cheese
¼ cup butter or margarine	½ cup chopped green pepper
¼ cup all-purpose flour	½ cup chopped onion
2 cups milk	½ cup mayonnaise
½ teaspoon salt	1 tablespoon chili sauce

Combine cabbage wedges and water in a large saucepan; bring to a boil. Cover, reduce heat, and cook 15 minutes. Drain well; place cabbage wedges in an ungreased 13- x 9- x 2-inch baking dish.

Melt butter in a heavy saucepan over low heat; add flour, stirring until smooth. Cook 1 minute, stirring constantly. Gradually add milk; cook over medium heat, stirring constantly, until mixture is thickened and bubbly. Stir in salt and pepper; pour over cabbage. Bake, uncovered, at 375° for 20 minutes.

Combine cheese and remaining 4 ingredients in a small bowl; stir well. Spread over cabbage. Bake, uncovered, at 400° for 20 minutes. Yield: 8 servings.   Bea Phillips

BMC on Our Menu
Baptist Medical Center Auxiliary of Volunteers
Columbia, South Carolina

Elegant Carrots

Toasted almond slices add a touch of class to these carrots.

1 pound carrots, scraped and thinly sliced	3 tablespoons honey
¼ cup golden raisins	1 tablespoon lemon juice
¼ cup butter or margarine, melted	¼ teaspoon ground ginger
	¼ cup sliced almonds, toasted

Cook carrot in a small amount of boiling water 8 minutes; drain. Combine carrot, raisins, and next 4 ingredients. Spoon into an ungreased 1-quart baking dish. Bake, uncovered, at 375° for 30 to 35 minutes or until carrot is tender, stirring occasionally. Sprinkle with almonds. Yield: 4 servings. JoAnn McDonnell

St. Stephen's Feast
St. Stephen Protomartyr Catholic Church
St. Louis, Missouri

Cauliflower au Gratin

1 large cauliflower, cut into flowerets	1 cup milk
4 slices bacon, uncooked and diced	¾ cup whipping cream
	¾ cup (3 ounces) shredded Gruyère cheese
¼ cup all-purpose flour	½ teaspoon salt
5 large eggs, lightly beaten	¼ teaspoon pepper

Place cauliflower in a steamer basket over boiling water. Cover and steam 10 minutes or until crisp-tender. Drain well; rinse with cold water. Place cauliflower in a greased 2-quart casserole.

Cook bacon in a skillet until crisp. Remove bacon, discarding drippings. Combine flour and remaining 6 ingredients in a bowl, stirring well with a wire whisk. Stir in bacon. Pour sauce over cauliflower. Bake, uncovered, at 350° for 45 minutes or until a knife inserted in center comes out clean. Yield: 6 servings. Joan P. Snyder

What's Cooking in Delaware
American Red Cross in Delaware
Wilmington, Delaware

Chinese-Spiced Eggplant

Delicious flavors of the Orient–sesame, garlic, and ginger–spice up this eggplant dish. Serve it as a side dish or over hot cooked rice for a main course.

2 **(1-pound) eggplants, peeled and cut into ¾-inch cubes**
2 **tablespoons sugar**
3 **tablespoons low-sodium soy sauce**
2 **tablespoons red wine vinegar**
1 **tablespoon dark sesame oil**
1 **teaspoon dry sherry**

¼ **teaspoon salt**
1½ **tablespoons minced garlic**
1 **tablespoon minced gingerroot**
1 **tablespoon peanut oil**
1 to 1½ **tablespoons sesame seeds, toasted**

Arrange eggplant in a steamer basket over boiling water. Cover and steam 15 minutes. Remove eggplant to a serving dish. Set aside, and keep warm.

Combine sugar and next 5 ingredients in a small bowl; stir well, and set aside.

Cook garlic and gingerroot in peanut oil in a large skillet over medium-high heat 1 minute, stirring constantly. Stir in soy sauce mixture. Bring to a boil; remove from heat. Pour sauce over eggplant; sprinkle with sesame seeds. Serve immediately. Yield: 6 servings.   Peggy Chung

Picnic in the Park
Atwood Community Center
Madison, Wisconsin

Sautéed Kale and Onion

In case you aren't acquainted with kale, it has a mild, cabbage-like flavor and is similar in texture to spinach.

1½ cups chopped onion
3 tablespoons olive oil
½ to 1 teaspoon dried crushed red pepper

7 cups chopped kale (about 2 bunches)
2 teaspoons balsamic vinegar
¼ teaspoon salt

Cook onion in oil in a large skillet over medium-high heat, stirring constantly, until tender. Add pepper and kale; cook, stirring constantly, 5 minutes or just until kale wilts. Add vinegar and salt; toss gently. Serve immediately. Yield: 4 servings.

Appealing Fare
Frost & Jacobs
Cincinnati, Ohio

Irresistible Aromatic Mustard Mushrooms

1 pound small fresh mushrooms, halved
2 medium-size green peppers, cut into 1-inch pieces
1 medium onion, chopped
½ cup butter or margarine, melted
¾ cup dry red wine

½ cup lightly packed brown sugar
2 tablespoons Worcestershire sauce
2 tablespoons Dijon mustard
½ teaspoon salt
Freshly ground pepper to taste

Cook first 3 ingredients in butter in a large saucepan over medium-high heat, stirring constantly, until vegetables are tender. Stir in wine and remaining ingredients; cook, uncovered, over medium heat 20 minutes. Serve with a slotted spoon. Yield: 6 servings.

Nothin' Finer
The Service League of Chapel Hill, North Carolina

Okra Fritters

These aren't your run-of-the-mill fritters–they're flavored with curry and studded with bits of okra, onion, and tomato.

1 cup thinly sliced fresh okra
½ cup chopped onion
½ cup chopped tomato
1 large egg, beaten
¼ cup all-purpose flour

¼ cup cornmeal
½ teaspoon salt
½ teaspoon curry powder
¼ teaspoon pepper
Peanut oil

Combine first 9 ingredients in a medium bowl, stirring well.

Pour oil to depth of 2 inches into a Dutch oven; heat to 360°. Using a tablespoon dipped in hot water, drop cornmeal mixture into hot oil. Fry 1 minute on each side or until golden. Drain on paper towels. Serve immediately. Yield: 16 fritters.   Millie Cathey

Sharing Recipes
Hook & Ladder Association of Holly Lake
Volunteer Fire Department
Big Sandy, Texas

Nutmeg-Onion Gratin

6 medium onions, cut into
  ½-inch-thick slices
3 tablespoons whipping cream
½ teaspoon salt

⅛ teaspoon ground nutmeg
½ cup (2 ounces) shredded
  Gruyère cheese

Cook onion in boiling salted water to cover in a large Dutch oven 10 minutes or until tender; drain.

Combine onion, whipping cream, salt, and nutmeg in a large bowl; toss well. Spoon into a buttered 11- x 7- x 1½-inch baking dish. Sprinkle with cheese. Broil 5½ inches from heat (with electric oven door partially opened) 5 minutes or until cheese melts. Serve immediately. Yield: 6 servings.   Edie Pennell

As You Like It
Williamstown Theatre Festival Guild
Williamstown, Massachusetts

Balsamic-Roasted New Potatoes

Balsamic vinegar is a bit expensive, but worth the cost. It's aged in wooden barrels to develop a rich color and unique flavor.

2 tablespoons olive oil
2 pounds small new potatoes, unpeeled and quartered
1 tablespoon minced garlic
1 tablespoon minced shallot
1 teaspoon chopped fresh thyme

1 teaspoon minced fresh rosemary
⅛ teaspoon ground nutmeg
¼ cup balsamic vinegar
½ teaspoon salt
¼ teaspoon pepper

Heat oil in a large skillet over medium-high heat. Add potato and next 5 ingredients; cook, stirring constantly, until thoroughly heated.

Place potato mixture in an ungreased 15- x 10- x 1-inch jellyroll pan. Bake, uncovered, at 400° for 25 minutes or just until potato is tender, stirring occasionally. Add vinegar, and toss well. Sprinkle with salt and pepper. Bake, uncovered, 7 additional minutes. Serve immediately. Yield: 4 servings.

Edward Asner

Today's Traditional: Jewish Cooking with a Lighter Touch
Congregation Beth Shalom
Carmichael, California

Potato Puff Soufflé

If you don't have time to prepare mashed potatoes from scratch for this recipe, use instant mashed potato flakes.

2 teaspoons minced onion
¼ cup butter or margarine, melted
¼ cup all-purpose flour
1 teaspoon salt

¼ teaspoon pepper
2 cups cooked, mashed potato
1 (8-ounce) carton sour cream
4 large eggs, separated

Cook onion in butter in a large skillet over medium-high heat, stirring constantly, until tender. Reduce heat to medium. Add flour, stirring until blended. Cook, stirring constantly, until thickened and bubbly. Stir in salt and pepper; remove from heat. Stir in mashed potato and sour cream.

Beat egg yolks until thick and pale. Gradually stir about one-fourth of hot mixture into yolks, and add to remaining hot mixture, stirring constantly.

Beat egg whites in a large bowl at high speed of an electric mixer until stiff peaks form; gently fold beaten egg white into potato mixture, one-third at a time. Spoon into a buttered 1½-quart soufflé dish. Bake, uncovered, at 350° for 40 minutes or until puffed and set. Serve immediately. Yield: 6 servings. Karen Johnson

St. Catherine of Siena Celebration Cookbook
St. Catherine of Siena Church
DuBois, Pennsylvania

Layered Sweet Potato and Cranberry Casserole

If you're looking for a new side dish for the holidays, we recommend this cranberry and sweet potato casserole.

4 **large sweet potatoes (about 3½ pounds)**
½ **cup firmly packed brown sugar**
1 **tablespoon butter or margarine**
1 **cup fresh cranberries, divided**
½ **cup orange juice**
½ **cup chopped walnuts**
2 **tablespoons butter or margarine, melted**
1 **tablespoon brown sugar**
½ **teaspoon ground cinnamon**

Cook potatoes in boiling water to cover 40 to 45 minutes or until tender. Drain; let cool slightly. Peel and cut into ¼-inch slices. Arrange half of potato slices in a greased 13- x 9- x 2-inch baking dish. Sprinkle with ¼ cup brown sugar; dot with 1½ teaspoons butter. Top with ½ cup cranberries. Repeat layers. Pour orange juice over top. Cover and bake at 350° for 45 minutes.

Combine walnuts and remaining 3 ingredients; stir well. Sprinkle mixture over potato mixture. Bake, uncovered, 10 additional minutes. Yield: 8 servings. Dorothy Ruthnick

The Richmond Museum of History Cookbook
Richmond Museum of History
Richmond, California

Plantation Squash

12 medium-size yellow squash
2 (10-ounce) packages frozen
  chopped spinach
1 (3-ounce) package cream
  cheese, softened
3 large eggs, lightly beaten
¼ cup plus 2 tablespoons
  butter or margarine, melted
1 tablespoons plus 1 teaspoon
  sugar
½ teaspoon seasoned salt
½ teaspoon onion salt
1½ teaspoons to 1 tablespoon
  cracked black pepper
¼ teaspoon salt
1 cup crushed round buttery
  crackers (25 to 30 crackers)
1¼ pounds sliced bacon,
  cooked and crumbled
Paprika

Cook squash in boiling water to cover 10 minutes or until tender. Drain and let cool slightly. Trim off stems. Cut each squash in half lengthwise; scoop out pulp, leaving a ¼-inch-thick shell. Set pulp and shells aside, and keep warm.

Cook spinach according to package directions. Drain spinach well, pressing between layers of paper towels. Add spinach, cream cheese, and next 6 ingredients to pulp; stir well.

Place shells in a greased 13- x 9- x 2-inch baking dish. Sprinkle with ¼ teaspoon salt. Spoon pulp mixture into shells. Sprinkle with cracker crumbs, bacon, and paprika. Cover and bake at 325° for 30 minutes or until heated. Serve immediately. Yield: 12 servings.   Betsy Harris

Shared Recipes Among Friends
The Junior Auxiliary of Russellville, Arkansas

Roasted Squash

2 medium zucchini, cubed
2 medium-size yellow squash,
  cubed
1 sweet red pepper, cubed
5 cloves garlic, crushed
2 tablespoons olive oil
1 teaspoon salt
½ teaspoon freshly ground
  pepper
1 tablespoon balsamic vinegar
2 tablespoons pine nuts,
  toasted
8 fresh basil leaves, cut into
  very thin strips

Combine first 4 ingredients in a large bowl; drizzle with oil, and sprinkle with salt and pepper. Toss well. Place vegetable mixture in an ungreased 15- x 10- x 1-inch jellyroll pan. Bake, uncovered, at 500° for

10 minutes. Remove vegetables from oven, and toss with vinegar, pine nuts, and basil. Serve immediately. Yield: 4 servings.   Betty Ray

Immacolata Cookbook
Immacolata Church Ladies Society
St. Louis, Missouri

Spaghetti Squash with Vegetable Sauce

1 (3- to 4-pound) spaghetti squash
⅓ cup water
1 (14½-ounce) can stewed tomatoes, undrained
3 tablespoons garlic-flavored tomato paste
2 tablespoons vegetable oil
1 cup chopped onion
1 cup sliced fresh mushrooms
¾ cup chopped zucchini
½ cup chopped yellow squash
⅓ cup finely chopped carrot
2 cloves garlic, minced
1 teaspoon dried basil
½ teaspoon salt
½ teaspoon dried oregano
¼ teaspoon dried thyme
¼ teaspoon pepper
½ cup freshly grated Parmesan cheese

Pierce spaghetti squash several times with a fork; place in a 13- x 9- x 2-inch baking dish. Microwave, uncovered, at HIGH 10 minutes. Cut in half lengthwise; remove and discard seeds.

Place spaghetti squash, cut side up, in baking dish; add water to dish. Cover with heavy-duty plastic wrap and vent. Microwave at HIGH 12 to 14 minutes or until tender, turning squash over every 5 minutes. Let stand 5 minutes. Drain; let cool.

Remove spaghetti-like strands, using a fork. Place strands in a large bowl; set aside, and keep warm.

Combine stewed tomatoes and next 13 ingredients in a large glass bowl; stir well. Cover and microwave at HIGH 15 minutes or until vegetables are tender, stirring every 5 minutes.

To serve, spoon vegetable mixture over spaghetti squash. Sprinkle with cheese. Yield: 6 servings.

A Slice of Paradise
The Hospital Service League of Naples Community Hospital
Naples, Florida

Stuffed Zucchini, Turkish Style

Feta cheese and fresh dill turn zucchini into a Turkish treat.

4 medium zucchini (about 1½ pounds)
¾ cup minced onion
3 small cloves garlic, crushed
3 tablespoons butter or margarine, melted
3 large eggs, lightly beaten
¾ cup (3 ounces) shredded Swiss cheese
½ cup crumbled feta cheese

2 tablespoons chopped fresh parsley
1½ tablespoons all-purpose flour
1 tablespoon chopped fresh dill
½ teaspoon salt
¼ teaspoon pepper
¼ teaspoon paprika

Cut zucchini in half lengthwise. Scoop out pulp, leaving ¼-inch-thick shells. Cook pulp, onion, and garlic in butter in a large skillet over medium-high heat, stirring constantly, until onion is tender. Remove from heat. Stir in eggs and next 7 ingredients. Spoon mixture evenly into shells; sprinkle with paprika. Bake at 375° for 30 minutes or until set. Yield: 8 servings.   Mary Ostwalt

Appalachian Appetites
The Service League of Boone, North Carolina

Hot Herbed Tomatoes

For dazzle, use red and yellow cherry tomatoes in this recipe.

2 pints cherry tomatoes, halved
¾ cup soft breadcrumbs
¼ cup plus 2 tablespoons minced onion
¼ cup plus 2 tablespoons chopped fresh parsley
1 clove garlic, minced

¼ cup chopped fresh basil
1 teaspoon chopped fresh thyme
¾ teaspoon salt
¼ teaspoon pepper
¼ cup plus 2 tablespoons olive oil

Place cherry tomato halves in a lightly greased 11- x 7- x 1½-inch baking dish.

Combine breadcrumbs and next 7 ingredients in a medium bowl, stirring well. Sprinkle breadcrumb mixture evenly over cherry tomato halves. Drizzle with olive oil. Bake, uncovered, at 400° for 7 to 9 minutes or until thoroughly heated. Serve immediately. Yield: 10 servings.

Be Our Guest
Trianon
Baton Rouge, Louisiana

Baked Dijon Tomato Cups

6 medium tomatoes
¼ cup Dijon mustard
⅛ teaspoon salt
¼ cup plus 3 tablespoons Italian-seasoned breadcrumbs
¼ cup plus 3 tablespoons freshly grated Parmesan cheese

¼ cup butter or margarine, melted
½ teaspoon dried parsley flakes
⅛ teaspoon ground red pepper

Cut tomatoes in half crosswise. Brush Dijon mustard evenly over cut side of tomato halves; sprinkle with salt. Combine breadcrumbs and next 4 ingredients; stir well. Spoon breadcrumb mixture evenly over tomato halves.

Place tomato halves, cut side up, in an ungreased 13- x 9- x 2-inch baking dish. Bake, uncovered, at 350° for 10 minutes. Turn oven to broil, and broil 8 inches from heat (with electric oven door partially opened) 5 minutes or until lightly browned. Serve immediately. Yield: 12 servings.   Christy Spence

Coastal Cuisine, Texas Style
The Junior Service League of Brazosport, Texas

Acknowledgments

Each of the community cookbooks listed is represented by recipes appearing in *America's Best Recipes*. Unless otherwise noted, the copyright is held by the sponsoring organization whose mailing address is included.

300th Anniversary Cookbook, All Hallows' Episcopal Church, 809 Central Ave., P.O. Box 235, Davidsonville, MD 21035

888 Favorite Recipes, Boy Scout Troop 888, Fairview United Methodist Church, 2505 Old Niles Ferry Pike, Maryville, TN 37803

Almost Chefs, A Cookbook for Kids, Palm Beach Guild for the Children's Home Society, 3600 Broadway, West Palm Beach, FL 33407

Altus "Wine Capital of Arkansas" Cookbook, Altus Chamber of Commerce, P.O. Box 404, Altus, AR 72821

Amazing Graces: Meals and Memories from the Parsonage, Texas Conference United Methodist Minister's Spouses Association, P.O. Box 3400, Palestine, TX 75802

American Buffet, General Federation of Women's Clubs, 1734 North St. NW, Washington, DC 20036-2990

Among the Lilies, Women in Missions, First Baptist Church of Atlanta, 754 Peachtree St. NE, Atlanta, GA 30365

Angel Food, St. Vincent de Paul School, 1375 E. Spring Ln., Salt Lake City, UT 84117

Another Taste of Aloha, Junior League of Honolulu, 1802-A Keeaumoku St., Honolulu, HI 96822

Appalachian Appetites, Service League of Boone, P.O. Box 2651, Boone, NC 28607

Appealing Fare, Frost & Jacobs, Suite 2200, 201 E. 5th St., Cincinnati, OH 45244

An Apple a Day, Knoxville Academy of Medicine Alliance, P.O. Box 10551, Knoxville, TN 37939-0551

As You Like It, Williamstown Theatre Festival Guild, P.O. Box 219, Williamstown, MA 01267

Back Home Again, Junior League of Indianapolis, Inc./J.L.I. Publications, 3050 N. Meridian St., Indianapolis, IN 46208

Be Our Guest, Trianon, 755 Highland Park Dr., Baton Rouge, LA 70808

The Bess Collection, Junior Service League of Independence, P.O. Box 1571, Independence, MO 64055

The Best of Wheeling, Junior League of Wheeling, Inc., 907½ National Rd., Wheeling, WV 26003

BMC on Our Menu, Baptist Medical Center Auxiliary of Volunteers, Taylor at Marion Sts., Columbia, SC 29220

The Bountiful Arbor, Junior League of Ann Arbor, P.O. Box 7704, Ann Arbor, MI 48107-7704

Briarwood Recipes to Crown Your Table, Women's Ministries of Briarwood Presbyterian Church, 2200 Briarwood Way, Birmingham, AL 35243

By Special Request, Our Favorite Recipes, Piggly Wiggly Carolina Employees, 4401 Piggly Wiggly Dr., Charleston, SC 29405

Cafe Oklahoma, Junior Service League of Midwest City, P.O. Box 10703, Midwest City, OK 73130

Candlelight and Wisteria, Lee-Scott Academy, 2307 E. Glenn Ave., Auburn, AL 36830

Cane River's Louisiana Living, Service League of Natchitoches, Inc., 446 Jefferson St., Natchitoches, LA 71457

Canticle of Cookery, St. Irenaeus Church Music Ministry, 5201 Evergreen, Cypress, CA 90630

Celebrated South Carolinians!, American Cancer Society, 128 Stonemark Ln., Columbia, SC 29210

Celebrating California, Children's Home Society of California, 7695 Cardinal Ct., San Diego, CA 92123

A Celebration of Food, Sisterhood Temple Beth David, 7 Clapboardtree St., Westwood, MA 02090

Champions: Favorite Foods of Indy Car Racing, Championship Auto Racing Auxiliary, 2915 N. High School Rd., Indianapolis, IN 46224

The Christ Church Cookbook, Christ Episcopal Church, 7305 Afton Rd., Woodbury, MN 55125

Classic Connecticut Cuisine, Connecticut Easter Seals, 152 Norwich-New London Tpke., P.O. Box 389, Uncasville, CT 06382-0389

Coastal Cuisine, Texas Style, Junior Service League of Brazosport, P.O. Box 163, Lake Jackson, TX 77566

Coe Hall Cooks!, Coe Hall, Planting Fields Rd., Planting Fields Arboretum, Oyster Bay, NY 11771

Collard Greens, Watermelons, and "Miss" Charlotte's Pie, Swansboro United Methodist Women, P.O. Box 771, Swansboro, NC 28584-0771

Come Savor Swansea, First Christian Congregational Church, P.O. Box 76, Swansea, MA 02777

Company's Coming, St. Charles Ladies Guild, 714 W. Union St., Morganton, NC 28655

The Company's Cookin', Employees of the Rouse Company, 10275 Little Patuxent Pkwy., Columbia, MD 21044

Conflict-Free Cooking, National Court Reporters Foundation, 8224 Old Courthouse Rd., Vienna, VA 22182-3808

A Continual Feast, St. Mary's Guild of St. Clement's Episcopal Church, 2837 Claremont Blvd., Berkeley, CA 94705

Cookbook 1893-1993, Friends of North Tonawanda Public Library, 505 Meadow Dr., North Tonawanda, NY 14120

Cooking Atlanta Style, Atlanta Community Food Bank, Longstreet Press, 2140 Newmarket Pkwy., Ste. 118, Marietta, GA 30067

Cooking in Alexander Valley: A Tradition of Excellence in Food, Wine and Education, Alexander Valley Parents Club, 8511 Hwy. 128, Healdsburg, CA 95448

Cooking in the Litchfield Hills, Pratt Center, 163 Papermill Rd., New Milford, CT 06776

Cooking on the Coast, Mississippi Gulf Coast YMCA, P.O. Box 430, Ocean Springs, MS 39566

Cooking Up a Storm, Florida Style, Brookwood Guild, 901 7th Ave. S., St. Petersburg, FL 33705-1998

Cooking with Class, Park Maitland School, 1450 S. Orlando Ave., Maitland, FL 32794-1095

Cooking with Fire, Fairfield Historical Society, 636 Old Post Rd., Fairfield, CT 06430

Cooking with Love, Standsfield Circle, 5276 Hawthorne Cir., Indianapolis, IN 46250

Cookin' with Fire, Milford Fire Department, 21 Birch St., Milford, MA 01757

Cooks by the Yard, Harvard Neighbors, Harvard University, 17 Quincy St., Cambridge, MA 02138

Cottonwood Cookbook, Cottonwood Elementary School, 925 Farm District Rd., Fernley, NV 89408

Creative Chef 2, Tourette Syndrome Association, Inc., 42-40 Bell Blvd., Bayside, NY 11361

Cuisine for Connoisseurs: Food Among the Fine Arts, Boca Raton Museum of Art, 10586 Stonebridge Blvd., Boca Raton, FL 33498

Daily Bread, Word of Life Women's Ministry, 565 Lovers Ln., Steubenville, OH 43952

Delicious Developments, Friends of Strong Memorial Hospital, 601 Elmwood Ave., Box 660, Rochester, NY 14642

Dining by Fireflies: Unexpected Pleasures of the New South, Junior League of Charlotte, 1332 Maryland Ave., Charlotte, NC 28209

Dining with Southern Elegance, Terrebonne Association for Family and Community Education, P.O. Box 627, Houma, LA 70361-0627

Door County Cooking, Bay View Lutheran Church, 340 W. Maple St., Sturgeon Bay, WI 54235

The East Hampton L.V.I.S. Centennial Cookbook, Ladies' Village Improvement Society, P.O. Box 1196, East Hampton, NY 11937. For more information call 516-324-1220.

The Educated Palate: The Hamlin School Cookbook, The Hamlin School, 2120 Broadway, San Francisco, CA 94115

The Elegant Cook, Friends of the Eastern Christian School Association, 50 Oakwood Ave., North Haledon, NJ 07508

Emory Seasons, Entertaining Atlanta Style, Emory University Woman's Club, 849 Houston Mill Rd., NE, Atlanta, GA 30329

Entertaining in Kingwood, Kingwood Women's Club, P.O. Box 5411, Kingwood, TX 77345

Essence of Kansas: 4-H Cookbook, Taste Two, Kansas 4-H Foundation, Inc., 116 Umberger Hall, Kansas State University, Manhattan, KS 66506

Ethnic Delights, Our Lady of Perpetual Help Byzantine Catholic Church, 1210 Spotswood Ave., Norfolk, VA 23507

Fabulous Foods, Children's Miracle Network, St. John's Hospital and Southern Illinois University School of Medicine, 800 E. Carpenter, Springfield, IL 62702

Family Favorites, Optimist Clubs of Alabama/Mississippi District, 1925 Still Oaks Dr., Montgomery, AL 36117

Fanconi Anemia Family Cookbook, Fanconi Anemia Research Fund, Inc., 1902 Jefferson St., Ste. 2, Eugene, OR 97405

Favorite Recipes, National Association of Women in Construction, Tri-County Chapter #317, 2250 S. Old Dixie Hwy., Vero Beach, FL 32962

Favorite Recipes, St. Isaac Jogues Senior Guild, St. Mary's of the Hills Catholic Church, 2675 John R. Rd., Rochester Hills, MI 48307

Favorite Recipes, Trinity United Methodist Women, 706 14th Ave. S., North Myrtle Beach, SC 29582

The Feast, St. Mary's Catholic Community, P.O. Box 399, 616 Dearborn St., Caldwell, ID 83606-0399

Feast of Eden, Junior League of Monterey County, Inc., P.O. Box 2291, Monterey, CA 93942

Feeding Our Flocks, The Shepherd's Fund, 7 Ash St., Hollis, NH 03049

Feeding the Flock, Holy Family Parish, 1926 N. Marquette, Davenport, IA 52804

Flavors of Fredericksburg, St. Barnabas Episcopal Church, 601 W. Creek St., Fredericksburg, TX 78624

Flavors of the Russian North, The Archangel, Russia & Greater Portland, Maine Sister City Committees, 15 Cragmoor, Cape Elizabeth, ME 04107

A Flock of Good Recipes, Shepherd of the Bay Lutheran Church, Hwy. 42, P.O. Box 27, Ellison Bay, WI 54210

Food for the Spirit, St. Thomas Aquinas Home & School Association, 14520 Voss Dr., Hammond, LA 70401

From Generation to Generation, Sisterhood of Temple Emanu-El, 8500 Hillcrest Rd., Dallas, TX 75225

Gaspee Days Cookbook, Gaspee Days Committee, P.O. Box 1772, Pilgrim Station, Warwick, RI 02888

Gatherings: A West Texas Collection of Recipes, Caprock Girl Scout Council, 2567 74th St., Lubbock, TX 79423

Georgia Hospitality, Georgia Elks Aidmore Auxiliary, 2394 Morrison Rd., Conyers, GA 30308

Global Feast Cookbook, Mystic Seaport Museum Stores, 47 Greenmanville Ave., Mystic, CT 06355

The Global Gourmet, Concordia Language Villages, 901 S. 8th St., Moorhead, MN 56562

Good Food, Good Company, Junior Service League of Thomasville, P.O. Box 279, Thomasville, GA 31799

Good to the Core, The Apple Corps of the Weller Center for Health Education, 2009 Lehigh St., Easton, PA 18042

Great Recipes from Great Gardeners, Pennsylvania Horticultural Society, 325 Walnut St., Philadelphia, PA 19106-2777

A Greek Feast: A Book of Greek Recipes, Daughters of Penelope, 2926 Cambridge Dr., Wilmington, NC 29403

Happy Memories and Thankful Hearts: Traditions Kept and Blessings Shared, St. Christina's Catholic Church, Box 261, Parker, SD 57053

Heard in the Kitchen, Heard Museum Guild, 22 E. Monte Vista Rd., Phoenix, AZ 85004-1480

Heavenly Recipes, Rosebud WELCA, Lemmon Rural Lutheran Parish, HCR 82, Box 81, Lemmon, SD 57638-9217

Here's What's Cooking at Standish Elementary, Standish Elementary Parents and Teachers for Kids, 583 E. Cedar St., Standish, MI 48658

Historic Spanish Point: Cooking Then and Now, Gulf Coast Heritage Association, Inc., 500 N. Tamiami Trail, P.O. Box 846, Osprey, FL 34229

Holiday Sampler, Welcome Wagon Club of the Mid Ohio Valley, P.O. Box 5365, Vienna, WV 26105

Holy Cow, Chicago's Cooking!, Church of the Holy Comforter, P.O. Box 168, Kenilworth, IL 60043

Homecoming: Special Foods, Special Memories, Baylor University Alumni Association, 700 S. University Parks Dr., 2nd Floor, Waco, TX 76706

Houston Junior League Cookbook, Junior League of Houston, Inc., 1811 Briar Oaks Ln., Houston, TX 77027

Immacolata Cookbook, Immacolata Church Ladies Society, 8900 Clayton Rd., St. Louis, MO 63117

The Impossible Diet Cookbook, Recovery Alliance, Inc., P.O. Box 561, Milford, CT 06460

In the Serving Tradition, Durham Woman's Club, Inc., P.O. Box 273, Durham, CT 06422

It's Not as Good as Patty Makes It, The San Francisco School, 300 Gaven St., San Francisco, CA 94131

It's Rainin' Recipes, Charles B. Hopkins Chapter, Telephone Pioneers of America, 1600 7th Ave., Rm. 2013, Seattle, WA 98191

The Kinderhaus Cookbook, Kinderhaus Children's Center, R.D. #2, Box 443, Williston, VT 05495

Lake Murray Presbyterian Preschool Cookbook, Lake Murray Presbyterian Preschool Parents Organization, 2721 Dutchfork Rd., Chapin, SC 29036

Living off the Land: Arkansas Style, Howard County 4-H Foundation, 421 N. Main St., Nashville, AR 71852

Look Who's Cooking, Temple Hesed Sisterhood, Lake Scranton Rd., Scranton, PA 18505

Madison County Cookbook, St. Joseph Church, 607 W. Green St., Winterset, IA 50273

The Maine Collection, Portland Museum of Art, 7 Congress Sq., Portland, ME 04101

Meals on Wheels Southwest Collection Cookbook, Meals on Wheels, 5900 Forest Hills Dr., NE, Albuquerque, NM 87109

Minnesota Times and Tastes, Recipes and Menus Seasoned with History from the Minnesota Governor's Residence, 1006 Summit Avenue Society, 1006 Summit Ave., St. Paul, MN 55105

Montana Celebrity Cookbook, Intermountain Children's Home, Box 5630, Helena, MT 59604

More Than Delicious, Erie Art Museum, 411 State St., Erie, PA 16501

Moveable Feasts, Mystic Seaport Museum Stores, 47 Greenmanville Ave., Mystic, CT 06355

New Additions and Old Favorites, Canterbury United Methodist Church, 350 Overbrook Rd., P.O. Box 130699, Birmingham, AL 35213

Not by Bread Alone, Catholic Committee on Scouting and Camp Fire for the Diocese of Lake Charles, 817 Azalea St., Lake Charles, LA 70605

Nothin' Finer, Service League of Chapel Hill, P.O. Box 3003, Chapel Hill, NC 27515

Our Best Home Cooking, Citizens of Zion Missionary Baptist Church Women's Ministry, 12930 N. Lime Ave., Compton, CA 90221

Our Favorite Recipes, Seasoned with Love, Neighborhood Bible Studies, c/o Patti Moore, 1814 Silver Pines Rd., Houston, TX 77062

Our History, Our Cooks!, Goshen Fire Department Local 1443, 209 N. 3rd St., Goshen, IN 46526

Pass It On . . . A Treasury of Tastes and Traditions, Delta Delta Delta National Fraternity, 2313 Brookhollow Plaza Dr., Arlington, TX 76006

Paws and Refresh, Virginia Living Museum, 524 J. Clyde Morris Blvd., Newport News, VA 23601

Pepper Lovers Club Cookbook, Volume I, Pepper Lovers Club of Virginia Beach, P.O. Box 848, Virginia Beach, VA 23455-0848

Perfectly Splendid: One Family's Repasts, McFaddin-Ward House, 1906 McFaddin Ave., Beaumont, TX 77701-1525

Picnic in the Park, Atwood Community Center, 2425 Atwood Ave., Madison, WI 53704

A Place Called Hope, Junior Auxiliary of Hope, P.O. Box 81, Hope, AR 71801

Presentations, Friends of Lied, Lied Center for Performing Arts, 301 N. 12th, Lincoln, NE 68588-0151

Preserving Our Heritage, Church of God Ladies Ministries, 6900 Wilkinson Blvd., Charlotte, NC 28266-8468

Queen Anne Goes to the Kitchen, Episcopal Church Women of St. Paul's Parish, ECW of St. Paul's Parish, P.O. Box 278, Centreville, MD 21617

A Quest for Good Eating, Cape Cod Questers, 40 Conservation Dr., Yarmouth Port, MA 02675-1416

Quilters Guild of Indianapolis Cookbook, Quilters Guild of Indianapolis, 910 Tecumseh Pl., Indianapolis, IN 46201-1944

Reading, Writing, Recipes, Literacy Volunteers of Greater Syracuse, 2111 S. Salina St., P.O. Box 27, Syracuse, NY 13205-0027

Recipes and Remembrances, Hospice at Grady Memorial Hospital, 561 W. Central Ave., Delaware, OH 43015

Recipes and Remembrances of Tolland, Tolland Historical Society, 52 Tolland Green, P.O. Box 107, Tolland, CT 06084

Recipes from a New England Green, Middlebury Congregational Church, The Green, Middlebury, CT 06762

Recipes from the End of the Road, Homer Special Olympics, P.O. Box 207, Anchor Point, AK 99556

Recipes on Parade, Calloway County Band Boosters, College Farm Rd., Murray, KY 42071

Ribbon Winning Recipes, South Carolina State Fair, 1200 Rosewood Dr., Columbia, SC 29201

The Richmond Museum of History Cookbook, Richmond Museum of History, 400 Nevin Ave., P.O. Box 1247, Richmond, CA 94801

Ridgefield Cooks, Women's Committee of the Ridgefield Community Center, 316 Main St., Ridgefield, CT 06877

River Road Recipes III: A Healthy Collection, Junior League of Baton Rouge, 9523 Fenway, Baton Rouge, LA 70809

The Roaring Fork, Gloria J. Deschamp Donation Fund, 124 Mount View Dr., Grand Junction, CO 81501

Ronald McDonald House of Burlington, Vermont, Anniversary Edition Cookbook, Ronald McDonald House, 16 S. Winooski Ave., Burlington, VT 05401

Sailing Through Dinner, Three Squares Press, 17 Oak St., L.P., Stonington, CT 06378

Saints Alive!, Ladies' Guild of St. Barnabas Anglican Church, 4795 N. Peachtree Rd., Atlanta, GA 30338

Savory Secrets: A Collection of St. Louis Recipes, Greater St. Louis Alumni Chapter of Sigma Sigma Sigma, 4710 Iroquois Trail, Godfrey, IL 62035

Saxony Sampler, GFWC Saxonburg District Woman's Club, P.O. Box 402, Saxonburg, PA 16056

Seaport Savories, TWIG Junior Auxiliary of Alexandria Hospital, P.O. Box 3614, Alexandria, VA 22302

Seasoned Skillets & Silver Spoons, Columbus Museum Guild, 1251 Wynnton Rd., Columbus, GA 31906

Sensational Seasons: A Taste & Tour of Arkansas, Junior League of Fort Smith, Inc., P.O. Box 3266, Fort Smith, AR 72913

Shared Recipes Among Friends, Junior Auxiliary of Russellville, P.O. Box 1011, Russellville, AR 72811

Sharing Recipes, Hook & Ladder Association of Holly Lake Volunteer Fire Department, Rte. 1, Box 72, Big Sandy, TX 75755

Sheridan School Brown Bag Cookbook, Sheridan School, 4415 Cheena Dr., Houston, TX 77096

Signature Cuisine, Miami Country Day School Parents' Association, 601 N.E. 107th St., Miami, FL 33161

Silver Selections, Catawba School Alumni, 1792 Sharonwood Ln., Rock Hill, SC 29732

Simple Elegance, Our Lady of Perpetual Help Women's Guild, 8151 Poplar Ave., Germantown, TN 38138

Simply Classic, Junior League of Seattle, 4119 E. Madison, Seattle, WA 98112

Simply Irresistible, Junior Auxiliary of Conway, P.O. Box 10322, Conway, AR 72032

A Slice of Paradise, Hospital Service League of Naples Community Hospital, 350 7th St. North, P.O. Box 413029, Naples, FL 33942-3029

Soroptimist Cooks, Soroptimist International of Dixon, c/o Jacqueline DuPratt, 910 Sievers Way, Dixon, CA 95620

A Southern Collection, Then and Now, Junior League of Columbus, 1440 2nd Ave., Columbus, GA 31901

Specialties of Indianapolis, Volume 2, Home Economists' Guild of Indianapolis, 7305 E. 55th St., Indianapolis, IN 46226

St. Catherine of Siena Celebration Cookbook, St. Catherine of Siena Church, 118 S. State St., DuBois, PA 15801

St. George Parish Cookbook, St. George Parish, 128 W. 4th St., Hermann, MO 65041

St. Stephen's Feast, St. Stephen Protomartyr Catholic Church, 3949 Wilmington Ave., St. Louis, MO 63116

Stephens Remembered, Recollections & Recipes, Stephens College Denver Area Club, 117 S. Reed St., Lakewood, CO 80226

Sterling Performances, Guilds of the Orange County Performing Arts Center, 600 Town Center Dr., Costa Mesa, CA 92626

Still Fiddling in the Kitchen, National Council of Jewish Women, 30233 Southfield Rd. #100, Southfield, MI 48076

Sun Valley Celebrity & Local Heroes Cookbook, Advocates for Survivors of Domestic Violence, P.O. Box 3216, Hailey, ID 83333

Sweet Home Alabama Cooking, 44th National Square Dancing Convention, 484 Planters Rd., Montgomery, AL 36109-1832

Tasteful Treasures, Docent Guild, Bowers Museum of Cultural Art, 2002 N. Main St., Santa Ana, CA 92706

A Taste of the Past and Present, First Baptist and Pastor's Sunday School Class, 606 Church St., P.O. Box 45, Philadelphia, TN 37846

Tastes and Traditions: The Sam Houston Heritage Cookbook, The Study Club of Huntsville, P.O. Box 6404, Huntsville, TX 77342-6404

Taste the Good Life, Assistance League of Omaha, 3569 Leavenworth, Omaha, NE 68105

Taste Without Waist, Service League of Hickory, P.O. Box 1563, Hickory, NC 28603

Tell Me More, Junior League of Lafayette, 100 Felecie Dr., Lafayette, LA 70506

Tempting Southern Treasures Cookbook, Riverchase Women's Club, 2166 Baneberry Dr., Hoover, AL 35244

Texas Temptations, Texas Association for Family and Community Education, 1050 Jan Lee Dr., Burkburnett, TX 76354-2942

Timeless Treasures, Junior Service League of Valdosta, P.O. Box 1582, 305 N. Patterson St., Valdosta, GA 31603

Today's Traditional: Jewish Cooking with a Lighter Touch, Congregation Beth Shalom, 4746 El Camino Ave., Carmichael, CA 95608

Town Hill Playground Cookbook, Town Hill Playground Committee, RR 1, Box 71-5, Deerhill Rd., Whitingham, VT 05361

Traditions, First United Methodist Church/United Methodist Women, 1 Jordan Ave., P.O. Box 147, Tallassee, AL 36078

Treasured Gems, Hiddenite Center Family, Inc., Church St., Hiddenite, NC 28636

Trinity and Friends Finest, Women of Holy Trinity, P.O. Box 25, Churchville, MD 21028

Tri-State Center for the Arts Celebrity Cookbook, Tri-State Center for the Arts, P.O. Box 712, Pine Plains, NY 12567

A Ukrainian-American Potpourri, St. Stephen Ukrainian Catholic Church, 1344 White Oak Bottom Rd., Dover Township, NJ 08753

Virginia Fare, Junior League of Richmond, 205 W. Franklin St., Richmond, VA 23220

Watt's Cooking, Oasis Southern Company Services, Inc., 64 Perimeter Center E., Atlanta, GA 30346

We Like It Here, Mukwonago High School, 605 W. School Rd., Mukwonago, WI 53105

West of the Rockies, Junior Service League of Grand Junction, 425 North Ave., Ste. B, Grand Junction, CO 81501

What's Cooking at Allied, Allied Services Nurse Retention and Recruitment Committee, 1804 Bundy St., Scranton, PA 18508

What's Cooking at Cathedral Plaza, Cathedral Plaza, 1575 Pennsylvania Ave., Denver, CO 80203

What's Cooking at Chico State, Staff Council/California State University, Chico, 1st and Orange Sts., Chico, CA 95929-0160

What's Cooking in Delaware, American Red Cross in Delaware, 910 Gilpin Ave., Wilmington, DE 19806

The William & Mary Cookbook, College of William and Mary, Alumni Society, P.O. Box 2100, Williamsburg, VA 23187-2100

With Special Distinction, Mississippi College Cookbook Committee, P.O. Box 4054, Mississippi College, Clinton, MS 39058

Women Cook for a Cause, Women's Resource Center of Schoolcraft College, 18600 Haggerty Rd., Livonia, MI 48152

Years and Years of Goodwill Cooking, Goodwill Circle of New Hope Lutheran Church, 8555 4th Ave., NW, Upham, ND 58789

Community Cookbook Awards

The editors salute the three national, six regional, and three special merit winners of the 1995 Tabasco® Community Cookbook Awards competition sponsored by the Walter S. McIlhenny Company, Avery Island, Louisiana.

- **First Place Winner:** *The East Hampton L.V.I.S. Centennial Cookbook*, Ladies Village Improvement Society, East Hampton, New York
- **Second Place Winner:** *The Artful Table*, Dallas Museum of Art League, Dallas, Texas
- **Third Place Winner:** *True Grits: Tall Tales and Recipes from the New South*, Junior League of Atlanta, Inc., Atlanta, Georgia
- **New England:** *Maine Ingredients*, Junior League of Portland, Inc., Portland, Maine
- **Mid-Atlantic:** *Delicious Developments*, Friends of Strong Memorial Hospital, Rochester, New York
- **South:** *Cajun Men Cook*, Beaver Club of Lafayette, Lafayette, Louisiana
- **Midwest:** *Women of Great Taste . . . A Salute to Women and Their Zest for Food*, Junior League of Wichita, Inc., Wichita, Kansas
- **Southwest:** *The Authorized Texas Ranger Cookbook*, Fort Fisher Texas Ranger Hall of Fame and Museum, Hamilton, Texas
- **West:** *Jewish Cooking from Here and Far*, Congregation Beth Israel, Carmel, California
- **Special Merit Winner:** *Gove County Gleanings*, Gove Community Improvement Association, Gove, Kansas
- **Special Merit Winner:** *Living off the Land: Arkansas Style*, Howard County 4-H Foundation, Nashville, Arkansas
- **Special Merit Winner:** *Stirring Up Yesterday*, Peter Becker Community, Harleysville, Pennsylvania

For information on the Tabasco® Community Cookbook Awards or an awards entry form send a self-addressed stamped #10 (legal size) envelope to:
Tabasco Community Cookbook Awards
c/o Hunter & Associates, Inc.
41 Madison Avenue
New York, NY 10010-2202

For a free booklet about producing a community cookbook send a self-addressed stamped #10 (legal size) envelope to:
Compiling Culinary History
c/o Hunter & Associates, Inc.
41 Madison Avenue
New York, NY 10010-2202

Index